From Text to Hypertext

Penn Studies in Contemporary American Fiction
Emory Elliott, Series Editor

A complete list of books in the series is available from the publisher.

From Text to Hypertext

Decentering the Subject
in Fiction, Film, the Visual Arts,
and Electronic Media

Silvio Gaggi

PENN

University of Pennsylvania Press

Philadelphia

Copyright © 1997 University of Pennsylvania Press
All rights reserved
Printed in the United States of America on acid-free paper.
10   9   8   7   6   5   4   3   2   1

Published by
University of Pennsylvania Press
Philadelphia, Pennsylvania   19104-6097

Library of Congress Cataloging-in-Publication Data

Gaggi, Silvio.
   From text to hypertext   :   decentering the subject in fiction, film,
the visual arts, and electronic media   /   Silvio Gaggi.
      p.   cm. — (Penn studies in contemporary American fiction)
   Includes bibliographical references and index.
   ISBN 0-8122-3400-6
   1. Creation (Literary, artistic, etc.)   2. Arts — Themes, motives.
I. Title.   II. Series.
NX160.G35 1997
700'.1—dc20   96-41219
                                                                         CIP

For my mother and father

Contents

Plates

Preface

It is a commonplace of structuralist and poststructuralist criticism that the subject is socially constructed, a product of language and discourse rather than an essential psychological-spiritual center that uses language for its own transcendental purposes. Emil Benveniste writes, "It is in and through language that man constitutes himself as a *subject*, because language alone establishes the concept of 'ego' in reality, in *its* reality which is that of the being" (224). As a construction, the subject is susceptible to deconstruction—a laying bare of its multiplicity and contradictions and a revealing of the social nature of what might otherwise be regarded as a natural, self-evident foundation of purpose and meaning. The rhetoric of "structure" and "construction" suggests a metaphor of architectural construction, involving bricks, lumber, and nails, or of some other kind of *structural* engineering; thus, the clever deconstructor need only identify the rhetorical sutures—the mortar holding the bricks together—to expose the fact that the house or church was *made* and did not grow from a seed.

Although it is generally acknowledged that language and representation play a crucial role in the formation of the subject, there are differences regarding the extent of this role. Is the subject entirely a product of representation, linguistic or otherwise, or does the critic hedge and by this hedging implicitly acknowledge the possibility of some pre- or extra-linguistic subject or proto-subject, inaccessible to language though it may be, some originary material that is shaped by representation? Recent debate has suggested that there may be dangerous implications to the view that the subject is entirely a construction. For if the subject is wholly a construction, what ethical constraints on that construction could be possible? In an age characterized by the ubiquity of mass media representations and by the unprecedented cultural power of those representations, might the deconstruction of the subject, regardless of the ethics and politics of those who theorize the subject, license the construction of social subjects who behave and consume in ways most beneficial to those who control representation? Given the power of the media, the subject deconstructed inevitably will be reconstructed in some form, old or new, and if so, on what basis shall that reconstruction be conducted?

Whether representation shapes or creates, few doubt its power to influence the selves we feel ourselves to be. Thus, critical analysis of representation, representation of the subject in particular, remains an urgent issue. The critic's role, then, is examining how texts speak to the social subject, how they imply or construct a subject to which they speak, or how they deconstruct that always already spoken subject.

The word "subject" will be used here much as it often is in contemporary criticism, conflating several different sources of meaning. Mikkel Borch-Jacobsen traces the current use of the term to Jacques Lacan, who takes it over from philosophy, where it designates "the *hypokeimenon*, the 'underlying' or 'subjacent' goal of basic, founding philosophical inquiry." The word becomes associated with the *cogito* of Descartes, and Lacan appropriates it, along with its Aristotelian and Cartesian history, applying it to the psychoanalytic "subject" ("The Freudian Subject," 62–63).

Most obviously, the word simply implies a "subject"—in the sense of a "topic"—under discussion or being represented. But more to the point here, it suggests the idea of a human subjectivity. "Subject" is preferred to "self" because "self" is likely to be taken to suggest an essentialist notion of subjectivity that is antithetical to poststructuralist and other contemporary thinking. The word "subject" also evokes the idea of being "subject" to a larger force or forces: a king, a dictator, or a totalitarian state, perhaps. Of course, in the poststructuralist world the larger force to which one is subject is not an individual or human agency but language itself, which contains all of us in its prisonhouse, makes subjects of us all. Finally, "subject" suggests the idea of the grammatical "subject" of a sentence. One is made a subject when one is represented in language—by a pronoun, by a proper name—when one is inscribed in language, hailed by ideology, constructed as a subject, and subjected to the force of representation.

At the present time there seems to be a particular sense of crisis in the theorizing of the subject and the relationship of that project to wider social, economic, and political realities. This sense of crisis was pointedly made in a letter sent to individuals invited to participate in the 1992 inaugural session of the Oxford Amnesty Lectures. The speakers were all renowned contemporary critical theorists: Hélène Cixous, Frank Kermode, Wayne Booth, Paul Ricoeur, Terry Eagleton, Julia Kristeva, and Edward Said presented lectures, and Jacques Derrida granted an interview. Proceeds went to benefit Amnesty International's work on behalf of individuals "imprisoned solely for their beliefs, color, ethnic origin, sex, language, or religion" ("Preface to the Oxford Amnesty Lectures," Johnson, vii). The letter that invited the participants read, in part,

Our lecturers are being asked to consider the consequences of the deconstruction of the self for the liberal tradition. Does the self as construed by the liberal tradition still exist? If not, whose human rights are we defending? (Johnson, 2)

The Amnesty lectures, as well as numerous other statements of recent years, represent a number of different kinds of responses to pointed challenges like this one: those responses may be assertions that there *can* be a basis for ethical action in the face of the deconstruction of the self or even that ethical action can *only* be taken if the self is first deconstructed, they may involve struggles to discover some minimal humanism that may survive the most rigorous deconstruction, or, on the other hand, they may be outright reactions against deconstruction and poststructuralism generally. Thus, the Amnesty lectures make explicit the fact that the present seems to be a critical juncture in the relationship between those committed to poststructural critical theory and those committed to ethical political action. The relationship may not be one of irreconcilable difference, but the space available for negotiating difference is clearly rather small.

For another reason, the question of the subject is particularly compelling at this time. The past two decades have witnessed a revolution in communications and information technology that is altering the way in which individuals relate to each other and to themselves. Engagement with electronic networks involves an extension of the individual that is potentially both empowering and enfeebling. One is empowered because one has free movement within an electronic space in which one can access information of all kinds and communicate with diverse individuals and groups, regardless of their physical location. The Internet and World Wide Web are complex spaces that are not physical spaces but which are navigated quickly and safely, without having to move one's physical body. On the other hand, in this space the individual, as he or she existed, can get lost, and the fixity of identity suggested by one's association with one's name or material body is diminished. Wonderfully indifferent to race, gender, beauty, and station in life outside the Web, the network absorbs the individual into an interactive dialogue in which the conversation assumes a life of its own and threatens to eclipse the participants who provide its content. Moreover, the Internet, democratizing and emancipating because of the anarchic freedom of information and relationships that it makes possible, is certainly not immune to control and censorship, so that the freedom and equality one is able to achieve on it could, indeed, become specious, offering users a large quantity of qualitatively insignificant choices.

This study is an examination of selected examples of different kinds of texts in the light of this issue, in an attempt to determine what those texts say or imply about the subject, by their explicit representation of characters or figures, by their presentation of themselves as enunciations that may or may not seem to emanate from a unified source, and by their implications regarding the reader or the viewer they seem to address. The word "text" is used in the broadest way possible and might apply to any representation—a verbal text, a painting, a photograph, a film, or an e-mail conversation.

The first chapter treats examples of static, visual representation—painting and photography—moving from Renaissance works, which suggest a coherent, unified subject, and proceeding to examples of modern and postmodern works, which challenge that classical conception of the subject. The second chapter treats literary examples, which may imply a fixed subject but which more easily suggest flux, elusiveness, and transformation. The third chapter deals with film, which, because of the nature of the medium and because it is historically situated in the modern period, is likely to suggest a fluid, moving, ineluctable subject. Film, in fact, through editing and camera movement, invites the subversion of the classical subject, and only by developing specific, highly conventionalized strategies can it create and maintain the illusion of a fixed subject. The final chapter treats new means of representation and communication—hypertextual systems that seem to be empowering for readers and writers but also, both theoretically and practically, are challenging the classical subject, decentering it, and demanding that we redefine our notions of individuality, authorship, and responsibility. An epilogue will explore some of the ethical and political implications of challenges to and redefinitions of the subject.

Although the organization of this study is itself a construction, the various readings arranged at least partly for rhetorical effect, it is not merely so. It would be difficult to deny that something has changed or that our conception of the subject is in the process of being radically challenged and revised. If the classical subject was quietly confident in its fixity, the modern subject—as has often been noted—is not so sure of itself. For where exactly is this "self" that was the locus of Cartesian certainty and, even more so, of Romantic assertion, with its huge investment in individuality and genius? If the modern subject doubts itself, senses its diminution, the postmodern subject is more systematically challenged by philosophy and linguistics, which threaten finally to eliminate it entirely, except as a construction that can be deconstructed and reconstructed at will. Moreover, in the postmodern world the ubiquity of mass media representation—where the subject is reduced to a surface, a mask, and a commodity—shifts the challenge of philosophy and linguistics from the level of theory to that of the lived experience of everyday life. The modern subject bemoans the diminution of the self, in the face of mass society, industrialization, and closer Cartesian scrutiny; the postmodern subject finds this bemoaning an embarrassment, wondering if there ever was anything there whose loss is now to be grieved.

It is difficult to predict what impact electronic networking will have on this trajectory of challenge and diminution. Although it is likely that in the future video and the Internet, each appropriating characteristics of the other, will become less distinguishable, at this moment they remain quite different, the former centralized and one-way, the latter decentralized and interactive. As suggested above, the newly emerging subject of hypertext is ambivalently huge and small, spreading out from the material subject until it encompasses a dimensionless virtual universe within which it freely moves, accessing information, constructing new kinds of relationships, and redefining itself, while the older subject, physically positioned in front of a keyboard and monitor, is reduced to a code in that larger electronic network.

Acknowledgments

I would like to thank the University of South Florida for a Research and Creative Scholarship Award (Summer 1993) and a one-semester sabbatical (Fall 1993), during which I wrote most of the first draft of this book. Two sections have appeared previously, in slightly different form. Part of Chapter 1 appeared as "The Tie That Binds: *Arnolfini's Wedding* and Ideology," in *Word & Image, A Journal of Verbal/Visual Enquiry*, 8, no. 4 (October–December 1992): 344–350, reprinted by permission. Part of Chapter 3 appeared as "Rush's *The Stunt Man*: Politics, Metaphysics, and Psychoanalysis," in *Post Script: Essays in Film and the Humanities*, 4, no. 1 (Fall 1984): 18–34, reprinted by permission. I also want to thank David Erben for making me aware of the multimedia journal *Perforations* and loaning me a copy of the issue that included Stuart Moulthrop's interactive narrative, "Dreamtime," which I discuss in Chapter 4. I would like to give special thanks to Jerome E. Singerman, acquisitions editor for the University of Pennsylvania Press, and the outside reviewers of the manuscript, who did their best to get me to get it right. I want to thank Mindy Brown, project editor at UPP, who has been most pleasant to work with, as well as Jennifer Shenk, for her extremely meticulous copyediting. Finally and above all, I want to thank Pat, Marisa, and Olivia, who, throughout much of this writing, had to put up with my too often absent presence.

Chapter 1
The Subject's Eye

The Tie That Binds

It is a painting of a couple exchanging vows in a nuptial chamber. Light streams in through a window on the left, and the space of the picture opens back three-dimensionally, though it is a slightly odd space, in a way that is hard at first to define. Just as odd are the figures themselves, which seem to be represented realistically, and yet are stiff and mannequin-like, not quite human somehow. The room is presented with obsessive detail, an almost hallucinatory excess, more than what could be seen if one had been actually present, if one had been a real witness to a real event. The man faces the viewer, right hand raised; the woman faces him, her right hand resting on his left, her left hand touching her belly.

Two of the standard observations regarding this painting involve the unusual signature on the back wall, "Johannes de Eyck fuit hic, 1434," and the mirror below that signature, which reflects not only the couple but two witnesses, one of whom is probably the artist himself. Thus Jan van Eyck is doubly inscribed in the painting, utilizing a redundancy of two different semiotic modes, one visual, the other verbal, the first iconic and motivated, the second symbolic and arbitrary. Not insignificantly, these two modes correspond to the two key Lacanian psychoanalytic orders of subject formation: the imaginary and the symbolic. Analogously, van Eyck's status as an artist, who views the world and paints its representation, and his position as a citizen, who witnesses agreements and signs contracts, are brought together to create a powerful cultural valorization of his significance as an individual. Vision—apprehending an image of oneself as a unified physical coherence—and language—accepting and

Plate 1. Jan van Eyck, *The Wedding of Arnolfini*, 1434. Tempera and oil on wood, approx. 32″ × 23½″. The National Gallery, London. Reproduced by courtesy of the Trustees, the National Gallery, London.

Plate 2. *The Wedding of Arnolfini*, detail. Reproduced by courtesy of the Trustees, the National Gallery, London.

using the name by which one is identified—confirm an understanding of the individual subject as an existential given.

*   *   *

Erwin Panofsky, in his seminal study of the painting, published exactly five hundred years after the painting itself was completed, makes two points that are relevent here. He argues that the type of marriage represented is a *per fidem* marriage, that is, a marriage, fully legitimate before the Council of Trent, administered by two individuals to one another, requiring neither the presence of a priest nor that of witnesses. Couples could marry *per fidem* by means of a simple ritual—the taking of an oath while the groom raised one hand, a pledge (such as a ring for the bride), and the joining of hands ("Jan van Eyck's 'Arnolfini' Portrait," 196–198).

That this system, rooted in individual honor and honesty before God, produced problems was inevitable, allowing as it did plausible deniability for anyone wishing to withdraw from a marriage so effected. Thus, the institutionalization of a ritual requiring priest and witnesses. But even then (and now) the priest was a formal requirement and not the one who administered the sacrament. For a *per fidem* marriage, a personal vow between two individuals in the presence of God should be enough.

And yet it is not. For, as Panofsky also argued, the painting functions as a pictorial marriage certificate ("Jan van Eyck's 'Arnolfini' Portrait," 198). Van Eyck's unusual signature on the painting appears, as if on the wall, above the mirror at the back of the room. "Johannes de Eyck fuit hic" are words quite different from more typical signatures involving phrases such as "me fecit," "complevit," or Flemish equivalents (Baldass, 74). The wording of the signature here implies that van Eyck not only painted the picture but witnessed the wedding. The legalistic connotation of the signature is reinforced by the calligraphic style of its script, which one might expect in a legal document. Moreover, as if the words are not enough, the verbal symbol is reinforced by a visual signature—the image in the mirror that seems to confirm the fact that the artist was there, that further testifies to his presence as witness to the wedding. Finally, the style of the painting suggests—but only imperfectly—the existence of a coherent space viewed from a specific position. That is, even without the mirror the existence of a witnessing subject is implied.

Thus, the painting involves a great deal of redundancy. Various levels of sign and representation testify to the marriage and mutually reinforce one another. *The Wedding of Arnolfini*, in fact, exists as a *supplement*, presenting itself as a necessary completion for something that is presumably complete in itself (Derrida, *Of Grammatology*, 144–145). Marriage *per fidem* requires no witnesses. The couple simply takes its vow according to conventional words and gestures that signify its commitment. But the intensely legalistic nature of the painting subverts the nonlegalistic nature of *per fidem* marriage as well as the sense of individual human agency as in itself sufficient to guarantee such a marriage. The mere illusionistic representation of the marriage—implying as it does the existence of a witness—begins the subversion. However, as if this formally implied witness were insufficient, that insufficiency is compensated by the redundant verbal and visual signatures that make explicit the artist's role as witness, that articulate the painting as a quasi-legal document, and that bring the viewer into a complicity binding the couple not only in its own eyes and the eyes of God but also in the eyes of human society. Artist, viewer, and pictorial subject are all constituted as free subjects freely participating in a ritual that binds them absolutely. The painting thus subverts the nature of the very thing it claims to represent. Its existence as supplement suggests the insufficiency of the thing it would "merely" supplement. Panofsky all but said it himself: a painting of a *per fidem* marriage functions as a pictorial marriage certificate.

In this light, *The Wedding of Arnolfini* can be seen as representing a transition from the medieval vow to the Renaissance contract, from individual honor to legal accountability, and as an attempt to use the written word to pin down, fix, keep in place the more elusive vocal commitment.[1] Jan van Eyck and Giovanni Arnolfini had ties to both the nobility and the bourgeoisie. Both worked for Philip the Good of Burgundy. Van Eyck was a court artist, but he also went on numerous diplomatic missions for Philip. In Bruges, where he established himself permanently after 1430, he combined "the office of a court artist with the normal activities of a bourgeois master painter who would not consider it beneath his dignity to accept such commissions as the coloring and gilding of the statues on the facade of the Town hall" (Panofsky, *Early Netherlandish Painting*, 178). Arnolfini, a merchant from Lucca, was one of the many residents representing Italian business interests in Bruges, but he also was made knight and councillor to Philip. The extremely legalistic aspect of van Eyck's depiction of a personal and nonlegalistic marriage convention, in the context of the entrepreneurial world both men succeeded in and in the context of the relationship between Flanders and Italy at the outset of the Renaissance—represented respectively by the artist and subject of the painting—suggests that more is going on than the painting of a wedding portrait. The particular contract involved is a wedding contract, but it also connotes contracts in general. It is not simply that the painting may function as a "pictorial wedding certificate," binding Giovanni Arnolfini and Giovanna Cenami. The painting also valorizes contracts themselves.

Although some recent readings of the painting have argued that the subject cannot be assumed to be Arnolfini and Cenami or that the marriage is not, in fact, a *per fidem* marriage,[2] the painting's powerful imposition of legal and contractual force on personal honor and accountability to God is something that cannot be denied. Linda Seidel relates the content of the painting to Tuscan marriage rituals and the intensely legalistic aspects of such marriage arrangements, with their emphasis on strictly correct and explicit agreements regarding dowries and exchanges of money and women, as well as to the "increasing commercialization of fourteenth-and fifteenth-century life." She suggests that the painting very literally may have had legal status, offering testimony for Giovanna's father that he had transferred the dowry, guaranteeing its future return to Giovanna when necessary, and thereby protecting his estate from possible future claims (70–71).

Although Seidel's reading may be overly literal, inappropriately "attributing specific documentary significance to the image" and assuming it to have a legal force it could not possibly have had (Harbison, "Sexuality and Social Standing," 251–254), her emphasis on the economic aspect of the work is no doubt correct and explains the legalistic *tone* of the painting, which exists whether or not the work might *actually* have had legal force. It is not so much that the painting might have really been used as a wedding certificate, nor is it even so important that the painting be seen as depicting exactly an event that actually occurred—enabling later commentators to infer from details such as the joining of hands the precise marriage convention involved or the relative social status of the couple. Rather, what is important is the documentary and legalistic *effect* of the whole, the verbal and visual rhetoric that creates the *impression* of a documented truth—*like* a notarized legal document; *like* photographic documentation; and the enhanced documentational force that results from the rhetorical redundancy of word and image. The relationship between *The Wedding of Arnolfini* and a legal contract is analogous to the relationship between some nineteenth-century art and science. The narrative voice of a novel and the cool, "objective" documentation of light in an Impressionist painting seem to emulate the (presumed) disinterested objectivity of a scientist, though neither the writer nor the painter was a scientist and their works were not science. But such works nevertheless contributed to an ideology that valorized science and the scientific attitude. Similarly, *The Wedding of Arnolfini* may or may not have been capable of legal force in an actual court of law, and it may or may not have documented literally an actual event. Nevertheless, its legalistic and documentary tone corroborate an ideology that valorizes the contract as a document that mediates and informs all human relationships: marriages, business arrangements, agreements between artist and patron.

In van Eyck's painting two semiotic modes, one verbal, the other visual, are used to reinforce one another, like a notarized statement combined with a documentary photograph, in order to dispel any doubts regarding the essential truth of the couple's marriage and to suture any possible gaps between sign and referent.[3]

And yet the suture is not so perfect. In the relationship between the verbal and the visual "signatures," each in different ways testifying to the presence of the artist as witness, there is an uneasy relationship between two kinds of semiosis. The struggle to synthesize the iconic (in the Peircian sense) [4] and the iconographic (in the Panofskian sense), the illusionistic and the symbolic, the "motivated" and the "arbitrary," is only partly successful. The image in the mirror and the words above it may be equal partners, alternative semiotic modes that each testify to the presence of van Eyck as witness to the event. But the balance is almost too equal to be stable. Michel Foucault, discussing the relationship between words and images in Western painting, writes,

In one way or another, subordination is required. Either the text is ruled by the image . . . or else the image is ruled by the text. . . . True, the subordination remains stable only very rarely. What happens to the text of the book is that it becomes merely a commentary on the image, and the linear channel, through words, of its simultaneous forms; and what happens to the picture is that it is dominated by a text, all of whose significations it figuratively illustrates. (*This Is Not a Pipe*, 32–33)

The problem with the dual "signatures" in *Arnolfini* is that they are too equal for comfort. One tends to want to hierarchize them, to regard the image as an illustration for the words or the words as a caption for the picture, to regard one as dominant and the other as marginal.

A similar ambivalence exists in other aspects of the painting as well. The ambivalence between the iconic and the iconographic, between a semiotics based on resemblance and one based on convention, is evident in the contradictory way in which the objects of the painting can be regarded. If the objects symbolize moral or religious qualities or truths because of iconographic conventions, areas of paint are read as objects by means that are presumably less arbitrary and more illusionistic. The illusionistic or "motivated" and the iconographic or conventional partly reinforce each other, it is true.[5] But the painting seems so intensely committed to both that there is a competition between them as well, as if it is uncertain which is the privileged mode, which is most forceful in testifying to a "truth." After all, if an object functions primarily as a symbol, why should so much effort be expended in representing it in all its material specificity? On the other hand, if representation of the visual and textural details of the material world is the goal, the symbolic status of objects must be seen as a distraction, implying that the importance of an object is not its unique materiality but an abstract quality toward which it points. If the main purpose of the dog is its function as a symbol of fidelity, do we need to see each of its hairs? On the other hand, if it functions as an example of the lush materiality associated with a bourgeois world, doesn't its symbolic status in the marital portrait act as an anachronistic and barely necessary religious rationalization?

And since, in painting, motivated, illusionistic signs tend to be associated with realism and the secular, and iconographic and conventional signs with religion and the sacred, this uneasiness is echoed on that other level as well. Is the social and legalistic recording of the marriage vow, meticulously depicted through van Eyck's hyperrealistic style, simply the pragmatically necessary documentation of an essentially sacred vow? Or is the religious dimension of the work, revealed largely through iconographic implications of the objects present in the room, used ideologically to valorize something that is primarily secular, used to mystify what is, after all, a legal arrangement. As Seidel states, the merchant-banker class "accommodated its commercial activities to meet requirements of religion, and it adjusted matrimonial ritual to reinforce market practice," using "art's persuasive powers to put a good, 'spiritual' face on the matter" (84–85).

There are other uneasinesses and ambiguities in the painting. Perspective is handled in such a way as to effectively create an illusion of three dimensions; at the same time, it does not precisely follow the rules of linear perspective that had recently developed in Italy. Although the *Arnolfini* portrait seems at first glance to conform to the rules of single point perspective, there are at least two separate, inconsistent vanishing points in the painting. The orthogonals of the ceiling converge near the upper edge of the mirror, and the orthogonals of the floor in the area of the couple's joined hands.[6] The result is an uneasiness, a subtle distortion the cause of which is difficult to identify. On an intuitive level an illusion of three dimensions is effectively created. At the same time, there is something a little "off" about the perspective and, consequently, something a little off about the position of the viewer. The split vanishing points split the viewer's position, leave the viewer ambiguously situated, disturbingly decentered, albeit only slightly. It is as if the painting is "hailing" the subject, to use Louis Althusser's word, saying to the viewer, "Hey, you there!" (Althusser, 162–164), struggling to fix the viewer, to constitute the viewer as a subject, as an individual occupying a specific place at a specific time who can be relied upon, held responsible. But the painting is not *quite* doing so, or doing so imperfectly.

The mirror image also creates a disturbance to that viewing subject who at first seems to be so clearly and unambiguously hailed. In illusionistic painting it is assumed that the viewer, stepping before the work, in effect displaces the artist, assumes more or less the position the artist occupied (actually or imaginatively) when viewing the scene. Standing before this painting, however, one sees two individuals reflected in the mirror, in approximately the position the viewer actually occupies. Thus, the viewer first displaces the artist but is subsequently displaced by the artist, who impossibly reasserts himself, forces himself by means of the reflection back onto the spot the viewer occupies. The viewer's identity is affirmed only to be rejected, denied, and replaced by that of the artist, whose presence and authority is doubly affirmed by image and inscription.

Finally, the human figures, their expressions, gestures, and postures, seem stiff and mannequin-like. This presentation of the human seems especially odd in a work that exists at the outset of that epoch that has been characterized as "humanistic." According to Panofsky, the price of the rigorous visual discipline of van Eyck's mature or "classical" work was stasis and emotional restraint (*Early Netherlandish Painting*, 182). He compares the *Arnolfini* figures with those on medieval slab tombs, which he suggests are a possible antecedent for van Eyck's composition. Although his comparison is made on the basis of the "statuesque" quality of the figures, the composition consisting of two full-length figures, and the presence of a dog ("Jan van Eyck's 'Arnolfini' Portrait," 199), there is something poetically correct about comparing van Eyck's figures to stone figures associated with death.

Thus, this extremely legalistic painting, which presents individuals freely submitting to a commitment to which they will be subsequently bound, seems a perfect illustration of Althusser's description of the subject interpellated in ideology:

the individual *is interpellated as a (free) subject in order that he shall submit freely to the commandments of the Subject, i.e. in order that he shall (freely) accept his subjection,* i.e. in order that he shall make the gestures and actions of his subjection "all by himself." *There are no subjects except by and for their subjection.* That is why they "work all by themselves." (169)

*   *   *

Traditional criticism of *The Wedding of Arnolfini* has emphasized its "realistic" aspects, both visually and in terms of its subject matter. Thus, it has been seen as a precursor to seventeenth-century genre painting. Since Panofsky, on the other hand, its religious iconography has also been emphasized. However, besides its realistic and religious dimensions, the painting is also an allegory of bourgeois ideology. The wedding taking place is as much a wedding between the north and south as it is between the individuals represented: northern artist, southern subject; the northern medium of oil, the perspective being developed by the Italians; Gothic naturalism, Renaissance illusionism. Most significantly, the painting stands as an emblem for all the legal contracts articulating business arrangements that bound Italy and Flanders. This painting of what is nominally the taking of a marital oath by two individuals in the presence of God has a subtext that valorizes the written contract as a legal document that informs and controls all human relationships. It is an ideological support for the ideology of contracts.

But in order for that ideology to work its first operation must be the construction of subjects who conceive of themselves as such, subjects who freely accept their subjectivity. Althusser writes that "with the rise of bourgeois ideology, above all with the rise of legal ideology, the category of the subject . . . is the constitutive category of all ideology" (160). The word subject here connotes both the idea of an individual human subjectivity and the idea of that subject being "subject" to a larger force or forces. The subject is "hailed" and "interpellated" by ideology when it becomes a subject of discourse, when it can be represented in language and other representational systems. Subjects properly constituted by ideology freely submit to their subjection because they see it not as a social construction but as something natural and appropriate. Thus, an "ideological" state apparatus makes it possible to avoid more overt means of coercion by the "repressive" state apparatus, coercion, that is, that would resort to utilizing police, courts, or the army.

[T]he subjects "work," they "work by themselves" in the vast majority of cases, with the exception of "bad subjects" who on occasion provoke the intervention of one of the detachments of the (repressive) State apparatus. But the vast majority of (good) subjects work all right "all by themselves," i.e. by ideology. . . . They "recognize" the existing state of affairs (*das Bestehende*), that "it really is true that it is so and not otherwise," and that they must be obedient to God, to their conscience, to the priest, to de Gaulle, to the boss, to the engineer. . . . Their concrete, material behaviour is simply the inscription in life of the admirable words of the prayer: "*Amen—So be it.*" (169)

The *Arnolfini* portrait illustrates the ideological functioning of representation in that it involves a certain kind of subject construction in relation to three different subjectivities: that of the artist, doubly inscribed into the work; that of the subjects represented, the mannequin-like Arnolfini and Cenami freely accepting their own subjectivity; and that of the viewer, who becomes also a witness to the wedding, becomes complicitous in binding the couple that freely binds itself.

Perhaps most significant is that the painting interpellates the subject both visually and verbally, thus elegantly juxtaposing Lacan's imaginary mode, instigated by the Mirror Phase (a notion of subject construction that results from the infant's identification with a visual image of coherence and unity) with his symbolic mode (a notion of subject construction that arises with the entry into language and discourse). The presence of the artist is attested to by both the inscription and the mirror reflection, and this doubly inscribed subject is echoed confusingly in the viewer of the painting. The painting's visual plenitude is a seductive appeal to the imaginary, and the verbal inscription an appeal to the symbolic. Those two modes echo the contrast between motivated and arbitrary signs, the iconic and the iconographic, which work in concert, complementing but also competing with each other, in an attempt to fix and hold a subject (artist, viewer, figure) and dispel any lingering doubts regarding the undeniable and essential presence of that subject.

However, the painting has a number of cracks and contradictions that make its ideological project less than seamless. If the words and gestures that constitute the marital vows and commitments are the things that are central to a marriage, why should such a legalistic representation of the event be necessary at all, especially one that involves such obsessive detail, the inclusion of witnesses, as well as redundant verbal and visual confirmation of one of those witnesses? Renaissance "realism" and medieval iconography do not fully merge; the "motivated" and "arbitrary" aspects of the painting's semiotics—word and image, symbol and illusionistic representation—are mutually subversive, even when they seem to support one another. The three-dimensional space is effective but inconsistent, suggesting a coherent viewing subject but simultaneously fracturing and decentering that subject. Moreover, that viewing subject is denied and negated by the mirror, which returns not his or her image but that of the artist and some other authority. And the figures in the painting are dehumanized, static, like automatons, suggesting a conflicting view of the human being: the agent who freely engages in a contract is the subject who is bound by it; once signed, the social contract becomes like a law of nature, and human beings, like objects, must obey that law.

The Keys of Power

Althusser, arguing that the formal structure of ideology is always the same, chooses religious ideology as a model to illustrate the operations of ideology generally. God is the Subject above all other subjects, who speaks through ideology (manifest through scripture, tradition, and institutional authority) to name individuals and constitute them as free and responsible subjects.

[Ideology] says: I address myself to you, a human individual called Peter (every individual is called by his name, in the passive sense, it is never he who provides his own name), in order to tell you that God exists and that you are answerable to Him. It adds: God addresses himself to you through my voice (Scripture having collected the Word of God, Tradition having transmitted it, Papal Infallibility fixing it for ever on "nice" points). It says: this is who you are: you are Peter! This is your origin, you were created by God for all eternity. . . . This is your place in the world! This is what you must do! (165–166)

Echoing Lacan, Althusser argues that ideology and the constitution of subjects by the Subject is "specular"; it involves a mirroring of the Subject by the subjects. "[A]ll ideology is *centered* . . . the Absolute Subject occupies the unique place of the Centre, and interpellates around it the infinity of individuals into subjects in a double mirror-connexion such that it *subjects* the subjects to the Subject" (168).

One is reminded of Perugino's Sistine Chapel fresco, *Giving the Keys to St. Peter* (1481), which valorizes the scriptural, traditional, and institutional forces that carry religious ideology. Like *The Wedding of Arnolfini*, it is a depiction of a contract of sorts, and, as in van Eyck's painting, linear perspective functions—more coherently here—to hail the viewing subject and to constitute the viewer as an involved witness to the event.

In the foreground center Christ hands the keys of heaven and earth to a kneeling Peter, who receives them. The keys—analogous to the exchange of tokens that might be part of a marriage ritual—occupy the exact foreground center of the painting, midway between the two main protagonists of the visual narration. Two groups of figures flank Christ and Peter. The piazza is formally divided into a perspective grid consisting of large rectangles whose orthogonal sides converge at a vanishing point behind a Renaissance church—domed and centrally organized—that dominates the background of the painting. The symmetry thus continues from the foreground through the middle ground into the background. In the middle ground are two biblical scenes, each also containing the figure of Christ as the main character. On the left is the "render unto Caesar what is Caesar's" scene and on the right is the stoning of Christ. The church in the back is flanked symmetrically by two identical classical triumphal arches.

Christ and Peter, involved in an ideological transfer of religious authority, are centrally located, surrounded by the groups on their left and right, by the (anachronistic) scenes in the middle ground (the figures of

Plate 3. Perugino, *Giving the Keys to St. Peter*, 1481. Fresco. Sistine Chapel, Vatican, Rome. Reproduced by courtesy of the Vatican Museums.

which might almost be mistaken for bystanders on the piazza, if one did not look at them too closely), and by the viewer, whose position in front of the scene is implied by the single-point perspective. The Absolute Subject and his representative, a subject who will become a stand-in for the Absolute Subject, thus occupy the appropriate place at the center of the scene.

Giving the Keys is a painting that involves Catholic religious ideology, it is true. But implicit in the intellectualized perspective of the painting and in the contractual connotations of the painting's subject (the transfer of religious authority from God to his representative) is a valorization of the individual subject and the binding force of contracts on individuals that is akin to van Eyck's *Arnolfini* painting. The relationship between Christ and Peter, the rock upon which the church is founded, is a kind of contract, and the viewer—localized in space and time in front of the painting, constituted as an individual who is also an imaginary witness to the event—is brought into a binding complicity. The viewer, as a member of the Christian community, is consequently bound by the terms of the contract—bound, that is, to recognize the Church as the rightful, "authorized" purveyor of Christ's teachings on earth. But the valorization of contracts that bound individuals—individuals understood as *individuals*—on the basis of honor and legal force was also essential to the effective workings of trade and commerce at a time when the bourgeoisie was growing as a major social force.

At the same time, although the perspective in this painting is logically coherent optically, there is nevertheless something stiff about it. As is often the case with Quattrocento space, it is a highly intellectualized space that lacks a sense of natural recession from foreground through middleground into background. There are four spatially distinct areas of activity or interest: Christ, Peter, and the flanking groups in the foreground; the biblical scenes in the middle ground; the church and arches of the background; and the distant landscape in aerial perspective. No figures or forms, apart from the orthogonals of the perspectival grid laid out on the piazza, mediate spatially among those areas.

Moreover, in spite of the logic of the perspective, the position of the viewer of the painting is unnaturally high. No doubt the reason for this not-quite-human point of view was Perugino's desire to present the entire scene, from foreground through middleground to background. If the point of view had been "normal," the figures in the forgeround would block the figures and forms of the middleground and background. Thus, the impulse to create a convincing, human-centered illusion of the events represented and the impulse to create a full and complete picture of those events come into conflict with one another.

The artist chooses totality and in doing so compromises the illusion of a human perspective. As a result, the humanistic project is subtly subverted from within.

That "project" might be summarized: Christ is God incarnate; he comes to earth and, in anticipation of his death, transmits temporal and spiritual power to a representative. His manner of doing so connotes other contractual obligations that, similarly, must be obeyed: render unto Caesar that which is Caesar's and unto God that which is God's.

This message would be most forceful when, as much as possible, it is expressed in representations that create an illusion of the world, viewed from a human perspective, thus subtly implicating the viewer into the obligations suggested by the scene. Optical perspective is useful in achieving this implied interpellation of the viewer by the work. However, here the need to present the scene fully results in an abnormally high vantage point, an unnatural, not-quite-human, position for the viewer.

This is a common tension in classic realist texts. The impulse to include all of the information relevent to the world that the text represents suggests a desire to present an omniscient, godlike point of view. But this impulse must be balanced with the need to present that world as—at least with reasonable suspension of disbelief—*humanly* comprehensible. If the devices necessary to represent a total world become too extreme or obvious, the illusion will be subverted. The impulse of classic realism to present a complete world and to present its apprehension as a human possibility are at odds with one another. If skillfully negotiated this tension may not be noticed and the viewer will achieve a sense of mastery that confirms logocentricism—his or her sense of being a centered consciousness capable of intellectually apprehending the world. However, if not successfully negotiated, the artifice of the entire construct will become evident and the ideological force of the representation will be compromised.

The Flattened Subject

If the ideology of individuality, individual responsibility, and the binding force of contracts gropes toward articulation in van Eyck's *Arnolfini* and Perugino's *Giving the Keys*, Pablo Picasso's *Demoiselles d'Avignon* (1907) gropes to de-articulate it, to decenter the subject. *Demoiselles* is a painting that is frequently taken as an announcement of modernism, a visual manifesto that is an example of the thing it proclaims, a declaration that the old painting of illusion is dead. Certainly one can find earlier antecedents to modern painting—in the work of Manet and Cézanne, especially—but in spite of earlier antecedents, *Demoiselles* has such a dis-

Plate 4. Pablo Picasso, *Demoiselles d'Avignon*, 1907. Oil on canvas, 8′ × 7′8″ (243.9 cm × 233.7 cm). The Museum of Modern Art, New York. Acquired through the Lillie P. Bliss Bequest. Photograph © 1996 The Museum of Modern Art, New York. © 1996 Succession Picasso/Artists Rights Society (ARS), New York.

ruptive potential, even today, that it is often used as a convenient marker for the beginning of modern art. Moreover, the formal problems it announced (evident earlier in Manet and Cézanne and more contemporaneously in Matisse and the *Fauves*) are problems that artists have continued to grapple with until very recently.

Picasso's painting decenters the subject—both the represented subject and the viewing subject. Renaissance space is self-consciously subverted, the various planes pushing forward to create an approximate congruence of illusionistic pictorial space and the actual flat surface of the canvas, like the sides of a cardboard box unfolded and flattened into a messy two-dimensionality. Different parts of the faces are seen simultaneously frontally and in profile, and the table in the foreground (to the extent that one can legitimately speak of a foreground in this painting) tips forward unnaturally, as if viewed from above rather than from the angle one might expect, given the eye-level viewpoint of the painting generally.

Demoiselles calls to mind Laura Mulvey's description, in "Visual Pleasure and Narrative Cinema," of the threat the image of a woman presents in narrative film—threatening because its erotic appeal and its evocation of castration anxiety tend to subvert the forward movement of narrative representation. Close-ups of legs and faces present, for Mulvey, fragmented images that work against the visual and narrative illusionism of the film. "One part of a fragmented body destroys the Renaissance space, the illusion of depth demanded by the narrative, it gives flatness, the quality of a cut-out or icon rather than verisimilitude to the screen" (309). For Mulvey, the cinematic image of a woman threatens to flatten things both spatially and temporally. Close-ups minimize the possibility for deep space and, at the same time, the narrative, dominated by a controlling male protagonist, tends to stop while the camera obsessively scrutinizes the erotic object. The lure of the imaginary threatens the phallocentrically dominated symbolic order.

In *Demoiselles*, the women—who, not insignificantly, represent prostitutes in a brothel, presented for the scrutiny of a client—push toward the surface in an obvious spatial flattening. Painting can, of course, only suggest narrativity, and therefore narrative flattening is less significant; it is, in fact, the norm in painting to "flatten" narrativity around a key incident in a larger story that may be evoked. Nevertheless, in preliminary studies for *Demoiselles*, the painting's "narrative" was more fully suggested. In these studies one or both of two potential clients—a sailor and a medical student—were included.

An examination of several of these studies alongside the final painting shows a progressive flattening of the space of the painting and a final decision to eliminate the clients (Rubin, 86–87, 98–99). There is still the implication that the women, at least the two most central figures, are being presented to a client, but that client is no longer visibly present in the pictorial space. In fact, it is the viewer who now assumes the client position. This positioning is not a spatially coherent position, resulting from Renaissance perspective, which implies the viewer's presence through the geometry of optics, but is a result of the eye contact the central women make with the viewer. The figure on the left pulls back a curtain revealing those women to us, explicitly presenting them as objects for our visual scrutiny.

The flattening of the painting, conjoined with the viewer's displacing the clients previously depicted explicitly in the painting, pushes the women threateningly toward the viewer. The women are presented as objects of desire, perhaps, but also of fear—as evidenced by the African-esque figures on the right. Mulvey, accepting Freud's explanation of the anxiety the female figure evokes in the male viewer, writes,

> the woman as icon, displayed for the gaze and enjoyment of men, the active con-trollers of the look, always threatens to evoke the anxiety it originally signified. The male unconscious has two avenues of escape from this castration anxiety: preoccupation with the re-enactment of the original trauma (investigating the woman, demystifying her mystery), counterbalanced by the devaluation, pun-ishment or saving of the guilty object . . . ; or else complete disavowal of castra-tion by the substitution of a fetish object or turning the represented figure itself into a fetish so that it becomes reassuring rather than dangerous. ("Visual Plea-sure," 311)

Although Mulvey, in this essay, is using psychoanalytic ideas to explain aspects of narrative film, the first strategy she describes—preoccupation, investigation, demystification, and devaluation—could easily apply to *Demoiselles*. Mulvey is perhaps too uncritical in her acceptance of Freud's explanation of the cause of male anxiety over female genitalia. Why not explain it as a fear of women's power rather than a fear of women as images of emasculation? But regardless of its cause, the painting suggests the anxiety as well as the attempt to come to terms with it through obses-sive scrutiny and devaluation. The Africanesque faces, for all their im-portance as formal innovation and exploration, still are threatening. And the (male) viewer, thrust into the client position, is disrupted. De-pending on the viewer, of course, the painting might be seen as an invi-tation to critically examine the image of woman as an object of desire and dread, or it might be taken as a confirmation of misogyny.

A common way of evading the entire issue is to treat the painting solely as a study in formal organization and the reconstruction of pictorial space. It would, however, be disingenuous to argue that Picasso's incor-poration of such brutal and garish distortions of form and color are *merely* the result of such experiments, stimulated by his exposure to Afri-can sculpture or paintings by artists like Cézanne and Matisse. Certainly many writers have noted the connections between Picasso's artistic ca-reer, its various styles and themes, and his relationships with women. Pi-erre Daix, acknowledging cultural and political factors in the creation of *Demoiselles*, has also said of it, "it is impossible not to infer that it is Fernande [Fernande Olivier, Picasso's mistress at the time] whose image he was now destroying" (72). This is not to reduce the reading of the painting to one that is grounded in artistic intentionality, but only to suggest that its aggressiveness toward women is obvious.

If there is aggression in the painting, there is also dread, and that dread implies a vulnerability on the part of the viewer of women. The viewer of *Demoiselles* (like the viewer of disruptive segments of Mulvey's narrative film) is thrust into an incomprehensible space of crumbling facets, segments of female form that one moment allure, another moment disrupt, and tumble toward him, so that his own position analogously threatens to dissolve across a plane in front of the canvas. The image of the female—because of its own power and because it suggests the possibility of an erotic dissolution into the imaginary—threatens the integration of the viewer's ego and his sense of mastery.

The stylistic discontinuity of Picasso's painting—suggesting variously African, Iberian, and Egyptian, as well as Cézannian, sources—similarly suggests an incoherence and incongruity of the depicted subject, just as the spatial inconsistency suggests an incoherence and incongruity in the viewer, in stark contrast to the logical coherence implied by Renaissance space. In later, more fully developed works of analytical cubism, Picasso further fragments and dissolves the subject—the human subject and the subject of the work.

The Gendered Subject

Barbara Kruger utilizes various visual-verbal strategies that challenge and confuse the voyeuristic viewer and deconstruct the image of woman as sexual object, sometimes utilizing techniques partly derived from cubism: fragmentation, collage, and the juxtaposition of verbal and visual elements. In Kruger's work, of course, the critique of gender construction—along with that of consumerism, violence, and the imagery, slogans, and catchphrases of contemporary mass media—is explicit. In an untitled work of 1982 (called, for convenience, *You Are Not Yourself*), an image of a woman's face is reflected in a shattered mirror. Her hand, in the lower left, holds the mirror and the fragmented image it reflects. The words, "You are not yourself," are collaged over the picture. Significantly, the letters that spell out those words are placed in separate, individual blocks. Thus, the constructed nature of the linguistic sign is emphasized. The alphabetic elements that make up the written words, suggesting the phonetic components of their vocal construction, are foregrounded. The pronoun "you" is ambiguous, referring to the fragmented woman in the painting but also a direct address to the viewer,

Plate 5. Pablo Picasso, *Portrait of Ambroise Vollard*, 1909–10. Oil on canvas, 36¼″ × 25⅝″. The Pushkin State Museum of Fine Arts, Moscow. © 1996 Succession Picasso/Artists Rights Society (ARS), New York. Photograph: Giraudon/Art Resource, New York.

Plate 6. Barbara Kruger, *Untitled* (*You Are Not Yourself*), 1982. Photograph, 72″ × 48″. Collection Edward R. Downe Jr. Courtesy of Mary Boone Gallery, New York.

conflating the two. The image itself also confuses representation and viewer in that (as in the *Arnolfini* portrait) the mirror image the painting reflects back to the viewer is not her or his own.

The gender of the viewer, the "you" who is often addressed by Kruger's slogans and ironic epigrams, varies, depending on the phrase in which the pronoun is embedded and the image with which it is juxtaposed. In this case, the viewer/reader is assumed to be female. And that female subject—represented subject conflated with viewing subject— who is denied her subjectivity is represented both visually and verbally by absence. The word "not" appears directly in the middle of the picture, and above and slightly to the left of it is the hole—another absence— left by the bullet (we assume it was a bullet) that caused the shattering of the mirror.

What is suggested is a binarism that is capable of conceiving of a woman only as a negation, as a man who is lacking. This binarism has been often discussed, usually, directly or indirectly, in the context of Freud's discussions of female sexuality and fetishism. The word "not," located in the center of Kruger's work, between sections of the fragmented face, suggests this subject constructed around an absence, and the hole above it—an opening, an absence, created and penetrated simultaneously by a bullet—echoes that absence. Craig Owens writes,

The critique of binarism is sometimes dismissed as intellectual fashion; it is, however, an intellectual imperative, since the hierarchical opposition of marked and unmarked terms (the decisive/divisive presence/absence of the phallus) is the dominant form both of representing difference and justifying its subordination in our society. What we must learn, then, is how to conceive difference without opposition. (191)

Gender, when construed in binary terms, can only be understood as a function of the difference between a positive term—the phallus—and its absence. The possibility of two contrasting but not contradictory terms, different but not logically opposed or hierarchized, is not recognized.

The aggression represented in Kruger's work is a phallic aggression, suggested by the bullet hole—guns and bullets being major cultural signs of phallic power—but it is also a power of the visual image and the verbal slogan, both ubiquitous aspects of a society saturated by mass-produced imagery, most of it devoted to encouraging consumption and constructing identities that view consumption as essential. The bullet itself creates the absence, the hole (an empty space, not an organ); it castrates woman and organizes her identity around an absence by defining her only as a negation. And verbally that identity is indicated by the word "not," located in the middle.

Freud, in "Female Sexuality," insists on defining feminity in terms of the absence of a phallus even though in the same essay he also acknowledges the double aspect of female genitals—comprised of both a clitoris ("analogous to the male organ") and a vagina ("the female organ proper"). Freud's own anatomical description implies fairly clearly what he refuses to acknowledge: that they are not mere absences but organs in their own right (227–235).[7]

Freud's binary understanding of gender is, of course, a standard target for feminist theorists, who frequently provide alternative views of the supposed lack that exists in female biology. Luce Irigaray describes the denial of women's sexuality as a "castration": "How could she be anything but suggestible and hysterical when her sexual instincts have been castrated, her sexual feelings, representatives, and representations forbidden?" (59–60). Irigaray argues, in fact, that woman's sexuality is not simply double (based on the clitoris and the vagina) but plural, many areas and organs of her body capable of providing erotic pleasure. For theorists like Irigaray and Hélène Cixous woman's pleasure is fluid, multiple, diverse, and nonhierarchical, in contrast to the defined, limited, and hierarchical male pleasure (Marks and de Courtivron, 90–106). Taking a rigorous nonessentialist position, Kaja Silverman argues that the symbolism attached to biology is not the result of any innate or inevitable response but is itself cultural. Possessing or not possessing a penis doesn't in itself create psychologies of power or weakness, but the penis becomes associated with power and value *because* men, who have penises, also have power.

We must consequently understand the attribution of superiority to the penis and inferiority to the clitoris as occurring from a point fully within patriarchal culture. It is only after the subject has arrived at an understanding of the privileged status afforded men and the de-privileged status afforded women within the current symbolic order that sexual difference can be read in the way suggested by Freud. In short, it is only retroactively that anatomy is confused with destiny. (142)

Not only is phallocentrism manifest in the ability to control language, but it is also manifest in the power to control the visual world—to control and define by seeing, both through the gaze itself and by controlling the images that dominate the visual landscape in which we live. This struggle to achieve mastery by means of the gaze has been related to Freud's description of fetishism as resulting from the trauma experienced by a male child after seeing female genitals, which appear as a lack and provoke in the male child a realization of castration as a possibility. The fetish is a retreat from a visually apprehended truth, a signifier that stands in for the phallus and that conceals its absence (Freud, 152–157). The obsession with vision and visual mastery of the world is seen as a response to this trauma and to the realization of male vulnerability (Owens, 198–200).

Kruger's work reflects this construction of woman around a negative, a project evident in the mass media as well as Freud. The female subject is denied her own subjectivity and is an object of the gaze of others. *You Are Not Yourself* suggests a woman's psychological projection of herself out of herself onto an other who views her and the resulting fragmentation and decentering of the female subject.

Of course, according to Lacan, all subject construction—for both men and women, both in the imaginary and symbolic orders—is a misrecognition, an attempt to deny a fundamental lack. That lack results from a developmental prematurity characteristic of human infancy, an experience the individual has of lacking focus and control of his or her body. Lacan describes "a real *specific prematurity of birth* in man," and "a certain dehiscence at the heart of the organism, a primordial Discord betrayed by the signs of uneasiness and motor unco-ordination of the neo-natal months" (4). It is only the apprehension of a visual image of unity and, later, representation of the subject in language that provide the illusion of a coherent self. The difference between men and women is not a matter of fundamental lack or presence; both experience equally such a lack. Rather, with the entry into the symbolic—structured by the binary logic of phallocentrism, misrecognized as it may be—the male is represented (or misrepresented), recognized (or misrecognized) as a positive and the female as a negative.

In *You Are Not Yourself* the Lacanian misrecognition of a unitary self is destroyed by the shattered mirror that reasserts the primordial disunity of the subject. At the same time, the words "You are not yourself" affirm the alienation that results from both imaginary identification with a visual image and the symbolic interpellation of the subject by language.

In Kruger's art, keeping women locked in this binarism, in which they are always characterized by a lack, is tied in with the way they are represented in the mass media and with the need to continue an ideology of consumerism. Kruger's images are generally appropriated from mass media sources, which she sometimes modifies, sometimes presents intact, and they are juxtaposed with slogans, clichés, and catchphrases that are themselves sometimes altered and sometimes not. By means of these visual-verbal collages, she reveals the way mass-produced imagery is used to present consumption as a solution to the lack that defines woman.

There is often a wry wit in these visual-verbal juxtapositions: A large black-and-white hand holds a red rectangle on which the words "I shop, therefore I am" are printed. In this obvious joke on the Cartesian argument for the existential certainty of the self, consuming displaces thinking. In another work, the words "Buy me, I'll change your life" are juxtaposed with a horrific image of a fragmented and distorted doll or puppet—or possibly a ventriloquist's dummy. Of course, since woman is a negative not only in the originary disunity of the "hommelette"—a Lacanian pun, combining "omelette" and "little man" and suggesting the amorphous, fluid, formlessness of the infant (Coward and Ellis, 101)—but also in the negative position she occupies in symbolic representation, none of this will work. But producing and encouraging the desire to achieve an impossible completeness by buying something to fill an absence that can't be filled is effective marketing. Ironically, the fact that the desire cannot be fulfilled does not make it less effective a strategy but more effective; having consumed and been left unsatisfied, one remains vulnerable to the ideology that encourages one to consume again.

The representation of woman caught in the prisonhouse of media images is most pointed in a lenticular photograph—a photo whose image changes according to the angle viewed—of 1985. From an angle, the words "Help! I'm locked inside this picture" appear on a red ground. A direct viewing of the picture reveals the image of a woman holding a frame in front of her face. The words "We are astonishingly lifelike" appear in the frame, one word near each of the four corners. The frame, like a prison, encloses a "real" woman's face, and her hands are visible at the bottom holding it up. She stares directly at the viewer, like a real person, but the first person plural phrase implies her artificiality. The work thus combines two contradictory messages: "This is a representation of a real woman holding a frame in front of her face," and "This is a realistic, 'astonishingly lifelike,' illusion." What is implied is the existence of a submerged and marginalized other that lies behind the personae of women who successfully emulate their media images. Such a presence is threatening, certainly, implying that the women we seem to know are really masks worn by a more elusive, hidden, and dangerous other whom we do not know so well, a "dark continent" that lies outside of representation, "a real which threatens to submerge not only the female subject but the entire order of signification" (Silverman, 187).[8]

Kruger's work suggests Irigaray's strategy of mimicry, in which the individual parodically accepts the identity that is imposed on her in order to subvert that identity.

Through her acceptance of what is in any case an ineluctable mimicry, Irigaray doubles it back on itself. . . . Hers is a theatrical staging of the mime: miming the miming imposed on woman, Irigaray's subtle specular move (her mimicry *mirrors* that of all women) intends to *undo* the effects of phallocentric discourse simply by *overdoing* them. . . . Irigaray's undermining of patriarchy through the overmiming of its discourses may be the one way out of the straitjacket of phallocentrism. (Moi, 140)

This kind of mimicry, a parodic acceptance of images and roles imposed by the media, is a strategy also utilized by Cindy Sherman. Sherman's images are not so literally appropriated as are Kruger's; they are photographs of herself taken by herself. But they evoke various conventions of the mass media, including those of movies, fashion photography, and centerfolds.

Sherman's use of herself as her primary subject, presented in different ways in order to suggest one stereotype or another, results in a critique of the idea of the unitary subject. Sherman radically alters her makeup, hair color and style, and dress, in addition to the attitude and personality she performs. Because she presents such different "selves" in her photographs, the very notion of a self being portrayed is called into question. Her various series of self-photographs are, therefore, very different from the kinds of series of self-portraits one finds among canonized artists like Rembrandt or Van Gogh. In the latter, changes of condition, experience, age, and artistic development affect the appearance, mood, attitude, and artistic style of the representation. The differences among such self-portraits tend to be seen as changes in a unified subject rather than as challenges to the idea of a unified subject. In Sherman's photographs, the subject presented is so different in look and character that—even though we know that it is always Sherman herself, in one guise or another, who is the performer posed in front of the camera—it is very difficult to think of the various figures as images of the same person.

In a sense, Sherman's works are not really self-portraits, and her craft is not primarily photography. Arthur Danto says that her work must be positioned midway between photography and performance (11). Her makeup, her dress, the mise-en-scène, and her performed gestures, postures, and expressions are at least as important in producing the final work as the photographic process itself. In posing for the camera it is more as if she is playing a role the way an actor would than presenting an aspect of her "self."

On the other hand, the photograph is more central to her work than would be a photograph that functioned primarily as a *documentation* for a performance. Composition, light, graininess, and color are all carefully calculated to help evoke a certain milieu or convention. For Sherman the photograph is the final product and the goal. Thus, she is, in effect, a performer who performs primarily for the still camera. She does not perform live, but her performances are necessarily mediated by photography, which makes its own essential contribution to the effect of the work.

Although any individual work is a performance of a character and not a self-portrait, Sherman's work, taken as a whole, *is* about her, as Danto

Plate 7. Cindy Sherman, *Untitled Film Still #27*, 1979. Black-and-white photograph, edition of ten, 10″ × 8″. Courtesy of Metro Pictures and the artist.

argues (10). Sherman's decision to use herself as a model/performer cannot be ignored; after all, apart from a few exceptions, artists usually use models other than themselves unless they are doing avowedly "self" portraits. Probably never before has an artist used her or his own self so exclusively as a model for so many diverse personae. Although Sherman's masks are representations of different personae, the fact that it is Sherman herself behind those masks is not something that can be forgotten; part of our experience of any of her works hinges on this awareness. If her photographs were simply examinations of the various stereotypes of women that are presented in the media, they would be moderately interesting, but that's about all. The fact that she consistently casts herself in these various roles gives her photographs a deeper resonance and suggests a more fundamental challenge to the notion of a unified subject.

Sherman presents her "self" in extremely diverse guises, but those guises are, for the most part, limited to media stereotypes: the glamour girl, the earthy heroine, the femme fatale, the stalked victim, the "starlet," the whore with the heart of gold, the girl next door, for example. In the early 1980s, after her *Untitled Film Stills* series (1977–80), her first major series, she began including more fantastic and grotesque images, inspired in part by fairy tales, but also connoting B-horror films. Occasionally Sherman presents a persona who seems straightforward, honest, and frank—as in her *Untitled #18*, 1983, a photo that seems to depict a "nice," ingenuous, wholesome looking young woman. However, in the context of her work generally, the straightforward image and the wholesome unaffectedness of the woman are problematized, and we must ask whether or not artlessness and candor may not themselves be roles that people learn to play.

The idea of the film still is ideal for Sherman's purposes: the film still captures a blatantly staged and provocative moment, highly conventionalized and, by virtue of that extreme conventionality, very legible. But it also interests her because it hedges ambiguously between being an independent image, complete in itself, and being a moment lifted out of a larger narrative context (Sherman, quoted in Smagula, 210). Sherman never has to provide that larger context or even think closely about its details: the stories have already been written, over decades of films and mass media images, as well as over centuries of older kinds of narrative and visual representation. Thus, a single moment is sufficient to suggest a larger story that is absent.

Because Sherman's images draw on cultural conventions in a very obvious way, they illustrate the point that no work of art is, in fact, the work of an individual artist acting alone. All works are products of the traditions out of which they emerge. A sonata by Mozart is his own individual creation in a significant way, but in another way it is a work that is created by the musical tradition out of which the conventions of the sonata evolved. There is, therefore, a radical intertextuality to all art that, when acknowledged, forces us to recognize that cultures create works as much as individuals. There is a social unconscious in any work that may or may not be adequately acknowledged by the artist who created it or by its audience.

In Sherman's early photographs there is considerable ambivalence in the attitude toward media stereotypes that is suggested. Whereas the "speaker" in Kruger's photos—the "we" or "I" indicated in her epigrams—suggests a subversive and dangerous, little known presence behind the visible roles women assume, Sherman's early photos, which contain no verbal component, are more ambiguous. They are images of masks, evident as such because they allude to conventionalized imagery that is obvious to anyone acquainted with movies and other mass media, but there is little hint of an other marginalized self that lies behind those masks. Kruger presents women's confinement within the roles that define them as a victimization by phallocentric power to control representation, and many of Sherman's images are of women as stereotyped victims—in positions that suggest sexual vulnerability and accessibility, hair disheveled, seemingly battered physically or emotionally. But Sherman's work seems less critical of that victimization. Because of the extremely stereotypical nature of her images, because they are so obviously staged, the sense of a victimized, angry, or wounded subject behind the mask is weakened. Critical distance is established in her work, but that critical distance does not result in a forceful rejection of stereotypes. Certainly there is something subversive about treating stereotyped roles in a way that makes overt their theatrics and conventionality, that makes obvious the mimicry and the masquerade. But the theatrics seem almost playful and suggest the possibility of playing roles, even victim's roles, as a tongue-in-cheek game, one that relates to cultural images and conventions but has little to do with real victimization. Thus, any outrage or feeling that such images might relate to serious injustices in the real world tends to be defused.

Clearly, as with other artists, the beholder's eye is central in determining the significance of Sherman's photographs. One viewer might, indeed, find them most interesting as critical examinations of stereotypical representations of women, as parodic masquerades of those stereotypes, or as deconstructions of the unitary subject. On the other hand, another viewer might find them wholly compatible with a kind of chic superficiality and fashionable victimization (overtly staged) associated with the rich and privileged. Thus, it was possible for Sherman to be hired in the early eighties by clothing designer Diane Benson to create ads for her company (Smagula, 213).

Sherman's relationship with the fashion industry was not completely satisfying, however, and this may explain the more obviously parodic anti-fashion photographs she did in 1983. This shift also initiated the darker and more disturbing turn her work took after that, first the surreal monsters, finally culminating in her more recent photographs of the most disgusting substances—vomit, blood, rotten food, and so forth. Mulvey relates the development of Sherman's work throughout the eighties to Julia Kristeva's notion of the "abject" and the failure of the fetish. Sherman's development is, for Mulvey, an unveiling of a truth from which the fetish and the female masquerade are designed to shield the male psyche (Mulvey, "A Phantasmagoria," 143–148). Sherman's abject images can also be related to Lacan's "hommelette" and "primordial discord." They suggest an unformed real that perpetually threatens the subject constructed in the symbolic order.

Twinning and Cloning the Subject

Mike and Doug Starn are identical twins who work as a single artist. They are usually regarded as photographers, though their work challenges the boundaries of photography and has aspects of collage and sculptural construction as well. Photographs, sometimes of major works from the history of Western art, are folded, creased, crumpled, or otherwise defaced, perhaps cut or torn into segments and reconstructed with visible tape or tacks, and attached to a support that is never concealed. Thus, their works relate in an obvious way to the modern and postmodern tendency toward stylistic opacity—a calling of attention to the processes and techniques by which representations are constructed. Probably never before has this tendency manifested itself so forcefully in photography, however.

The fact that the Starns are identical twins who collaborate itself problematizes issues of identity and authorship. Not only are they nearly indistinguishable visually, their collaboration is so complete and apparently unproblematical that it is impossible to determine which of them is responsible for any aspect of any particular work. One has the impression that they function as a collaborative unity throughout their artistic process—from the photographing itself (if one of them looks through the lens and snaps the shutter, very likely the other is at his side) through the darkroom procedures to the construction and mounting of the final work. Indeed, descriptions of the way they work together (e.g., Grundberg, 39–41) suggest something stronger than mere "collaboration": As artists they seem almost to be a single personality coexisting in two identical bodies. Of course, they *are* separate organic entities and personalities, and they *do* have their own distinct personal lives. But their identical appearance, the fact that they are monozygotic, their presentation of themselves as a single artistic entity, and their apparently effortless and seamless collaboration create the feeling that they are, in fact, a doubled individual rather than two similar individuals.

As might be suspected, doubled images—sometimes images of two different though similar things, sometimes two images printed from the same negative—are common in their work: horses, Rembrandt portraits, the *Mona Lisa*, a crucified Christ created by turning upright a dead Christ painted by Philippe de Champaigne, their own self-portrait. Issues of identity and authorship are further questioned when a photograph of one of them is identified as a "self-portrait." How can an image of a single person be a "self-portrait" of two collaborative artists? Of course it hardly matters which one of them it "really" is since, being monozygotic, they are themselves like two prints from the same genetic negative. On the other hand, even a work that identifies which of them is represented can create problems. The title of *Portrait of Doug* (1986) seems to resolve the problem of who is represented. However, it is a doubled image of Doug, and this doubled image suggests the inevitable presence of his twin.

Two-Headed Swan (1989) is derived from a seventeenth-century painting by Jan Asselijn. The Starns photographed the original, printed it on several individual sections of photographic paper, and reconstructed the image from those sections. The reconstruction is messy and casual, with tears, creases, and irregularities throughout. Part of the actual frame of the original painting is photographically included along the left and bottom left sides. There is a casual formality in the organization of the image and the individual photographic segments that comprise it.

The image of the swan's head is doubled, a second mirror image of the first created by reversing the negative. The mirrored heads thrust in opposite directions and appear to fight each other, beaks open as if in panic. Thus, the doubling suggests a difficult duality, characterized by struggle and conflict. This certainly is different from the playful tensions and more attenuated ambivalences that one senses in some of the Starns' other doubled images.

In the upper portion of the work is a piece of shiny metal, a mirror, in effect, that reflects the viewer. As in the *Arnolfini* portrait, the viewer is inscribed in the work, though here more literally. Thus, the doubling of the swan may be taken to apply to the viewer, who becomes part of the work, as well as to the Starns themselves. The subject is divided, even if one does not happen to be a twin. Looked at from this perspective, the doubling of Doug in *Portrait of Doug* need not be read merely as a reference to his status as a twin but may be taken at face value; it can suggest a doubling within his own subjectivity, apart from his relationship to his brother.

When the Starns appropriate canonized images from art history they usually do so by photographing the works in situ, in the museums where they hang. They do not set up special situations so that a quality art reproduction is produced, nor do they, on the other hand, simply rephotograph images from art books. Thus, the frame is indicated in *Two-Headed Swan*, and the *Mona Lisa* of their *Double Mona Lisa with Self-Portrait* (1985–88) is photographed through the glass shield that protects it, so that one sees superimposed the reflections of the artists. The image of the *Mona Lisa*, in its frame, is presented twice, on the left and on the right, and below it are the reflections of the twins—also twice, producing a doubling of doubles, a twinning of twins—apparently in the process of snapping the very picture we are looking at.

The Starn twins have been criticized because of aspects of their work that seem regressive from a more rigorous poststructural perspective, one that would tend to incorporate traditional artistic values like beauty, form, and expression only in quotation marks, subjecting them to critical, deconstructive scrutiny. The Starns' works suggest and their public statements acknowledge an unapologetic concern for "beauty" (Grundberg, 23). They often employ romantic, evocative images—horses, swans, and landscapes, usually mediated by the imagery of art history—that are often associated with transcendental sentiments and expressionist styles. The organization of their work, moreover, often involves the kind of casual formalism, subtle and nuanced, that one finds at times in the combines and photo-transfers of Robert Rauschenberg as well as in the fragmented surfaces of cubism. The organization of the photo-facets in *Double Stark Portrait in Swirl* (1985–86) is, in fact, not unrelated to the organization of the cubist facets in Picasso's *Portrait of Ambroise Vollard* (1909–10; see Plate 5). Its near monochromaticism further confirms this connection with analytical cubism. At the same time, the doubled image, the figure on top staring down at itself, as if in a pool, connotes Narcissus and carries with it a degree of sentimentality.

No doubt there is some truth in the criticisms of the Starns' work. Nevertheless, the Starns do manage to convey their humanistic tendencies in forms that problematize representation and the subject—both of which are central concerns of postmodern art and criticism. Certainly the common conventions and presuppositions of photographic representation—ideas of realism, aesthetic unity, and permanence—have rarely been subjected to such a thoroughgoing critique as they are in the work of the Starns, and the decentering of the subject is suggested not only in their work but in the public persona(e) they present.

Plate 8. Mike and Doug Starn, *Double Stark Portrait in Swirl*, 1985–86. Toned silver print, tape, 99″ × 99″. © 1996 Mike and Doug Starn/Artists Rights Society (ARS), New York. Photo courtesy of Castelli Photo Archives, New York.

Moreover, there is a strong social and political dimension to their work. Their appropriation and re-presentation of Champaigne's *Christ* connotes a concern for victimization in general, a view confirmed by other works that deal with victimization. *Lack of Compassion*, an ongoing and growing project, consists of a series of wooden planks with images of famous martyrs attached to them: Anne Frank, Malcolm X, JFK, Bobby Kennedy, and Gandhi, for example. The presence of additional planks without images attached suggests the martyrs yet to come, those whose names are not yet known. The planks lean against the wall or lie in piles on the floor, human subjects presented as building materials used in an ongoing construction of violence and victimization.

Suggesting that something as simple as "lack of compassion" may be responsible for the evils of the world is not profound politics. On the other hand, since it is really not clear what form of art or artistic representation, at this point, *might* be politically effective, perhaps the Starns' efforts, which at the very least are highly evocative tributes, should not be summarily dismissed. For better or worse, the Starn twins join aspects of conventional humanism—which permits and respects things like compassion and beauty—with the problematizing of representation and subjectivity that is so much a part of postmodern art and poststructural thought.

Chapter 2
The Subject of Discourse

Conrad and the *Mise-en-Abîme*

In *Heart of Darkness* (1902) Kurtz is close to being Marlow's mirror image. Not quite, perhaps, since Marlow maintains his connection with his fellow men—white, European, and male—while Kurtz's single-minded commitment to the goals of European colonialism causes him to adopt extreme and "unsound" methods that result in his break with the society he so effectively serves. Marlow's journey up the Congo River is an attempt to locate and come to terms with this double gone astray, is—among other things—a quest for the truth of the self, an attempt to come as close as possible to that self—primitive and horrible though it may be—without quite losing himself in it, without quite abandoning himself wholly to its dangerous and seductive potential. The allure of power and sexuality are evident in Kurtz himself, the jungle, and the exotic black "goddess" who seems to be Kurtz's African wife.

Joseph Conrad has been called a "harbinger of the current debates about language, meaning, and selfhood" (Trethewey, 102). For who exactly is this "Kurtz" whom Marlow seeks? Kurtz is, in fact, not an entity but a creation of discourse itself; perhaps he *is* nothing more than discourse, an eloquence that surrounds a nothing, a glow surrounding a haze, to use the frequently quoted metaphor used to describe Marlow's own narrative mode. Kurtz's eloquence echoes away from an absent center, replicating and transmitting itself centrifugally outward. It is evocative and mystifying, but refers to nothing, like the colonial idealism that justifies the horrors that belie that idealism. Marlow says of Kurtz,

"The man presented himself as a voice. Not of course that I did not connect him with some sort of action. Hadn't I been told in all the tones of jealousy and admiration that he had collected, bartered, swindled, or stolen more ivory than all the other agents together? That was not the point. The point was in his being a gifted creature, and that of all his gifts the one that stood out pre-eminently, that carried with it a sense of real presence, was his ability to talk, his words—the gift of expression, the bewildering, the illuminating, the most exalted and most contemptible, the pulsating stream of light, or the deceitful flow from the heart of an impenetrable darkness." (*Heart of Darkness*, 62)

Kurtz is nothing but the eloquence of his words. His "real presence" is belied by the eloquence that testifies to that presence. Kurtz's representation in *Heart of Darkness* is itself a deconstruction of the metaphysics of presence in relation to the human subject. Kurtz's voice produces an expanding aura that seems to originate in a transcendental subject—a genuinely remarkable man with immense power to do good and evil. But in fact there is no Kurtz behind the voice. His language is not the product of his subjectivity and power, but his subjectivity and power are the products of his language. Language is an instrument of politics rather than ontology. And Kurtz's language represents the power of discourse to do violence.

The power of Kurtz's language is also evident in his writing. Kurtz's eloquence is the characteristic that Marlow finds most remarkable in the report Kurtz writes for the "International Society for the Suppression of Savage Customs." The report is a moving and idealistic justification for colonialism, based on altruism and white supremacy. But it ends with the apparent non sequitur, appended as if an afterthought, "Exterminate all the brutes!" (66), just as Kurtz's life ends with the exclamation, "The horror! The horror!" (85), words that belie the idealism and altruism that are supposed to justify the atrocities that he and his fellow Europeans have created.

Of course the story's discourse is not that of Kurtz, nor is it that of Marlow either, strictly speaking. The actual narrator is an unnamed sailor who, along with Marlow and two others, is a guest of the "Director of Companies" aboard the *Nellie*, anchored at the mouth of the Thames. Marlow's narration, which comprises most of the novel, is thus mediated by that other narrator, about whom we know very little. *Heart of Darkness* thus involves the kind of telescoping of points of view that Conrad was fond of employing, the unnamed sailor narrating Marlow's narration of his journey, of Kurtz, and of Kurtz's actions, eloquence, and death.[1] Kurtz and Africa are simultaneously distanced and made closer by this technique: distanced by the telescoping narrative levels, but made closer because in a very literal way the setting of the novel is England more than Africa, the river is the Thames more than the Congo, the horror is European more than African, and Kurtz is, of course, us.[2] But also, Conrad's framing of the story in quotation marks foregrounds discourse as itself a major concern of the novel and provokes questions about the relationship between discourse and subjectivity. Those quotes, according to Vincent Pecora, "indicate that the language thus bracketed is precisely what is under examination" (999).

Kurtz is revealed to be an empty center surrounded by an eloquent rhetorical haze. Of course this is the way Marlow is described as well. The glow and haze metaphor appears originally as a description of the way meaning emerges when Marlow tells stories, and Marlow's narration is the one framed in quotation marks, suggesting that, like Kurtz, we know him almost exclusively through his discourse. Just as Marlow describes Kurtz as a voice, the unnamed narrator describes Marlow as a voice. Marlow becomes for him a disembodied narration unfolding on the dark deck of the *Nellie*:

It has become so pitch dark that we listeners could hardly see one another. For a long time already he, sitting apart, had been no more to us than a voice. . . . I listened, I listened on the watch for the sentence, for the word, that would give me the clue to the faint uneasiness inspired by this narrative that seemed to shape itself without human lips in the heavy night-air of the river. (42)

Not only is the subjectivity of Marlow and Kurtz problematized in the novel, but the reader's own ground is destabilized. Is the reader imaginatively listening to a story by the unnamed sailor, or is the reader listening directly to Marlow himself? Once the story gets rolling the exterior narrator largely—but not completely—drops out. Only the quotation marks and an occasional interjection from someone on deck draws us back to the original setting and reminds us of the *Nellie* and the original narrator. These telescoping narrative levels, together with the darkness at both ends—the unnamed narrator, who represents the widest narrative frame of the novel, and, at the dark center, Kurtz, who lacks a transcendental *cogito* but is instead centerless discourse itself—provoke in the reader a sense of the *mise-en-abîme*, a perpetually shifting and ultimately groundless narrative representation.

The point of view of *Lord Jim* (1900) is even more complex and shifting. The novel takes an overall third person point of view, but that third person narrator rarely describes events directly. Typically, Jim explains his experiences to Marlow, who—between quotation marks—relates to friends orally and in writing (in the last chapters) what he has learned. As in *Heart of Darkness* the multiple points of view correspond to multiple settings as well as to different interpretations and evaluations of Jim and his situation. Chapter 9, for example, from one perspective takes place on the *Patna* and involves the horror and confusion that leads to Jim's jump from the ship, the event that acts as a fulcrum for the action of the entire novel. At the same time, the chapter takes place on shore, after Jim's trial, as Jim describes the event to Marlow. And, from still another perspective, it takes place later, in London, as Marlow tries to "render in colourless words" the "innumerable shades" of Jim's experience to his friends (*Lord Jim*, 94). Moreover, throughout the course of the novel numerous other characters are introduced, each adding his own particular response to and evaluation of Jim. Thus, in *Lord Jim* various points of view are embedded within one another and have the effect of being presented simultaneously, but others follow one another sequentially. The novel involves a multiplicity of fictional narrators, fictional audiences, and imaginary subject positions, which the reader occupies sometimes simultaneously and sometimes consecutively.

Such complexities in the narrative voice—multiplicity of narrative perspectives and telescoping perspectives—create a complexity in the reader's position that is in strong contrast to the clear positioning of the reader in classic realist fiction. Classic realist fiction establishes a stable narrator—whether first or third person—as well as stable characters: characters that are stable insofar as they "make sense," even if they happen to be psychologically *un*stable or change as a result of the action of the story. But most significantly, there is a stable relationship between the narrator and the reader; they share certain values and assumptions that are simply taken for granted. The opening line "It is a truth universally acknowledged, that a single man in possession of a good fortune, must be in want of a wife" affirms a ground of common understanding, of common presuppositions between narrator and reader. And that common ground exists—or seems to exist—even if the line is understood as ironic and the reader recognizes, along with the narrator, that the proposition is really a silly prejudice of narrow minds.

Catherine Belsey, drawing on Barthes, Lacan, and Althusser, says that "classic realist fiction . . . 'interpellates' the reader, addresses itself to him or her directly, offering the reader as the position from which the text is most 'obviously' intelligible, the position of the *subject in (and of) ideology*" (56–57). The coherent positioning of the reader vis-à-vis the narrator and the stability of a consistent narrative voice, along with an entire ensemble of shared assumptions and values, are analogous to the unambiguous physical positioning of the viewer, the stability of an optically correct representation of a coherent spatial world, and the assumption of a commonality between the represented world of the painting and the world the viewer lives in, that are characteristic of Renaissance painting.

Classic realist fiction, according to Belsey, involves a "hierarchy of discourses" (70). The discourse of the characters will probably exist on a lower level in the hierarchy than that of an authorial, third-person narrator, and the reader will share—or come to share throughout the course of a novel—the authorial discourse. Within any such hierarchical narrative, any heterogeneity of voices is contained within a higher homogeneity—that of the author-reader—that overarches the diversity of lower level voices embedded in the text. Even if the narrator's voice is a limited one there will be an "implied author" (Wayne Booth's expression, which Belsey adopts), whose greater point of view the reader will share or come to share. As in Renaissance painting, the point of view of the viewer/reader converges with that of the artist/author.

This is in strong contrast to the disturbed hierarchy of works like *Heart of Darkness*. The unnamed seaman provides the widest narrative frame of the story—he speaks in first person without quotation marks—but Marlow's narration, formally embedded in the unnamed seaman's, is the focus of the story, and it is Marlow's insights—as well as his confusions—that we tend to rely on most. On the other hand, it is clear that the unnamed seaman is no fool. His description of Marlow is perceptive, though brief and inevitably partial. It is significant that he is the one who provides us with the "glow" and "haze" metaphor for Marlow's narrative mode. Nevertheless, he offers no interpretation or evaluation of the significance of Marlow's story itself.

Of course, Marlow also provides no clear explanation of that significance. Kurtz's last words, "the horror," which Marlow relays to us, are ambiguous. What is it, exactly, that is horrible? Is it death that is horrible or life itself? Is it the horror perpetrated upon the Africans or the (admittedly racist) horror of dark Africa itself? Is it a horror that proceeds from the recognition that, beneath the eloquence of the voice, there is no transcendental subject that provides its foundation? Pecora writes,

Only in this "shudder" [of Schopenhauer] can we begin to understand the full extent of Mallarmé's anxiety when he confronts the *abîme* that yawns beneath him after he has denied any transcendental signified and displaced language from its semantic moorings. Only at this point can we hear the full resonance of Kurtz's "horror" at the "heart of darkness" he stumbles upon in Conrad's story. (996)

Marlow's uncertainty and his inability to provide us with an answer to the significance of the story is underlined by the fact that, at the end, he betrays one of his own principles. Marlow is averse to lying, finding a bit of death in all lies (*Heart of Darkness*, 41). Nevertheless, he violates this principle by lying to Kurtz's "Intended" regarding Kurtz's last words. The novel thus ends without closure, without resolution, without the protagonist having found, for himself or the reader, a satisfactory solution to the dilemma it poses. The inevitable lie that is meant to conceal the horror contains the death it tries to hold at bay.

Once Marlow begins his embedded narration early in *Lord Jim*, the third-person narrator rarely intrudes or comments. As in *Heart of Darkness*, the widest narrative level (first-person in *Heart of Darkness*, third-person in *Lord Jim*) is largely abandoned—or remains a silent frame for lower level narrations, only the quotation marks and very brief and occasional intrusions reminding us of its presence.

Various characters, each with his own fixed ideas, with his own strategy for coping with the world, provide different perspectives on Jim and his dilemma. Not all these perspectives are equal, of course. Marlow and Stein certainly present "discourses" that are higher than those of the other characters in the novel. We have more respect for Marlow's fidelity and compassion and Stein's almost superhuman ability to accept the cruelty of life, his willingness to immerse himself in the "destructive element," than we do for Chester's amorality or Brown's moralistic vengefulness. But Marlow and Stein do not themselves represent the same solution, and this creates some uncertainty regarding which of their perspectives is best. Moreover, the cumulative effect of the multiple and telescoping points of view is a problematizing of all perspectives, a distancing of "facts" behind the discourse about facts, and an inability of the reader to find a conceptually or psychologically firm footing from which to evaluate the events of the novel. Marlow or Stein may, indeed, represent higher level discourses than most of the other characters, but the clear hierarchy Belsey describes as characteristic of classic realism gets obscured in the complexity and multiplicity of voices.

Two other characteristics of classic realist fiction that Belsey identifies—illusionism and closure—have fairly obvious correspondences in painting. In illusionistic painting the two-dimensional rectangle of the painting pretends to be a window opening onto a three-dimensional world—to use the often quoted phrase of Leon Battista Alberti, who in 1436 described the rules of optical perspective. Not only does a flat surface pretend to be a window opening onto a three-dimensional world, but paint applied to that surface is manipulated in such a way as to create the illusion of various materials—fabric, metal, glass, flesh, hair, and so forth. A classically realistic painting—like Perugino's *Giving the Keys*—is "closed" in the sense that its content and formal structure suggest that everything that needs to be included is included. Nothing of significance to the event or scene depicted has been left out.

Belsey describes the handling of scenes in realistic fiction in extremely visual terms, as if she were describing realism in a painting. Utilizing a segment of *Oliver Twist* as an example, she argues that scenes are described as if they are viewed from a particular spatial position. This is an interesting point, since it is obviously not a constraint of verbal art that it assume a particular physical position in describing a scene. Even freer than what is permitted by the codes and conventions of visual perspective, literary perspective can easily shift, moving about a scene without necessarily assuming the point of view of a character. However, in the example Belsey chooses, the scene is described as if from Oliver's visual point of view, even though, conceptually, the narrator's and reader's consciousness is higher than that of the character (76–77). The omniscient, third-person narrator provisionally assumes the limited perspective of an individual character, the protagonist, without, at the same time, giving up its own wider perspective. The reader's sense of comprehension and mastery is valorized by the overall third-person perspective, but the temporary limiting of that perspective, in order to relate more clearly what the major character is experiencing, valorizes individual experience and confirms our understanding of the individual as the primary existential entity.

This is in contrast to narratives like those of Conrad. When such narratives localize themselves around a particular consciousness the sense of the partiality of that consciousness is overwhelming and the reader's attempt to understand clearly what is happening is frustrated. The reader's perspective becomes *limited* to that of the character; this limited perspective may coexist with other limited perspectives presented in the work, but it will not (as in the Dickens passage Belsey describes) coexist with a broader perspective offered by a narrator or "implied author" who has an adequate understanding of the novel's events. Throughout *Heart of Darkness*, except in the beginning when we get a brief description of Marlow on board the *Nellie*, our experience of events is limited to that of Marlow, and nothing in the novel provides clues to an understanding of events that might be broader or more accurate than what he can provide himself. When Marlow is confused about the odd "ornamentations" on top of the fence posts at Kurtz's outpost, later correctly identifying them as human heads, the reader's understanding of what they are is limited to and entirely dependent on Marlow's. And in the passage in which Marlow catches Kurtz attempting to escape, the reader's perspective is absolutely limited to that of Marlow. Marlow does manage to act effectively, it is true, but his comprehension and successful action are very local in scope. Surrounding them there is a wider world where darkness, danger, confusion, and ignorance prevail:

" . . . at my back the fires loomed between the trees, and the murmur of many voices issued from the forest. I had cut him off cleverly; but when actually confronting him I seemed to come to my senses, I saw the danger in its right proportion. . . . It was very awful. I glanced back. We were within thirty yards of the nearest fire. A black figure stood up, strode on long black legs, waving long black arms, across the glow. It had horns—antelope horns, I think—on its head. Some sorcerer, some witch-man, no doubt: it looked fiend-like enough." (81)

In *Lord Jim* there is a free and confusing dispersal of consciousness across and through various subjectivities. Under such circumstances one gets a sense of a network of discourses, a network of perspectives, some of which may, indeed, be broader or deeper than others, but none of which can contain the totality of truth the novel struggles to represent. Not even the narrator who represents the widest perspective formally can provide such a totalizing perspective. The unnamed seaman in *Heart of Darkness* and the third-person narrator of *Lord Jim* are not stupid, but they are not smarter than Marlow, whose discourse they contain. And they largely drop out of the discourse, their silent presence indicated only by quotation marks. There may be a purely formal hierarchy of discourses—a narrator contains the discourse of Marlow, who contains the discourse of Marlow, Jim, and others—but that formal hierarchy does not reflect corresponding levels of understanding.

Faulkner's Dying "I"

Perhaps nowhere does one get a better sense of this dispersal of consciousness across and through various subjectivities than in William Faulkner's *As I Lay Dying* (1930), which avoids even the kind of formal hierarchy present in Conrad's novels. Instead of embedding narratives inside narratives, Faulkner's novel juxtaposes, without hierarchizing them, sections presented from the points of view of various of its characters. Since each section is headed by the name of the character whose point of view it presents, the reader quickly gets the general idea behind the narrative system of the novel. However, it soon becomes clear that there are contradictions and inconsistencies in the way this system is actually applied.

Some sections read like straightforward first-person narrations, as if the character is telling the story to an audience in a conventional narrative fashion, but most of them read as stream of consciousness, a discourse that is far less "formed" than a conventional narration and more likely to betray the more incoherent workings of an individual's presumably private experience. Generally the monologues of the members of the Bundren family, whose experiences provide the story of the novel, tend toward stream of consciousness, while those of others tend to be more conventional narrations.

Tull, a neighbor of the Bundrens, sounds like someone relating the events of the story to friends, at some point in the future, after the events of the novel have taken place.

It was nigh to midnight and it had set into rain when he woke us. It had been a misdoubtful night, with the storm making; a night when a fellow looks for most anything to happen before he can get the stock fed and himself to the house and supper et and in bed with the rain starting, and when Peabody's team come up, lathered, with the broke harness dragging and the neck-yoke betwixt the off critter's legs, Cora says "It's Addie Bundren. She's gone at last." (65)

The handling of this voice is quite different from that of Vardaman, Addie's youngest son. Vardaman, young, uneducated, unstable, and traumatized, confuses his mother's death with that of a fish he caught, and he holds the doctor, who arrived shortly before she died, responsible for her passing.

Then I begin to run. I run toward the back and come to the edge of the porch and stop. Then I begin to cry. I can feel where the fish was in the dust. It is cut up into pieces of not-fish now, not-blood on my hands and overalls. Then it wasn't so. It hadn't happened then. And now she is getting so far ahead I cannot catch her. . . . If I jump off the porch I will be where the fish was, and it all cut up into not-fish now. I can hear the bed and her face and them and I can feel the floor shake when he walks on it that came and did it. That came and did it when she was all right but he came and did it.
"The fat son of a bitch." (52–53)

Not only are there inconsistencies in the handling of voice among the monologues, there are also inconsistencies within the individual monologues themselves. On occasion a character's voice modulates to a kind of diction that would be impossible for that character, a sophisticated and literary diction that one tends to identify as "authorial." After Vardaman beats the doctor's horse, in an irrational rage directed against an animal associated with the individual he believes is responsible for his mother's death, there is a shift of voice:

It is dark. I can hear wood, silence: I know them. But not living sounds, not even him. It is as though the dark were resolving him out of his integrity, into an un-related scattering of components—snuffings and stampings; smells of cooling flesh and ammoniac hair; an illusion of a co-ordinated whole of splotched hide and strong bones within which, detached and secret and familiar, an *is* different from my *is*. I see him dissolve—legs, a rolling eye, a gaudy splotching like cold flames—and float upon the dark in fading solution; all one yet neither; all either yet none. (55)

Vardaman, in a nearly psychotic state, experiences the dissolution of the horse into separate spatial and temporal components. But the passage involves a diction and syntax articulating that experience that is far different from what would be possible for the confused, panicked, uneducated boy. And yet the "I" of the passage *is* Vardaman's "I"; it is Vardaman's experience that is being articulated. It is as if the author—or his narrative surrogate—comes to the boy's rescue, as if the consciousness of the passage creates a bridge between a boy who is incapable of grasping and mastering what he is going through and an authorial narrator who can—or who can, at least, come closer to articulating what can't be fully articulated by anyone, since what is occurring is the dissolution of perceptual and conceptual categories themselves and the failure of words to identify such categories and keep them in place.

Another violation of the coherence and consistency of the individual monologues occurs when events are related that the individual whose point of view is represented could not logically know. The section describing Addie's death is attributed to Darl, the second oldest son. Darl is intelligent and unstable, and it is his voice that most easily modulates into that of the "authorial" voice that obtrudes, more obviously, into the monologues of some of the other characters. Although the section is identified as Darl's, it is logically impossible for him to describe his mother's death because, at the time of her death, he has gone with his brother Jewel to deliver a load of wood. Toward the end of the section there is an additional confusion. In italics, the point of view modulates to that of Dewey Dell, Darl's sister and the second youngest sibling. Only at the very end of the section is the point of view unambiguously Darl's, when he informs Jewel that their mother has died—confirming for the reader his "clairvoyant" knowledge. Thus, the text requires that we accept contradictions in its construction, contradictions that have obvious thematic implications. Segments of monologue, on one hand, present themselves as originating in specific individuals; on the other hand, they challenge our understanding of individuals as coherent subjects, unified and separate from other individuals.

What the novel suggests is the notion of a larger, heterogeneous discourse that surrounds and engulfs and moves through and about individual subjects. This larger discourse, which does not honor the boundaries that separate individual discourses, does at times modulate into an authorial narrator. But this authorial voice is not that of a "higher" consciousness or an omniscient narrator, since it does not synthesize the lower level discourses into a larger coherence. Within this larger discourse contradictions and irresolutions remain, unresolved. Daniel Ferrer describes the relationships among the various monologues: "[They] seem to communicate between themselves, like apparently closed wells joined by a subterranean stream" (31). That communication is not an act of individual intelligence or will, but a psycholinguistic spilling of one subject into another that challenges the integrity of the subject.

Perhaps the most obvious impossibility in the novel's point of view is the section entitled "Addie." Because it is Addie who dies early in the story, her single section, more than halfway through, makes little logical sense. The problematical nature of this section is anticipated in the novel's title, which suggests a story told from the point of view of a dead or dying person, a difficult conceit, at best. Moreover, most of the story takes place not as she dies but after she is, in fact, physically dead.

Unlike the other sections, Addie's section does not relate directly to the main action of the story—her death and the family's darkly comic struggle to transport her decomposing body during nine days of summer heat, hampered by flood, fire, and hungry vultures, to the cemetery in her hometown. Addie's section is delivered as a first-person past tense narration, in contrast to the interior monologues of the other members of her family. It reveals some important background information, including the fact that Jewel is not her husband's child but the illegitimate son of Whitfield, the preacher. Aspects of Addie's character are revealed, especially her deep bitterness and alienation. It is in Addie's section that some of the existential themes of the novel are underscored: the isolation of individuals in their subjectivities and in their physical bodies; their vulnerability and the suffering they experience when they do touch, as they do in sex, childbirth, and physical violence; and the elusiveness of a subjectivity that slips away from language and the proper name.

The inconsistencies and ambiguities in the narrative system that Faulkner establishes in *As I Lay Dying* are not sufficient to invalidate that system, however. Recognizing the novel's point of view as a construction of individual monologues by different characters, indicated by whatever name heads each section, is essential to understanding the novel's action, characters, structure, and themes. However, the inconsistencies and ambiguities *do* problematize the novel; they are aspects of the novel that can't be contained by its own system.[3]

It is the inconsistencies and ambiguities, the slidings of voice from character to character, the unexpected intrusions of alien voices, that challenge the integrity of the *cogito* and threaten the reader's own confidence in his or her ability to fully master the text. Benveniste argued that the subject really "is only the emergence in the being of a fundamental property of language" and not really a "psychic unity that transcends the totality of the actual experiences it assembles" (224). The very structure of *As I Lay Dying*—including the inconsistencies and contradictions within that structure—challenges the idea of the subject as a "psychic unity."

In numerous monologues characters describe disruptions of sensibility that explicitly problematize the relationship of language to subjectivity. Vardaman experiences a disruption of his sense of himself as an agent who controls even his own body. After his mother's death, he experiences his crying not as something he is doing but as something that is simply happening. "The crying makes a lot of noise. I wish it wouldn't make so much noise" (53). It is not simply that Vardaman cannot control his crying, which would be a common enough experience. Rather, his crying seems to be something that is not even happening to him, an agentless event, no different from other events in nature that happen outside of himself. Shortly thereafter he experiences the doctor's horse as disintegrating into "an unrelated scattering of components." The category, "horse," is dissolved not simply as a verbal category (associated with the symbolic) but as a visual category (associated with the imaginary). Vardaman's crisis suggests a pre-imaginary mode in which linguistic and perceptual categories that imply a coherent world and a unified subject and agent aware of that world are not operative.

Dewey Dell also experiences disruptions in the "normal" sense of her self as an agent identified by and organized around a body, a gender, and a name. Her understanding of humans as radically incarnated, as fully and fundamentally bound to their physical existences, is powerful and profound. She has an existential sense of herself and others as "tub[s] of guts." At the same time, she is intensely aware of the fact that her body can tear, be penetrated, and become painfully unalone. "I feel my body, my bones and flesh beginning to part and open upon the alone, and the process of coming unalone is terrible. Lafe. Lafe. 'Lafe' Lafe. Lafe" (59). Lafe is the name of the boy who got her pregnant, and his appearance here suggests the penetrability and vulnerability of the body that occurs in sexual union. Of course that challenge to the body's integrity also occurs in gestation and childbirth. For the two major women in *As I Lay Dying*—Addie and Dewey Dell—the radical isolation of the individual is juxtaposed to a vulnerability and pain that results from and is the condition of not-aloneness.

In Dewey Dell's monologue the third "Lafe" in the series is enclosed in quotation marks, suggesting her awareness of the problem of proper names and their relationship to identity. Obviously Dewey Dell would not use quotation marks in an internal monologue, but the use of them in the text suggests that she is, in effect, thinking, "that person or thing to which the name 'Lafe' has been attached, but which is really separate from him." When she uses the name without quotes, she identifies the subject and his name, as we usually do. When the quotes are present, she notices the disjunction. With the quotes we become aware of the terrible juxtaposition of distance and closeness between individuals. Lafe, as "an *is* different from my *is*," seems nearly inaccessible, distant and invisible behind his name. At the same time it is he who has penetrated her, gotten her pregnant, and made her so painfully unalone.

Addie grapples with the same problem in her discussion of her husband, Anse, and his name.

Sometimes I would lie by him in the dark, hearing the land that was now of my blood and flesh, and I would think: Anse. Why Anse. Why are you Anse. I would think about his name until after a while I could see the word as a shape, a vessel, and I would watch him liquify and flow into it like cold molasses flowing out of the darkness into the vessel, until the jar stood full and motionless: a significant shape profoundly without life like an empty door frame; and then I would find that I had forgotten the name of the jar. I would think: The shape of my body where I used to be a virgin is in the shape of a   and I couldn't think *Anse*, couldn't remember *Anse*. It was not that I could think of myself as no longer unvirgin, because I was three now. And when I could think *Cash* and *Darl* that way until their names would die and solidify into a shape and then fade away, I would say, All right. It doesn't matter. It doesn't matter what they call them. (165)

What Addie might wish for would be "not-Anse," that ineffable subjectivity behind the name. But Addie never asks Anse for not-Anse, and she regards her not asking for it as a fulfillment of her duty to him. Anse himself, naively identified with his name, is unaware of a problem, and she permits him to continue in his ignorance. "I would let him be the shape and echo of his word. That was more than he asked, because he could not have asked for that and been Anse, using himself so with a word" (166).

Derrida describes the violence associated with the proper name:

[S]uch is the originary violence of language which consists in inscribing within a difference, in classifying, in suspending the vocative absolute. To think the unique within the system, to inscribe it there, such is the gesture of the arche-writing: arche-violence, loss of the proper, of absolute proximity, of self-presence, in truth the loss of what has never taken place, of a self-presence which has never been given but only dreamed of and always already split, repeating, incapable of appearing to itself except in its own disappearance. (*Of Grammatology*, 112)

For Derrida "not-Anse" is not a possibility. The subject is "always already" inscribed in writing. There never was an unsplit subjectivity present to itself and whole, because there never was a "subject" before it was named and inscribed and split. For Derrida difference precedes and produces "entities" that differ, not the other way around.[4] For Addie, however, "not-Anse" may not be a possibility for Anse, but we have the impression that she may regard it as a possibility for someone, that there is a realm of subjectivity, of selfhood, ineffable though it may be, that lies below or behind language and naming. She simply permits Anse to remain in his naivety and ignorance, in his defensive self-reduction, allows him to continue "using himself so with a word." But for Addie, as for Derrida, the process of naming is a violence, an inadequacy of the name to a subject, whether that subject is originary or "only dreamed of," constructed and deferred at the moment of its splitting, at the moment of its inscription.

Not only are proper names dissociated from their referents, other words like "sin and love and fear" are as well. These words are used only by individuals like Cora, Tull's wife, who, according to Addie, can never really sin or love or fear. Addie thinks about "how words go straight up in a thin line, quick and harmless, and how terribly doing goes along the earth, clinging to it, so that after a while the two lines are too far apart for the same person to straddle from one to the other . . . " (165). For Addie sin and fear and love exist, but they exist silently, outside of discourse, and they disappear as soon as they are spoken.

Addie can only represent herself as a blank. This blank can be associated with her gender, and she uses it specifically to refer to her anatomy, "the shape of my body where I used to be a virgin." The blank space on the page where Addie indicates but does not represent herself is like the word "not" and the bullet hole in Kruger's *You Are Not Yourself.*

On the other hand, if all representation of the subject in language is, in fact, a symbolic misrepresentation, the blank could apply to all subjects, regardless of gender. It is a way of indicating the subject without claiming to represent it. The blank that Addie uses to indicate what can't be represented is similar to the "not-Anse," which also indicates the subject behind the name Anse. The sentence that begins with the clause in which she indicates herself with a blank ends with a clause describing her inability to conceive of *Anse* as a person behind the name Anse.

On a couple occasions in the novel, characters attempt to describe a condition of subjectlessness or a state of being a proto-subject prior to or outside of the establishment of subjectivity. Such descriptions tend to be associated with states of mind that exist between sleep and consciousness, when waking up or just before falling to sleep. Dewey Dell describes such a state:

> When I used to sleep with Vardaman I had a nightmare once I thought I was awake but I couldn't see and couldn't feel I couldn't feel the bed under me and I couldn't think what I was I couldn't think of my name I couldn't even think I am a girl I couldn't even think I nor even think I want to wake up nor remember what was opposite to awake so I could do that I knew that something was passing but I couldn't even think of time then all of a sudden I knew that something was it was wind blowing over me it was like the wind came and blew me back from where it was I was not blowing the room and Vardaman asleep and all of them back under me again and going on like a piece of cool silk dragging across my naked legs (115–116)

Of course this passage does nothing to clarify the "nature" of this silent, unspoken, subjectless subject. When one is outside of discourse, one cannot speak; when one is in discourse, one cannot speak the subject that is outside of it.

Darl also engages this paradox in the context of grappling with sleep. Dewey Dell's experience is one of having woken up, but not quite. Darl describes the experience of falling asleep in a strange room:

And before you are emptied for sleep, what are you. And when you are emptied for sleep, you are not. And when you are filled with sleep, you never were. I dont know what I am. I dont know if I am or not. Jewel knows he is, because he does not know that he does not know whether he is or not. He cannot empty himself for sleep because he is not what he is and he is what he is not. Beyond the unlamped wall I can hear the rain shaping the wagon that is ours, the load that is no longer theirs that felled and sawed it nor yet theirs that bought it and which is not ours either, lie on our wagon though it does, since only the wind and rain shape it only to Jewel and me, that are not asleep. And since sleep is is-not and rain and wind are was, it is not. Yet the wagon is, because when the wagon is was, Addie Bundren will not be. And Jewel is, so Addie Bundren must be. And then I must be, or I could not empty myself for sleep in a strange room. And so if I am not emptied yet, I am is. (76)

Darl's thoughts about his brother Jewel are like Addie's thoughts about Anse. Jewel knows himself to be only because he naively assumes an identity with his name and is incapable of conceiving his existence in any way other than his definition in the symbolic, just as Anse is incapable of recognizing or giving to Addie "not-Anse."

Darl's obsession with the transformation of subjectivity while falling asleep proceeds by association to other kinds of transformation. The load of wood he and Jewel are delivering is in the process of changing ownership. Darl associates Addie's imminent transformation from life to death with the transferal of ownership of the wood, as if the two are connected in some significant way. Darl's experience of rain on the wagon also involves what we would normally regard as a confused understanding of relations. For him, the rain does not strike the wagon, which interrupts and redirects its fall; rather, it is the rain's movement that produces the shape of the wagon. Darl's obsessive attention to transformations, borders, and gaps between categories and conditions, his attribution of significance to conditions that are merely synchronous, and his inversions of causal relationships result in a destabilizing of conventional categories and a challenge to conventional understandings of how things in the world are connected.

The discourse of *As I Lay Dying* plays around, dances around, that which cannot be stated, indicating its existence without claiming to actually represent it. If discourse differs from and defers what it seems to represent rather than provides access to it, how can one talk about anything at all, let alone something as ineffable, mercurial, and intangible as the subject? Addie represents herself by a blank and speaks of an unreachable "not-Anse" behind her husband's name. Darl and Dewey Dell grope with the dissolution of consciousness in sleep. Vardaman loses all sense of his own agency, and he and Darl experience fragmentations and dispersals of perceptual and conceptual categories. The autonomy of individual subjectivities is disturbed psychologically, when one character's monologue intrudes on another's, and physically, when there is transgression of the limits of the body, as in sex, childbirth, violence, and, of course, the decomposition of death itself.

The reader's own sense of mastery is also challenged. Simply piecing together the monologues in order to construct a coherent narrative is difficult. This task is complicated by the fact that the major characters are uneducated, that they speak a dialect of English, and that they are at times unstable, young, or in desperate emotional states. Moreover, their monologues frequently contain pronouns without antecedents, allusions to characters whose identities are unclear, and references to incidents that have not yet been explained.

One tends to assume that the "I" of the novel's title refers to Addie. But clearly the novel is a more general challenge to the transcendental subject. The "I" that is dying is the self itself, at least the understanding of the self as a coherent, unified, separate, and self-sufficient entity. A humanism remains, but it is of a different type, one that provokes in the reader sympathy without arrogance and a recognition of the individual as vulnerable, penetrable, and mortal.

Calvino and the Traveling Subject

Probably no novel destabilizes the reader's position so systematically as Italo Calvino's *If on a winter's night a traveler* (1979, English translation 1981). The trajectory of *Heart of Darkness* is centripetal, the interrogation moving closer and closer to a center that reveals itself finally as an absence. In Faulkner it is centrifugal, the various subjects spilling through their body skins and ego skins and mixing messily with other not so separate subjects. In Calvino's novel, however, there is no center that is emptied of content or that spills away from itself, no self to be challenged. Rather, Calvino's subject is fluid, freely changing roles and shifting positions as if effortlessly, as if there is no essential locus to hamper such movements and metamorphoses.

The novel begins by utilizing the unusual second-person voice. The reader is thus incorporated into the story, becomes in fact the protagonist of the novel. The "you" of Calvino's novel becomes a character in a metafictional frame tale in which numerous framed tales are embedded. The reader of *If on a winter's night a traveler* is, at the outset, fractured and experiences a loss of mastery. The reader is an individual reading the novel (and presumably in control of his or her self) as well as a character in the novel (over which he or she has no control).

The novel begins with a playful direct address to the "Reader," the protagonist who is projected onto and confused with the real reader.

You are about to begin reading Italo Calvino's new novel, *If on a winter's night a traveler*. Relax. Concentrate. Dispel every other thought. Let the world around you fade. Best to close the door; the TV is always on in the next room. Tell the others right away, "No, I don't want to watch TV!" Raise your voice—they won't hear you otherwise—"I'm reading! I don't want to be disturbed!" (3)

The first chapter describes various details of the Reader's struggle to begin Calvino's novel: his ("your") decision to read the book, buying the book, his attempts to find a comfortable, quiet place to read, and so forth. In fact, the first chapter establishes the conflict that informs the entire organization of the novel: the Reader's struggle to read the novel—or some novel, since the novel being read undergoes numerous permutations throughout—and the various obstacles to his doing so. Because some of the problems, discomforts, and obstacles may be similar to ones the real reader of the novel has actually experienced, the real reader's identification with and confusion with this second-person protagonist is strengthened.

At the end of the first chapter the Reader is finally ready to start reading, and the next section—titled but not numbered as a chapter—begins. The title of this first embedded section, "If on a winter's night a traveler," corresponds to that of the novel as a whole, and its author has already been identified as "Italo Calvino." This story, like all the other embedded stories the protagonist reads, has little to do with the framing story, at least on the surface. Although certain themes, character types, names, kinds of situations, and images at times resonate among the framed stories and between the framed stories and the framing story, the fictional worlds they conjure are not the same. The novel proceeds by alternating between numbered chapters and titled embedded stories, until the last two chapters, when the pattern is broken. Each of the embedded stories is interrupted for some reason or other, so that the Reader, the "you" of the framing story, is continually frustrated in his attempts to finish reading the various novels he begins.

The major conflict of the framing story involves this struggle, foreshadowed by the problems in getting started described in the first chapter but formally instituted at the end of the first titled section, when the Reader cannot continue because of a printer's error. In each numbered chapter the frustrated reader attempts to procure the rest of the last interrupted novel. He gets a hold of a novel or manuscript that he believes is the continuation he seeks, begins reading it, discovers that it is actually part of an entirely different novel, becomes engrossed in it anyway, and then is inevitably interrupted once again. Various reasons for the interruptions are contrived—printer's errors, incomplete manuscripts, books being stolen, and so forth.

The embedded stories usually involve some degree of ambivalence in their point of view. They seem to be, on one hand, narrative fragments contained within the larger novel and, on the other hand, *descriptions* of those fragments seen from the point of view of the Reader:

The novel begins in a railway station, a locomotive huffs, steam from a piston covers the opening chapter, a cloud of smoke hides part of the first paragraph. In the odor of the station there is a passive whiff of station cafe odor. There is someone looking through the befogged glass. (10)

Passages like this read partly as descriptions of the embedded novel, paraphrased but not directly quoted, and partly as passages of the embedded novel itself, quoted directly and exactly. From the former perspective there is no shift in point of view between the framing story and the numbered chapters: We are reading *about* what the Reader/protagonist of the framing story is reading, we are reading *about* his experience of reading, we are not reading the exact text he is reading. However, as the stories proceed and as the reader (the fictitious Reader *and* the real reader) becomes increasingly engrossed, references to the reading of the story tend to become rarer, and we begin to respond as if we are reading the exact text of the embedded story. By the time the inevitable interruption occurs, the real reader of Calvino's novel feels a frustration analogous to that experienced by the fictitious Reader.

An "Other Reader" is introduced, a woman, with whom the first Reader forms an alliance. Both Readers bought the same flawed printing of Calvino's novel, experienced the same frustration, and returned to the bookstore to get a correct copy. It is there that they meet. The first Reader is attracted to the woman and therefore has a double motivation for developing the relationship. The quests for narrative and sexual closure are parallel, and conflating the two is a motif that recurs throughout the novel. Both closures, happily, are eventually achieved. The two Readers make love in chapter 7, and the novel ends with a double closure of narrative and matrimony. The twelfth, final chapter, is brief:

Now you are man and wife, Reader and Reader. A great double bed receives your parallel readings.
   Ludmilla closes her book, turns off her light, puts her head back against the pillow, and says, "Turn off your light, too. Aren't you tired of reading?"
   And you say, "Just a moment, I've almost finished *If on a winter's night a traveler* by Italo Calvino." (260)

The parallel between patterns of narrative and those of lovemaking is something that has been noted by critics and exploited by authors. Robert Scholes writes, perhaps too sweepingly, "The archetype of all fiction is the sexual act," and he compares the tension in fiction between the movement toward resolution and impediments toward that movement with the tension in sex between the movement toward orgasm and impediments that delay orgasm and prolong pleasure (26). And Calvino writes (addressing his first Reader), "The pursuit of the interrupted book, which instilled in you a special excitement since you were conducting it together with the Other Reader, turns out to be the same thing as pursuing her, who eludes you in a proliferation of mysteries, deceits, disguises" (151).

Linda C. Badley discusses the connection between Roland Barthes's "lyrical meditation on the erotics of reading the decentered or reader-written text of 'bliss' " and the relationship between reading and eroticism in Calvino's novel (Badley, 105). Nowhere is this connection more evident than in chapter 7, where the Readers' lovemaking is described as an erotic, Barthesian "reading" of one another.

> Ludmilla, now you are being read. Your body is being subjected to a systematic reading, through channels of tactile information, visual, olfactory, and not without some intervention of the taste buds. . . . And you, too, O Reader, are meanwhile an object of reading: the Other Reader now is reviewing your body as if skimming the index, and at some moments she consults it as if gripped by sudden and specific curiousities, then she lingers, questioning it and waiting. (155)

Calvino also presents an apparent *contrast* between reading and lovemaking, arguing that, in contrast to reading texts, the reading of lovers

> starts at any point, skips, repeats itself, goes backward, insists, ramifies in simultaneous and divergent messages, converges again, has moments of irritation, turns the page, finds its place, gets lost. A direction can be recognized in it, a route to an end, since it tends toward a climax. . . . But is the climax really the end? Or is the race toward that end opposed by another drive which works in the opposite direction, swimming against the moments, recovering time? (156)

But what Calvino is really contrasting is not so much lovemaking and reading as two kinds of reading (as well as two kinds of lovemaking). These two modes are those encouraged by what Barthes calls the text of pleasure (*plaisir*) and the text of bliss (*jouissance*) (*Pleasure of the Text* 14). Classical texts produce pleasure by means of a linear movement toward climax and closure, but bliss results when that linearity is disrupted, when one gets lost in the process, forgets the goal, lingers on some parts, skips others, disregarding the "point" of the whole thing. *If on a winter's night a traveler* plays off this tension; it has an overarching plot that impels the reader forward, but it is structured around a series of digressions that are enticing enough to encourage blissful attention and forgetfulness of their relation to the whole.

In all sorts of ways, on a variety of levels, Calvino's novel splits and disperses the subject, whether we take the "subject" to be the narrator, a character, the reader, or, even, the author. Usually, in fact, there is confusion between at least two of those four terms. In the framing story, at the outset, there is confusion regarding the "you" who is both character and reader. And although at first we tend to take the narrator for granted, as we might take for granted the narrator of a third-person novel, confusions regarding that narrating voice begin in the first embedded story and intensify throughout the novel.

Each embedded story emerges as a first-person narration, the "I" of the story being both its narrator and protagonist. Because the numbered chapters modulate into these titled, first-person embedded sections, that "I" can, in fact, be seen as a continuation of the more anonymous narrator of the second-person chapters. If one takes the novel's pronouns at face value, then, the third-person narrator of the novel as a whole assumes numerous different first-person identities throughout; the narrator who speaks the "you" in the framing story becomes a whole series of diverse "I"'s in the framed stories. The following lines are from the first embedded story:

The lights of the station and the sentences you are reading seem to have the job of dissolving more than of indicating the things that surface from a veil of darkness and fog. I have landed in this station tonight for the first time in my life, entering and leaving this bar, moving from the odor of the platform to the odor of wet sawdust in the toilets, all mixed in a single odor which is that of waiting. (11)

The first sentence suggests a continuity with the first chapter, a narrator narrating a "you" who bought Calvino's novel, got himself comfortable, and is now reading it. That narrator uses the first-person pronoun in the next sentence. But when he speaks in the first-person at this point, it is not simply to acknowledge himself as a narrator and utilize a conventional direct address to the reader, but to establish himself now as a character in a new story, a first-person story, the story "If on a winter's night a traveler" by "Italo Calvino." This character, this "I" who narrates a story about his own experiences, enters the train station of a provincial town, apparently involved in some obscure assignment for an unidentified organization, and confused and paranoid because the connection and exchange of suitcases he was supposed to make haven't proceeded according to plan.

This pattern of metamorphosis, of modulating the narrative voice from a noninvolved, more or less omniscient narrator of the framing tale to an involved first-person narrator of an embedded story and then back to the anonymous narrator when each embedded story is interrupted, continues throughout the novel. In each embedded story the narrating

"I" can be seen as a new incarnation of the anonymous narrator of the framing story. Thus, the narrator of *If on a winter's night a traveler* is fractured and multiplied into a series of heterogeneous voices.

The various narrative voices are to a great extent separate and independent, but not totally so. Although the protagonists of the embedded stories are different—a criminal, a professor, a spy, a corporate leader, a writer, for example—there are resonances among their characters and situations. There is a recurring paranoia in these characters regarding the larger organization (police, espionage, criminal?) for which they may or may not be working; there is a recurring sense of guilt on their part, the result of some crime or indiscretion; there is sometimes the suggestion that the narrator himself has become the hunted, the likely victim of the organization for which he may have been working; often there is a woman who may be his ally but who turns on him or whom he himself victimizes.

Such continuities and resonances preclude our completely dissociating the different "I"'s who tell the various embedded stories. Moreover all those "I"'s are extensions or mutations of the narrator of the novel as a whole. The narrating subject of the novel presents a problematically interesting ambivalence between unity and multiplicity: It is not a single persona, but not quite a set of clearly different personae, either.

There are other complexities and ambiguities regarding the "you," the Reader, besides the obvious confusion between that "you" and the real reader of Calvino's novel. They arise when the Other Reader, Ludmilla, becomes herself addressed by the narrator. For about half the novel she is identified as another reader, but only in the third person, in contrast to the second-person first Reader. Then, early in the chapter in which the two Readers consummate their relationship,

What are you like, Other Reader? It is time for this book in the second person to address itself no longer to a general male you, perhaps brother and double of a hypocrite I, but directly to you who appeared already in the second chapter as the Third Person necessary for the novel to be a novel, for something to happen between that male Second Person and the female Third, for something to take form, develop, or deteriorate according to the phase of human events. (141)

Not only might she be the "you" who is addressed, rather than he, but the two of them may be merged and addressed together using the second-person plural pronoun.

You are in bed together, you two Readers. So the moment has come to address you in the second person plural, a very serious operation, because it is tantamount to considering the two of you a single subject. . . . Maybe afterward you will go your separate ways and the story will again have to shift gears painfully . . . ; but now, since your bodies are trying to find, skin to skin, the adhesion most generous in sensations, to transmit and receive vibrations and waves, to compenetrate the fullnesses and the voids . . . , you can be addressed with an articulated speech that includes you both in a sole, two-headed person. (154)

That "sole, two-headed person" is at once an organic being with two heads, two bodies fused into one in sexual intimacy, and the doubling of antecedents in the second "person" plural pronoun "you" (explicit in Italian as *voi*, distinct from the singular *tu*). The narrator's awareness of the gravity of his act, of its challenge to our commonsense understanding of the subject as identified with a single organic individual, is clear: it is "tantamount to considering the two of you a single subject."

In other of its aspects the novel presents a sense of subjectivity as metamorphic, provisional, and shifting. A name used in one story may be used for a different, unrelated character in another story. The figure of a young woman reading occurs on numerous occasions, often being watched, perhaps secretly, by a man. This figure is especially associated with Ludmilla, the Other Reader, whose reading suggests a kind of focused and unselfconscious absorption in literature, a "special bliss" (176) that fascinates other characters, including the First Reader. This female reader is elsewhere incarnated as a sultan's wife, who reads translations of Western literature, possibly receiving treasonous messages secretly encoded in them, and a woman in a deck chair, watched through a spyglass by Silas Flannery, the apparent author of some of the embedded stories. In a further variant, presented as a story idea of Flannery, two writers watch the woman reading from their respective chalets in Switzerland, each imagining that she is reading a novel written by the other.

Calvino creates confusions regarding his own identity. Italo Calvino is a real author who wrote the novel *If on a winter's night a traveler*. In that novel is the fragment of a different novel entitled "If on a winter's night a traveler," written by a fictitious writer named "Italo Calvino." Of course "Calvino" the character is no more the real Calvino than the real reader is the second-person protagonist of the novel. And the fragment, "If on a winter's night a traveler," is not the novel *If on a winter's night a traveler*, though the latter does contain the former. But the correspondence of the authors' names, along with the identical titles for their works, creates an almost inevitable confusion between the real and the fictional Calvino.

In other ways the notion of authorship is subverted. Ermes Marana is a putative translator who manages to obtain highly desirable manuscripts, often by elusive but important writers, including Flannery, along with the rights to those manuscripts. In fact Marana often misrepresents what he sends to publishers, submitting manuscripts incorrectly titled and attributed and sometimes passing off insignificant works as major works. Marana is a kind of anti-authorial terrorist. He is associated with the OEPHLW (Organization for the Electronic Production of Homogenized Literary Works), and, presenting himself as its representative, he offers Flannery "technical assistance to finish his novel" (122) when Flannery encounters writer's block. Marana is also the founder of the OAP (Organization of Apocryphal Power), a terrorist organization that tries to steal important literary manuscripts. Marana has left the OAP, which itself has split into two competing factions, but he continues to use theft, forgery, and misrepresentation to create such a chaos in world literature, such a proliferation of incorrect and misattributed manuscripts and editions, that reading will be freed from the constraints imposed on it by the aura of authorship.

When confronted by a publishing agent, a Mr. Cavedagna, regarding his misrepresentation of texts, Marana argues that the names that appear on book jackets are irrelevent. Ironically, Cavedagna himself comes to sympathize with Marana's position, and the Reader realizes that the most important authors, the "true authors" for Cavedagna, are those who are not known at all as individuals but are simply names on book jackets. Even Flannery, whose own works have been the object of Marana's terrorism, ends up sympathizing with Marana.

> How is it possible to defeat not the authors but the functions of the author, the idea that behind each book there is someone who guarantees a truth in that world of ghosts and inventions by the mere fact of having invested in it his own truth, of having identified himself with that construction of words? . . . Ermes Marana dreamed of a literature made entirely of apocrypha, of false attributions, of imitations and counterfeits and pastiches. If this idea had succeeded in imposing itself, if a systematic uncertainty as to the identity of the writer had kept the reader from abandoning himself with trust—trust not so much in what was being told him as in the silent narrative voice—perhaps externally the edifice of literature would not have changed at all, but beneath, in the foundations, where the relationship between reader and text is established, something would have changed forever. (159)

This freeing up of texts from the constraints of authorship is identical to that imagined by Foucault in his essay "What Is an Author?". Foucault often uses the expression "author-function" rather than "author," arguing that the author-function is a construction that imposes ideological constraints upon the reading of a body of texts identified as being by a certain "author." For Foucault the subject itself—and the subject of the author in particular—is a product of discourse rather than the origin of discourse (158). Historically, the author becomes significant when property rights and legal accountability become important; writing becomes a kind of property itself, and the author-function, like laws that impose constraints on the flow of property and wealth, imposes limits and conditions on reading.

> The author allows a limitation of the cancerous and dangerous proliferation of significations within a world where one is thrifty not only with one's resources and riches, but also with one's discourses and their significations. The author is the principle of thrift in the proliferation of meaning . . . he is a certain functional principle by which, in our culture, one limits, excludes, and chooses; in short, by which one impedes the free circulation, the free manipulation, the free composition, decomposition, and recomposition of fiction. (158–159)

It is this Foucauldian desire for "the free circulation, the free manipulation, the free composition, decomposition, and recomposition" of texts that Marana seeks to establish through forgery, theft, and misrepresentation. One might add that it is this free circulation and manipulation of writing and the resulting threat to traditional notions of authorship and intellectual property that are enhanced by new electronic means of replicating, revising, transmitting, and exchanging textual material.

Flannery, the elusive author who should be most threatened by this possibility, comes to look favorably upon it. His individuality, his "[s]tyle, taste, individual philosophy, subjectivity, cultural background, real experience, psychology, talent, tricks of the trade" all seem to be impediments to his writing. "How well I would write if I were not here!" (171). "I, too, would like to erase myself and find for each book another I, another voice, another name, to be reborn; but my aim is to capture in the book the illegible world, without center, without ego, without I" (180). It is significant that Flannery emerges not only as the possible author of some of the stories embedded in *If on a winter's night a traveler*, but as the likely author/narrator of the entire novel, the "I" who narrates the second-person framing story and also the "I" who is "reborn" into various incarnations in the first-person embedded stories.

Flannery imagines an impersonal, subjectless form of writing, which might be envisioned by using the verb "to write" in the same impersonal way we use the verb "to rain." Instead of saying "I write" one might say "It writes." (176). This notion of an agentless discourse suggests a full-blown poststructuralist position, in which power and ideology arise from language itself rather than from a conscious, rational, individual *cogito*.

Conventional understandings of authorship and the subject are also challenged elsewhere in the novel. Although its language continues to incorporate terminology suggesting the distinctions between "truth" and "falsehood," "original" and "copy," its various depictions of the process of textual replication gone awry finally challenge those distinctions and instead suggest a Baudrillardian notion of "hyperreality." For

Jean Baudrillard the proliferation of images in mass, technological society has resulted in a situation in which the whole problem of reference, as traditionally framed, is no longer meaningful. It is no longer a question of whether a particular representation—be it a newscast or a commercial or a theme park like Disneyland—is true or false or even partly true or false, because those representations have become so ubiquitous that they create their own "hyperreality." It is, in fact, more accurate to think of them not even as representations but as simulacra—pure similitudes that refer to nothing more than what they create themselves. The resulting hyperreality of mass-produced images is not susceptible to judgments of truth in the way that older kinds of representation seemed to be, and it renders obsolete any conventional distinction between original and copy. The authority of simulacra is a result of their dominance and ubiquity and not of their grounding in a referent in a world that lies outside the process of representation itself.

Under such circumstances, where signs are simultaneously opaque—they are mere surfaces referring to no reality beyond themselves—and vertiginously transparent—they replicate themselves endlessly and those replications never terminate in a final ground of established truth—the possibility for effective action socially and politically is all but eliminated. For where exactly is the reality that one is supposed to act upon? For Baudrillard the most significant political action today is passivity itself, a strategy hit upon by the masses through the intelligence of an unconscious that is capable of humor, irony, and parody in the face of the mass media, which on one hand represents them as free subjects but also simultaneously makes them into objects, conducting opinion polls and turning back to the masses images of themselves. In a kind of ironic rebellion, the masses accept their status as objects, refuse, on the other hand, to pretend to be free and involved subjects, and they parodically turn back to the media the image of themselves the media represents.

[T]he object, the individual . . . is not only condemned to disappearance, but *disappearance is also its strategy*; it is its way of response to this device for capture, for networking, and for forced identification. To this *cathodic* surface of recording, the individual or the mass reply by a parodic behavior of disappearance. . . . They turn themselves into an impenetrable and meaningless surface, which is a method of disappearing. They eclipse themselves; they melt into the superficial screen in such a way that their reality and that of their movement . . . may be radically questioned. . . .

There is and there always will be major difficulties in analyzing the media and the whole sphere of information through the traditional categories of the philosophy of the subject: will, representation, choice, liberty, deliberation, knowledge, and desire. For it is quite obvious that they are absolutely contradicted by the media; that the subject is absolutely alienated in its sovereignty. . . . [T]he media and even technics and science . . . have muddled the cards and deprived any subject of the disposal of his or her own body, desire, choice, and liberty. (*Selected Writings*, 213–214)

Thus, for Baudrillard the mass replication of representations has radical consequences for the subject as well. Not only is the subject itself replicated by the media, just as other "objects" are, but the subject becomes so powerless in this ungrounded network of representations and so inscribed itself in the hyperreal that the only possibility for "action" is a negative one—a parodic emulation of the condition of objectness that characterizes its representation in the media.

But the passivity and capitulation of the objectified subject are not quite complete. Because of the parody and because that parody is described as a "strategy," a residual politics—as well as a residual subject and a residual sense of agency—is nevertheless implied. One does not fight one's representation but simply turns back to the media the image of oneself presented in the media—just as the women in Kruger's visual works sometimes parodically emulate the roles ascribed to them by phallic power, presenting the viewer with exactly what "he" wants. "I am your reservoir of poses," one of her works declares. This strategy was, of course, suggested earlier in the visual works of Andy Warhol, whose art— as well as life—turned back to the media stereotypes that the media created and disseminated.[5] Parody may be a politics of despair, but as long as there is parody, the despair is not complete. Baudrillard's belief in the inventiveness of a residual subject, enabling it creatively to engage in a strategic use of parody, is itself a kind of endgame humanism.

The poststructural challenge to reference and the subject, with its roots in philosophy and linguistics, is echoed by Baudrillard, who sees a similar challenge emerging from the sociology of everyday life in a world whose landscape is dominated by mass-replicated imagery. One might, in fact, argue that what might be called "high postmodernism" occurs with the convergence of these two sources of challenge to reference and authenticity: the poststructural source, drawing on linguistics and philosophy, and the social and psychological analysis of the impact of the contemporary landscape itself, dominated by mass-produced commercial and popular imagery.

Such issues are suggested in Calvino's novel by the free circulation of misattributed translations that Marana promotes, wherein any attempt to trace a work to its legal and authentic authorial source becomes ludicrous. But also in other ways the theme of multiplication and replication, to the point of disturbing the possibility of locating an authentic origin, recurs in the novel. One section, entitled "In a network of lines that intersect," is a segment of a novel possibly written by Flannery but possibly

a fake by Marana. In it a powerful businessman creates numerous doubles, actors posing as himself, whose movements and activities are choreographed so as to confuse his enemies. He also creates multiples of
both his wife and his mistress and arranges for "fake" liaisons between
his own doubles and those of his mistress. He eludes kidnappers by creating fake kidnappings, fake ransoms, fake payments, and, in fact, entire
fake criminal organizations which create plots and counterplots. Of
course, the best fake criminal organization is a real criminal organization, or a fake organization that carries out criminal activities so effectively that any distinction between it and a real criminal organization
dissolves. When the businessman is kidnapped and encounters his mistress, apparently herself a prisoner, as well as his wife, things have gotten
so confusing that he no longer knows what kind of reality to attribute to
the kidnapping, his mistress, his wife, or even himself. "Already I can
distinguish no longer what belongs to one and what belongs to the other,
I am lost, I seem to have lost myself, I cannot see my reflection but only
theirs" (168).

As in Baudrillard's analysis, the subject becomes lost in a mirror maze
of reflections and representations. When replication and multiplication
decenter the world by depriving it of a reference that grounds, that "authorizes" those replications and multiplications, the subject itself reflects
that decenteredness, as it does when viewing a painting that contains
multiple, inconsistent vanishing points or when reading a novel that
consistently shifts voice. In the end the subject cannot even distinguish
itself from the world that was previously viewed as object and reverts to a
pre-symbolic, imaginary identification with the world. Calvino's kaleido-
scopic businessman says, "Now it seems to me that everything that surrounds me is a part of me, that I have managed to become the whole,
finally . . . " (168). But if he is "whole," it is a different kind of wholeness
from that which we usually imagine. This wholeness is not that of an
independent, complete individual, separate from the rest of the world—
a Renaissance man, a self-realized *cogito*—but a "wholeness" in which
the subject dissolves into the world around it, in which the very distinction between subject and object is obliterated.

This loss of groundedness is also reflected in the financial transactions
of the narrator of "In a network of lines that intersect."

I have built my financial empire on the very principle of kaleidoscopes and catop-
tric instruments, multiplying, as if in a play of mirrors, companies without capital,
enlarging credit, making disastrous deficits vanish in the dead corners of illusory
perspectives. My secret, the secret of my uninterrupted financial victories . . . has
always been this: that I never thought directly of money, business, profits, but
only of the angles of refraction established among shining surfaces variously in-
clined. (162)

Any notion of wealth or value as rooted in labor or in "use-value" becomes lost. Money and certificates do not themselves stand for anything real that has value, but wealth results from the manipulation of representation itself, from the creation of "illusory perspectives." National and international electronic transfers and exchanges eliminate even the need for paper, creating even more abstract representations of value, even further removed from anything rooted in real human needs. Fredric Jameson and Baudrillard argue that representation itself becomes a source of value. Signs are themselves the things that are manufactured, sold, and circulated. In a world of imaginary relations to imaginary things, the world becomes obsessed with what Jameson calls "sheer images" and "pseudo-events." He writes,

> It is for such objects that we may reserve Plato's conception of the "simulacrum,"
> the identical copy for which no original has ever existed. Appropriately enough,
> the culture of the simulacrum comes to life in a society where exchange value has
> been generalized to the point at which the very memory of use value is effaced.
> (Jameson, 18)

Technological means of replicating and transmitting texts, images, and information are crucial in creating a postmodern "culture of the simulacrum." Computers figure significantly in Calvino's novel as a way of demystifying literature and the author. There is the suggestion that a properly programmed computer might emulate the work of famous writers. But there is also something about the entire structure of the novel that calls to mind computerized texts and electronic networks. The shiftings, slippages, and transformations of reading and writing subjects, the replication and transmission of texts, and the problematizing of the distinction between authenticity and forgery anticipate the transmission, replication, and revision of ideas in electronic networks, which also challenge traditional notions of self and authorship and problematize attribution and intellectual property.

In fact, Calvino's novel demonstrates a structure much like that which George P. Landow describes in his book *Hypertext: The Convergence of Contemporary Critical Theory and Technology.* In a fully developed hypertextual system the proliferation of nodes and links produces a web that finally subverts any original Aristotelian textual structure, possessing a clear beginning, middle, and end. The different narrative fragments in Calvino's novel—the different *lexias,* to use the term Landow borrows from Roland Barthes (*S/Z*, 13)—are linked together to create a branching and labyrinthine network through which the embedded Reader moves, in a way not unlike the way a different kind of reader, seated in front of a computer terminal, might navigate a hypertextual *network.* Two of Calvino's embedded stories are, in fact, entitled "In a network of lines that inter-lace" and "In a network of lines that intersect." In this kind of network the sense of a primary axis of movement gets lost, just as a fully developed hypertextual system subverts the sense of a single, primary path of move-ment from one lexia to another. Madeleine Sorapure describes the ex-perience of reading the novel in terms that could be used to describe a hypertextual reading experience.

Readers of *If on a winter's night a traveler* find themselves immersed in fragments of stories, clues that seem to lead nowhere, tangled complexities, and must ex-tract their own meaning, make their own connections between fragments, trace their own paths through the labyrinth of the text. (705)

Of course in Calvino's novel it is only the embedded Reader who does this fully, whose quest for narrative experience produces a linking of tex-tual fragments into a larger narrative structure that is no Aristotelian unity, to be sure, but is not quite random or arbitrary either. The real reader of the novel remains, in a more or less traditional way, controlled by the physical sequence of words, sentences, paragraphs, pages, and chapters. And, of course, Calvino does provide us with a perhaps facile, definitely tongue-in-cheek, somewhat abrupt, "Aristotelian" closure at the end. Calvino's novel is a book and not a hypertext.[6] Nevertheless, the experience his character/readers have and which the real reader vicari-ously shares—a series of partial narratives linked partly through accident and partly through choice—is similar to the Barthesian writerly reading that Landow imagines, and it can be seen as a forecast of the nonlinear joining of lexias in hypertextual systems. Landow sees the subject as freed and empowered by hypertext, in contrast to Baudrillard's nearly invisible subject, hypnotized into passivity by the cathode ray, reduced to parrot-ing and parody. It is possible that hypertext, with its demands for a more actively engaged reader who navigates and participates, may suggest at least the possibility of an antidote to the passivity encouraged by the spec-tator of traditional video.

*   *   *

Experimentation with point of view, with its implications regarding the subject, is a hallmark of twentieth-century literary art, not only in the examples treated here but in such seminal works as James Joyce's *Ulysses* and T. S. Eliot's *The Waste Land*, works that stand in relation to what came after them in the way that Picasso's *Demoiselles d'Avignon* stands in relation to the later development of modern painting. Both literary works involve collage constructions in which diverse voices alternate and compete, weakening the sense of a unified narrative voice. But if, in works like these, the sense of a coherent speaking voice is weakened, this weakening is not the result of a frontal attack on the classical subject but is carried out in the name of creating a new kind of collage-like art construct that reflects the complexity of subjectivity and intersubjectivity and the heterogeneity of modern life.

Moreover, through the agency of the artist—who, in spite of the narrative dissolution, remains implicit as a supreme fabricator behind the heterogeneous voices of the text—some unity is forged out of that complexity and diversity, even if it is a unity that can be achieved only in art. Such works—in spite of their ambivalences, complexities, and doubts— continue the Romantic tradition of the specialness of the artist and the importance of art as a vehicle that can bring meaning and order into a world in which meaning and order might not otherwise exist. Absent transcendental religious and metaphysical values, the artistic act that is required is even more creative: the artist must, as Stephen Dedalus says, "forge in the smithy of my soul the uncreated conscience of my race" (James Joyce, 525).

Belsey describes the continuity of the subject of the author between Romanticism and early modernism:

It is readily apparent that Romantic and post-Romantic poetry, from Wordsworth through the Victorian period at least to Eliot and Yeats, takes subjectivity as its central theme. The developing self of the poet, his consciousness of himself as poet, his struggle against the constraints of an outer reality, constitute the preoccupations of *The Prelude, In Memoriam,* or *Meditations in Time of Civil War.* The "I" of these poems is a kind of super-subject, experiencing life at a higher level of intensity than ordinary people and absorbed in a world of selfhood which the phenomenal world . . . either nourishes or constrains. (67–68)

Although she acknowledges that the Romantic and post-Romantic subject is not entirely unproblematical, that there is an "increasing despair as the contradictions in the Romantic rejection of the world became increasingly manifest" (123), Belsey argues for the primary importance of the authorial subject in this period. In fiction, where direct authorial intrusion becomes less overt, the author's presence nevertheless remains as a "shadowy authority" behind the text (68).

In *post*modern works the representation of the subject, even that of the artist, is the object of a more radical revision, and the art does not quite bring it all together anyway. If modernist novels like those of Conrad and Faulkner weaken and distance the subject or if their characters display a degree of slippage, the discourse of one making penetrations

into the consciousness of another, Calvino's novel more radically disperses the subject, vertically from reader to character and, within the
narrative, horizontally across characters, creating hybrids, authors and
forgers who shift identities, characters who pop up in different places
and may or may not be the same ones, as well as that "sole, two-headed
person" whom the two embodiments of the second-person protagonist
become. The various embedded narratives remain unclosed, and the apparent closure of the overall story is unconvincing, abrupt, leaving many
questions unanswered. *Heart of Darkness* challenges the subject at its elusive center, and *As I Lay Dying* challenges it at the skin that separates self
from other. In Calvino's novel, however, there is less a sense of loss or
threat because of this absence of center and separation and more the
sense that a new kind of centerless subject is being described, one that
freely metamorphoses from one role to another, from one position to
another, a traveling subject that is replacing the classical *cogito*. Moreover, artistic genius itself is challenged by the suggestion that a computer
might create works like those of major authors.

The classical subject is radically questioned as well in works by Samuel
Beckett, John Fowles, John Barth, Thomas Pynchon, Don DeLillo, and
Ishmael Reed, who, in *Mumbo Jumbo* (1972), mixes literary and non-
literary voices, voices from sources as diverse as jazz vernacular, the mass
media, and avant-garde literature, in order to create a hip heterogeneous subcultural (as opposed to individualistic) assault on the unified,
logocentric subject of Western man. Similarly, a work like Kathy Acker's
Empire of the Senseless (1988) mixes discourse levels, literary and non-
literary, intellectual and vernacular, lofty and obscene, and her protagonist, a black, female cyborg, is a "subject" that crosses boundaries that
usually define the "subject." [7]

Such works are overt challenges to the unitary subject. Interestingly,
David Carroll, in *The Subject in Question: The Languages of Theory and the
Strategies of Fiction*, deconstructs the unified subject in the works of Henry
James, an author whose works seem to valorize that subject. Carroll analyzes the Jamesian notion that a coherent subject must provide an indis-
pensable center of consciousness that informs and unifies the formal
structure of successful fiction. Whether that center is taken to be the
consciousness of a character or that of the author, the writings of
James—both his writings about fiction and the novels themselves—are
more complex and contradictory than is acknowledged by many of those
who see themselves as following in James's footsteps and who use his
ideas and example as a justification for a formalist approach to fiction.
The fictional subject, in James's theory, is really simply a vehicle, ultimately leading to the "real" subject of the work, the one who provides

the foundation for the work and whose point of view really counts, the author.

The fictional-subject as center and origin is not solid enough ground for the novel, not sufficiently substantial or autonomous. The author-subject will provide the definitive origin and center of the novel. . . . He will not speak in his own voice or see directly with his own eyes—but *his voice* and *his eyes* will be there behind the consciousness and voice of the fictional subject he has constructed. The author-subject is the "true," transcendent subject of what I would call James's phenomenology of fiction and form. (Carroll, 56)

However, when that "author-subject" is closely examined, he also fails to provide the firm foundation one might have expected. James acknowledges that he himself sometimes does not remember what he was thinking of when he began a work and, more importantly, that what his novels became was often far removed from his original intentions, whatever those intentions might have been. Works become "monsters" that grow into creatures that are far different from what anyone, even the author, might have anticipated, given the "germ" that got them started in the first place.

Thus, when readers identify an apparent unified center of consciousness in a novel, whether they take that center to be the consciousness of a character or that of the author, it is not a result of characteristics that exist in the novel itself but of theoretical positions they hold and impose on the novel. On the other hand, when Carroll discusses the challenge to the subject posed by structuralist theory and the French New Novel, especially the works of Claude Simon, he argues that the subject lingers, perhaps subtly, even among writers and theorists who seem to have done away with it. The subject, when closely examined, always is problematical. But it is not easily dispensed with. Therefore, rather than assume, with impunity, that the subject has been done away with, that we have somehow gone beyond it, it makes more sense to problematize, question, and analyze the way the subject manifests itself in literary works than to naively assume it can be eliminated entirely.

Certainly the works examined here demonstrate this grappling with a slippery subject, never quite catching it, testifying rather to the fact that it can't be caught, but not completely eliminating it either. In these works the discourse acts as the trace of that which eludes discourse. It is significant that even in Calvino's work, the subversion of textual and authorial authority that is carried out so rigorously is done at least partly in order to free up reading for the *reader*, the second-person protagonist in the novel and, we can assume, the real reader of the novel as well.

Chapter 3
The Moving Subject

Stunts and Other Masquerades

The protagonist of Richard Rush's film, *The Stunt Man* (1980), like the Reader of Calvino's *If on a winter's night a traveler*, finds himself enmeshed in a confusing labyrinth of reality and representation. Devices such as ambiguous perspectives, contradictory points of view, and the confusion of reality and illusion are used to provoke epistemological questioning and a problematizing of the self. The main action of the film is instigated by an early misunderstanding of events by the protagonist, and the film is subsequently structured around a series of Pirandellian confusions that occur during the making of a movie.

The introductory sequence of the film encapsulates aspects of the film's structure and themes. A buzzard flies off a telephone pole as a police car below honks at a dog that has been sleeping in the road. The dog moves off and, behind a shot of the police car, a helicopter enters the frame. The helicopter flies by two telephone linemen, who comment on how close it came to them. They throw something at the buzzard, now perched on a nearby pole, scaring it off. The buzzard flies into the helicopter. "That goddamn bird . . . just tried to kill us," the pilot remarks. "That's your point of view. Should we stop and ask the bird what his was?" the passenger, Eli Cross (Peter O'Toole), replies. He throws an apple out of the chopper, which bounces off the roof of a café and onto the roof of the parked police car, startling its two occupants. "Something hit the roof," one of them says. "So will the chief if we don't grab this guy Cameron," the other replies.

The cops, aroused by the bump on the roof of their car, go into a diner to make an arrest. On a television screen Nina (Barbara Hershey), who plays a major role later in the film, appears in a commercial. Cameron

(Steve Railsback), scruffy, paranoid, is arrested and handcuffed. But he escapes, runs into the woods, and encounters the linemen. He overcomes one of them, who tries to apprehend him, and he uses their tools to cut the chain of the handcuffs.

Cameron (whose name is a pun, "camera on") is a fugitive and a Vietnam veteran. After he escapes, he stumbles onto a bridge that is being used as a location in a film. He misinterprets the actions of a stunt man driving a Duesenberg and, believing that the man is trying to run him down, throws a large bolt at the car, breaking its windshield. The Duesenberg drives over the edge of the bridge and sinks. The plunge into the water was part of a stunt being filmed, but Cameron assumes he is responsible. When the driver fails to surface Cameron also assumes that he has caused the man's death. The stunt man has, in fact, been killed, although it remains unclear whether or not Cameron's breaking the windshield had anything to do with it.

Moments later the helicopter descends and hovers in front of Cameron. Cross, the passenger who earlier threw the apple startling the cops into action, stares out at him, like an omniscient god descended from heaven, aware of Cameron's transgression. The helicopter is suggestive of helicopters used in Vietnam; a camera, like a gun, is positioned in an opening.

By this point in the film a whole sequence of events has occurred. Sometimes those events are causally connected, as if they are part of a complex Rube Goldberg machine; other times there is no real causality between juxtaposed events but simply a spatial and temporal contiguity. More significantly, the individuals involved often are unaware of how their lives are implicated with one another's. The linemen startle a bird, which flies into the chopper. Cross drops an apple, which startles policemen below, reminding them that they have to arrest Cameron. Later, after he is arrested, Cameron encounters the same linemen in the woods, who are already indirectly implicated in his life because of a chain of events of which neither he nor they are aware. And when Cross descends to look at Cameron on the bridge, he also is already implicated in Cameron's life because of the apple he threw earlier, which was associated with Cameron's arrest and subsequent escape to that very bridge.

Not only are these interlinked individuals unaware of the silent, unspoken connections that exist among them, the audience is also very likely confused. The predominance of close-ups reinforces the partiality of the audience's vision. All perspectives are local—a dog snarls at a police car, a helicopter collides with a bird, a fugitive escapes—and it is difficult, perhaps impossible, to find a vantage point from which one might have a broad overview, from which one might see the interconnectedness of things, the kind of overview provided by establishing shots or panoramas in classical movies.

A series of metaphorical relationships begins to be established that is maintained and reinforced throughout the film. Helicopters used to make films are like helicopters used to make war. The whirling blades of the crane that carries Cross above and about the location of his film are similar to the blades of the helicopter that at other times carries him. Cross is a god-the-father figure, the master-of-the-spectacle, and the "system" that cannot be beaten. Cameron, who is "conscripted" by blackmail into Cross's film, is the son, a soldier, a stunt man, and a performer struggling to escape from the performance Cross plans for him, from the orders he must obey. Cameras point at people like guns. Shooting a film is like shooting a war. Having set up these associations, the manner in which the film deals with them and the way it develops and tries to resolve the Oedipal struggle between Cross and Cameron have implications regarding power, representation, and the subject.

After the incident on the bridge Cameron wanders into the seacoast town and beach area where most of the film is being shot. In an attempt to make himself less conspicuous among the tourists he cuts off the legs of his jeans and tries on a hat, checking his appearance in a mirror. When he does this he creates his first disguise and unwittingly performs an action that begins his movement into a world where his identity is regularly transformed and where the self that he is increasingly is indistinguishable from the representation he constructs.

Cross, having lost Burt, his own stunt man, persuades Cameron to take Burt's place, to pretend he *is* Burt. Thus, the filming will be able to proceed: there will be a replacement for the lost stunt man and there will be no investigation of a man killed or missing. Cross tells Cameron that he will be "a stunt man, who is an actor, who is a character in a movie, who is an enemy soldier." Pointing to the door of the makeup room, he says, "That door is a looking glass and inside it is Wonderland. Have faith, Alice . . . and enjoy." Cross offers Cameron a vertiginous world of delight, where dreams can be lived and illusions can become realities. But Cameron must, in exchange, accept Cross's position as the master manipulator who controls the machine of pleasure, fantasy, and identity. Cameron closes his eyes, and when he opens them he sees in a mirror his new face—a copy of Burt copying Raymond, the leading man, made up to play the role of a World War I hero.

The Stunt Man abounds in pyrotechnical confusions of art and life. Sometimes they are confusions on the part of Cameron; sometimes they are tricks on the audience. Cross, in his quest for spontaneity, sometimes alters the script of stunts without informing Cameron. Cameron, whose sense of his own fixed identity becomes increasingly subverted through-out the film, oscillates between consciously playing his role and becom-ing confused and reacting spontaneously and "authentically," as if he is involved in real situations and not merely acting. In one scene, he falls onto an awning that he has been told would hold him. It does not hold, he falls through it, and then through a skylight onto a bed where a couple lies. He is suddenly in a German brothel. Soldiers seize him, carry him out of the room, and strip him, cameras rolling all the while. He is confused, humiliated, and angered, but when Cross yells "Cut!" there is applause, congratulations, and a kiss from the leading lady. He is sud-denly transformed from a victim into a hero, and his anger and humilia-tion dissipate.

Cameron finds himself in a *mise-en-abîme*, a vertiginous hall of mir-rors, a network of representations without firm ground, that is Cross's creation. He resents Cross's domination, but there are advantages to Cameron's capitulation. In the cinematic world of illusions and perfor-mances, he is protected from the police. He is also a hero, one who is admired and who possesses a special mystique based on his physical abili-ties and his willingness to take risks. And only in Cross's cinematic world can he have Nina, the actress, the leading lady. Ironically, in that world he must engage in an Oedipal competition with Cross himself for her attentions.

Cameron becomes convinced that Cross, having gotten his use out of him as Burt's replacement, will kill him by having him perform the same stunt that killed Burt. A crucial aspect of our response to the film hinges on whether we view Cameron's fears as rational or paranoid. Although Cameron, as a Vietnam veteran and a fugitive, is predisposed to suspi-cion and mistrust, there is abundant evidence that his fear of Cross is not completely unfounded. Cross's altering of scripts without informing Cameron has contributed to Cameron's suspicions. When Nina con-fronts Cross about Cameron's fear that Cross is trying to harm him, Cross sidesteps the issue by stating, "Any number of people are trying to harm him." Henry, a cinematographer Cross fires, tells Cameron that when Burt was in trouble, Cross insisted that Henry keep shooting. Concern for Burt's life evidently took second place to Cross's obsession with com-pleting his film.

Cross's behavior in the case of Burt's death might be rationalized: There was nothing to be done about Burt so why not, at least, save the film? However, a later incident is harder to justify. Nina's parents are visiting and are invited to watch some rushes of their daughter. Somehow a nude love scene between her and Raymond has been included among the otherwise innocent shots. The parents are appalled to see their daughter perform such a scene. Later Cross prepares Nina for a scene in which she is supposed to express shame, and he tells her about the incident just before the cameras roll, exploiting it in order to put her in the right mood for her scene. It is also possible that he actually planned the entire thing.

Cross's language frequently suggests aggression and the need to control. He refers to the crane that carries him around the set as "Eli's killer crane." And in a conversation about the possibility of one of his scenes being cut, he assures Cameron and Sam, the scriptwriter, that it won't be cut because if it is "I'll kill them. And then I'll eat them." Ironically, Cross is passionately aggressive in a way that Cameron, who has had a much more direct experience with violence and who probably *has* killed, cannot be.

In spite of ample evidence suggesting that Cross is quite unscrupulous and willing to utilize whatever means are necessary to complete his film, at other times the film itself tries to persuade us otherwise, to persuade us that Cameron's fears are the result of paranoia and Cross is really a decent fellow trying to complete a worthwhile, moral project. Early in the film Cross seems genuinely grieved over what happened to Burt and says that no film is worth the death of an individual. Moreover, we may view Cross's Machiavellianism as justified, at least in part, by the importance of his goal, making an effective antiwar movie.

The problem is that Cameron never comes off as the dangerous, paranoid character with the "dark soul" that both Cross and Sam describe. To the extent that Cameron is paranoid, it is the paranoia of Joseph Heller's Yossarian—he is afraid that everyone is trying to kill him because everyone is trying to kill him. Even when Cameron threw the bolt at Burt's car, the "paranoid" misinterpretation that instigated his whole involvement in Cross's film, the car was speeding toward him in such a way that even a reasonable person might assume the driver was trying to run him over. Cameron *has* been to Vietnam; the police *are* after him; Cross *has* demonstrated himself to be unscrupulous when his film is at stake. And Burt, whom Cameron has not simply replaced but, in effect, *become*, did die while playing the same role Cameron is now assigned in Cross's film.

The various statements Cross and Sam make about Cameron's dangerous, paranoid character do not, in fact, jibe with most of the evidence we get from the film. It is as if the film is urging us to believe that Cameron is paranoid and Cross is a moral individual, highly committed to a virtuous goal, even as that view is subverted by the evidence of the film itself. Significantly, *The Stunt Man* does not have an unresolved, open ending, leaving the audience with two or more different but opposed, equally possible explanations for its events. Instead it attempts to dispel inevitable questions, close off possible interpretations, and eliminate ambiguity. In the end it in effect asserts that Cross is good and humane and that Cameron has been dangerous and misguided. But because Cameron has not really seemed *that* unstable and because Cross has frequently demonstrated himself to be unscrupulous, the film seems at odds with itself, asserting that it is about paranoia, but continually giving the impression it is about megalomania.

This abdication of the political is reinforced by an exchange, early in the film, among Cross, Sam, and Cameron.

SAM: The problem is, Eli, way back when, when you were all so charged up about making a great big antiwar statement, they wouldn't let you. Well, now they'll let you but you haven't got a war. What you do have, my friend, is a great deal of egg on your face. . . .

ELI: This film I'm making is not about fighting wars, Sam.

SAM: Oh?

ELI: No, its about fighting windmills. Appalling though it is, war isn't the disease, it's merely one of the symptoms.

SAM: Eli, what is the disease?

ELI: Ah, Sam, interesting. Define the disease. Write me a new scene. The egg will drop from my face and we shall have a relevant screenplay.

Eli asks Cameron to repeat a saying from Vietnam, about the need to assume that the man facing you is trying to kill you if you want to "get home for Thanksgiving." Eli then says, "Sam, perhaps that's what our film's about, being scared shitless, whistling in the dark, inventing enemies."

Thus, the choice the film makes: the problem is windmills, not wars; misjudgment, not the struggle for power; and paranoia, not megalomania. War does not produce paranoid individuals; paranoid individuals are themselves the problem. Enemies are invented. The film's potentially subversive content is thereby domesticated and contained.

In a prop room Cameron confesses his "crime" to Nina. After he returned from Vietnam, enraged over a broken commitment and a betrayal by his "old lady," he tears apart a friend's ice cream store, pouring different flavored ice creams and syrups all over. As he describes this he enacts the scene, knocking over cans of paint of various colors and creating a pile of spilled paint and paint buckets—comic metaphors for ice cream, ice cream buckets, and syrups—into which he and Nina fall. In the store it was a cop who fell into the mess, after Cameron knocked him out and left him with his head resting in an ice cream bucket. As a result the frostbitten cop lost the tip of his nose and an ear lobe. Although Cameron's crime is not insignificant, it does have a comic aspect, and certainly it falls short of the possible crimes one might have imagined were part of his supposedly dark and criminal past.

Cameron and Nina try to escape, but they cannot because a guard, acting under Eli's instructions, will not let anyone leave. Cameron then gives expression to the feeling that he is controlled by, that he is in fact constructed or *written* by, some power outside himself. "That son of a bitch knows whatever I'm thinking. I'm beginning to feel like something Sam wrote. I'm not real. I'm some jerk American flier from World War I who's got to go off a bridge and die because some goddamn script says so." Cameron's subjection to the script of Cross's movie corresponds to the subjection of a soldier required to obey orders, the "script" written for him by military and political authorities. Cameron's role in Cross's film is analogous to the role he played in Vietnam.

At this point Cameron and Nina simultaneously begin to get the same idea. There is a shot of Cameron, on the right side of the frame, from inside the Duesenberg. Nina's face dissolves into the shot on the left, as if it is reflected in the window. Both begin to smile as he continues: "If they just tore out that page, just ripped it out, you know, I'd be fine. If they crossed it out and wrote something else, like 'At the last moment he veers the big car from the railing and goes speeding off to live happily ever after.' " Cameron and Nina begin to recognize the possibility that it may not be inevitable that they live the story that Eli and Sam have authored but may be possible for them to rescript their lives themselves. "Hey, how about that, huh? Empty road, me out there all alone. The crew they're way back, they're breathless. As I approach the bridge . . . I can have fifteen minutes on them before they even know they're shooting a whole goddamn new version." Nina insists on locking herself in the trunk so that the next day, when the final stunt is filmed, they can escape together.

This rescripting by Cameron and Nina represents the only point in the film at which the potential for radical transformation is glimpsed and contemplated. Rescripting suggests the possibility of becoming one's own author, of becoming an agent, subject to oneself rather than to some other power.

The scene is shot in a way that evokes the Lacanian mirror phase and the instigation of the imaginary, the moment at which the individual first conceives of him or her self as an autonomous entity. Nina's face, reflected in the window through which Cameron's face is seen, calls to mind Lacanian descriptions of the mother holding the child up to the mirror so that both of them can be seen. In this scenario it is the mother who "authorizes" the child's birth into subjecthood.

In the mirror the child perceives the familiar household objects, and also its object par excellence, its mother, who holds it up in her arms to the glass. But above all it perceives its own image. This is where primary identification (the formation of the ego) gets certain of its main characteristics: the child sees itself as an other, and beside an other. This other other is its guarantee that the first is really it:

by her authority, her sanction, in the register of the symbolic, subsequently by the resemblance between her mirror image and the child's (both have a human form). (Metz, 45)

The moment at which Cameron imagines the possibility of independence is joined with his mirror reflection in the window. Significantly, Nina is also present, alongside him in that image, the "other other" who guarantees, authorizes, and sanctions his independence and coherence—and therefore significantly qualifies that independence and coherence. He is paradoxically dependent on her for his independence; his need for her to validate his wholeness suggests that he is incomplete.

Perhaps this original lack, which can't be filled or fully compensated, explains in part Cameron's continued vulnerability to paternal control— to seduction by Cross and the hyperreal world of film. In spite of Nina and the scene in the prop room, throughout the film it is the father whose power prevails and, in the end, is valorized. The imaginary wholeness associated with Nina and Cameron's reflection really functions to set the stage not for the overthrow of Cross but for his final victory. In the end the film withdraws from the notion of self-scripting and creates a "happy" ending in which a benevolent father is legitimized as master-of-the-spectacle and fabricator of subjects. Cameron accepts his position as a character in a world constructed by Cross. The power of the image, of the imaginary, is appropriated by Cross, who uses it to consolidate his own power. Cameron is enticed, seduced, and defined by the image, but in the end Cross controls the spectacle as well as the script, the image as well as the language.

The following day the cast and crew assemble at the bridge. Cross gives instructions that "once the action starts, no matter what happens, keep film rolling. We must have this shot. I therefore order that no camera shall jam and no cloud pass before the sun." The statement is presented as if it were hyperbole, but Cross's godlike power is nevertheless emphasized.

Raymond steps up to the Duesenberg and, referring to Nina, says, "No need to look. . . . If she loves you she's still there. If she doesn't then it really doesn't matter anyway." Again, Cameron's feeling of entrapment within a larger deterministic system that knows and controls even his thoughts is reinforced. Even his rebellion is contained within that larger determinism, is itself a planned part of the script, and is therefore no real rebellion at all. He panics and, before the cue is given, begins racing across the bridge. But the car has been rigged and a button is pushed, causing a blowout. The car swerves and plunges into the water, just as planned. Before finally sinking, it briefly surfaces and Cameron sees Cross and Nina looking down at him from the bridge above. A red light above the dashboard indicates that the camera behind Cameron's head is rolling.

However, Cameron, unlike Burt, escapes. He crawls ashore, exhausted, and actors, dressed as German soldiers, approach and surround him. Cameron is so disoriented that once again he confuses reality and performance. This confusion is enhanced by the fact that some of the soldiers are real policemen who had been hunting him earlier, now hired as extras. After Cross yells "Cut!" the soldiers' aggressive screams modulate into congratulations, as in the brothel scene. Cameron breaks into a loud full laugh. It is a laughter that is supposed to suggest insight and recognition: his situation is absurd, but that absurdity is the result of a kind of "cosmic" joke that has been played on him. Now that he understands the joke, he has comic distance on himself and his condition and will no longer take himself so seriously. And if this recognition is not enough to seduce him into acceptance, the beautiful Nina, enthralled once again by his courtship of danger, approaches him.

Cross descends, first in his helicopter, then in his crane. The presence of frogmen in the water, who would have saved Cameron if necessary, demonstrate that Cross has taken appropriate precautions and never meant to harm Cameron. Nina says that she was found five minutes after he left her in the trunk of the car. Cross explains to Cameron that he wouldn't let him leave the previous night because he wanted to "convince the world, with my movie, there is a reasonable and better way of getting home for Thanksgiving." Thus, the nobility of Cross's goal, which justifies any questionable means he may have employed, is emphasized at the end of the film. And the lesson he has taught Cameron is tied in with the goal of his film:

CROSS: I couldn't let you go through life, anonymous, paranoid, thinking I was trying to kill you, could I?
CAMERON: Paranoid?
CROSS: Sam, your screenplay has just become relevant again. The young man has named the disease.
SAM: Oh yeah? What is it?
CROSS: It's a social disease, quite common.
SAM: Yeah? Like crabs? The clap? Or what?
CROSS: Both. It's got from screwing your fellow man.

The message the film finally emphasizes, the end justifying all of Cross's questionable means, is that the problems of the world are a result of "screwing your fellow man." No doubt there is truth in such a statement, but it is of such a vague and general nature as to be practically meaningless. As an antiwar statement it is obviously useless. Thus, although the film broaches important and interesting issues relating to power, violence, and subjectivity, in the end it domesticates those issues by recasting power as benign and presenting a platitude as a valuable insight.

As Cross flies off (now back in the helicopter), he and Cameron bicker through a walkie-talkie about the pay for the stunt. But with lively, playful music in the background, Cross's dropping of colored smoke from the chopper, and his last joking statement—"Sam, rewrite the opening reel. Crush the little bastard in the first act"—the tone is light and comic. The conflict between Cameron and Cross, with all its political and psychological implications, is trivialized. In spite of this last, light disagreement over pay, we have little doubt that Cameron will accept his place in Cross's world. Like other conflicts between fathers and sons, theirs may go on forever, but there is no danger of a serious challenge to Cross's authority. Cameron has recognized the joke and now will accept his shifting identities within the hyperreality of movie making, along with the seductive advantages it offers.

The Stunt Man is a film that delights, through its vertiginous pacing, its *coups de théâtre* and sudden mood shifts, and its art-and-life pyrotechnics. Moreover, it sets up interesting thematic implications relating to power and subjection, the world and representations of the world, and the construction of subjects. However, having set up such issues, it attempts to close off and suppress certain dangerous interpretations. Cameron is (or has been) paranoid, and Cross is not, after all, brutal or monomaniacal. Just as Cross's brutality is suppressed at the end, Burt's death early in the film is forgotten, reconstructed by new representations. Film of the accident is manipulated in order to deceive the police, and Cameron becomes Burt. For all practical purposes, there has been no death. And, in spite of Cross's assertion that he wants to make a serious antiwar movie, the message that is finally delivered is that life is an absurd, metaphysical joke that, once you get, is really quite funny.

The problem posited by *The Stunt Man* is precisely one that has been treated in many recent discussions of the hyperreal. Should we reconcile ourselves to the world of simulacra, let, in fact, our selves be constituted by representations of selves, and despair of the possibility of seriously engaging the world? Or should we struggle to understand critically the world and affect it, difficult though that might be? The ending of *The Stunt Man*, with its retreat from serious engagement with the issues it raises, suggests a final victory of the hyperreal over the real.

Moreover, the understanding of the subject posited by the film and the film's politics suggest a dangerous possibility. The view that the subject is radically constructed is juxtaposed with a reactionary politics that valorizes authority and suggests that authority has the right to do the constructing. The serious and real aspects of Cameron's life prior to his involvement with Cross's movie—his experience in Vietnam, his involvement with killing and the risk to his own life, the betrayal he experienced upon his return, and the fugitive existence he has been living—all are repressed. We are simply supposed to forget about them and permit them to be eclipsed by the world of film and film representations and the notion that there is no abiding subject that needs, in the present, to be reconciled with such past experiences, regardless of what new roles the subject may assume.

Coppola's Lesson from Las Vegas: *One from the Heart*

In *Learning from Las Vegas*, Robert Venturi (along with his associates, Denise Scott Brown and Steven Izenour) argues that if one looks at the Las Vegas strip with an open mind, with eyes perhaps untainted by the austere high seriousness and utopianism of orthodox modernism, then one might see that such vernacular architecture, billboards and all, is, in fact, "almost all right" (6). And Baudrillard, for whom America is the epitome of hyperreality, a place where the simulacra of the city, the speed of the automobile, and the temporal and spatial distortions of air travel suggest an escape from all meaning and reference, similarly seems fascinated by this city of illusion, built in the middle of the desert:

> The secret affinity between gambling and the desert: the intensity of gambling reinforced by the presence of the desert all around the town. The air-conditioned freshness of the gaming rooms, as against the radiant heat outside. The challenge of all the artificial lights to the violence of the sun's rays. Night of gambling sunlit on all sides; the glittering darkness of these rooms in the middle of the desert. (*America*, 127–128)

The film *One from the Heart* (1982) suggests that Francis Ford Coppola shares with Venturi and Baudrillard this fascination with the city that epitomizes the artificiality and allure of America. As much as it embodies that which we despise—or thought or pretended we despised—the possibility of quick money, the ubiquitous signs of power and sex, the easy aesthetics of blinking lights, neon, and glitter, and the emotional release provided by rootlessness and motion, all have an intoxicating appeal that is hard to resist. With mixed feelings, not quite approving but not disapproving either, Venturi, Baudrillard, and Coppola, in different ways, offer their testimonials to, their qualified acceptance of, Las Vegas. It's "almost" all right.

No doubt it was the appeal of Las Vegas's hyperreality that caused Coppola to shift the setting of the original story, by Armyan Bernstein, from Chicago to Las Vegas. Rather than shoot the film on location, however— as if Las Vegas itself is not artificial enough to represent sufficiently well its own artificiality—Coppola's set designer, Dean Tavoularis, reconstructed the Las Vegas strip, along with lounges, restaurants, apartments, a suburb, and the airport, in Coppola's Zoetrope Studios, flaunting the artificiality of the film, itself a reflection, only slightly intensified, of the artificiality of the hyperreal world it represents.

Everything in the film is flat and stereotypical. Not only are the sets obviously sets, in spite of their detail and apparent authenticity, the characters themselves are characterless. When Hank (Frederic Forrest) and Frannie (Teri Garr) break up early in the film, they do so over not much in particular; we assume they are simply tired of each other and there is nothing holding them together. Why, in a flatly emotional, sentimental, and blatantly contrived conclusion, they come back together and seem to be so much "in love," after all, is a *complete* mystery. Of course such questions are irrelevant. There is no basis for anything in the film apart from adherence to the most blatant conventions: boy and girl separate but are reconciled in the end, after they each have superficial affairs and realize that they "really" love each other. What sets Hank and Frannie's love apart from the brief affairs they have is impossible to say—and unnecessary, since the film does not deal with real people but with Baudrillardian simulacra of people. In the hyperreal world the self disappears and what is left is the image of a self that is as flat as a cardboard figure in the lobby of an old movie theater. And individuals are complicitous in their own disappearance. The individual "is not only condemned to disappearance, but *disappearance is also its strategy*" (Baudrillard, *Selected Writings*, 213).

One from the Heart begins with the image of a curtain, which opens up on a globe. Then an aerial view of a city at night is seen through misty clouds. The clouds dissolve to images of sand and then to the sign of the "Sands" hotel, returning again to images of sand, this time with footsteps in it. The world we are entering—the world of Las Vegas, of America, of film, of hyperreality—is one that is blatantly staged and that has the shifting and liquid character of sand. The film, like footsteps in sand, is an indexical sign, the trace of an absent and inaccessible, possibly nonexistent, referent.

The genius of the film is the rigor of its tackiness. No set, no scene, not a line betrays anything more than the conventional and the clichéd. Even the spectacular visual effects—the camera movements, the transitions, the superimpositions and inserts—which are, in fact, innovative in a purely technological sense, are really high-tech spectacularizations of dated movie conventions. Nothing is allowed accidentally to enter that might betray any psychological, social, or philosophical depth, that might disturb the uncompromising superficiality of the statement.

Even a jazz musician playing a sax in a combo emerges as a cliché. This touch is a kind of tour de force: For what musical mode, if not jazz, *should*, one would think, be revelatory of depth of character, individuality, presence, and authenticity, spontaneously manifesting themselves? What kind of music should be heard as *speech* rather than read as *writing*, to put it in Derridean terms? And yet here the musician and his music, both conventionalized, have quotation marks around them and are thereby distanced, made ironic. This is not an individual speaking his self through his breath, his instrument, and his musical genre, as we might have thought, as we were led to believe when we read about the jazzmen playing in the Chicago clubs described in Kerouac's *On the Road*, but an image of such a person, like many other such images that populate our streets and screens. Jazz, existentialism, and authenticity of the individual have been conventionalized, reproduced, and flattened into depthless signifiers, simulacra.

Myriad details quickly betray the real content of the film—the fact that the film is *about* a world of flat conventions and not itself a mindless submission to those conventions. The dialogue is banal, the performances flat, the plot simplistic, and the cinematic structure blatantly conventional. Various shots and scenes call to mind conventional movie genres: the musical, the film noir, and the romance. The credits are presented as lights on glitzy Las Vegas signs (done with models), and at the end of the film the camera pulls back revealing the suburban Zoetrope set; a curtain, which opened at the beginning of the film, closes over it. Over the curtain the words "Filmed Entirely on the Stages of Zoetrope Studios" are superimposed. Such details clarify the metacinematic content of the film, the fact that it is *about* a world that has itself become a cinematic fiction.

The body of the film is broadly structured around crosscuts between the two main characters, as they meet with their best friends after their breakup and as their new romances begin and develop. This kind of parallel structure is fully conventionalized and obvious. Even the names of the characters, "Hank," "Frannie," "Maggie" (for Frannie's best friend), and, of course, the classical "Moe" (for Hank's best friend and business partner) bespeak a kind of art of the obvious and uninventive. If aspects like these are too subtle for some viewers, the name of the junkyard that Hank and Moe own, "Reality Wrecking," is another signal for the theme of the film, which is the perhaps irretrievable loss of "reality" behind a hyperreal surface of manufactured images.

Throughout the film lights change suddenly, as if by themselves. If such changes were subtler and less obtrusive, they might be regarded simply as expressive liberties. But here such shifts are sudden and obtrusive, calling attention to themselves. And when Hank conducts a pile of junked cars, which play a musical piece, "Usedcarlotta," on their horns while Leila (Nastassia Kinski) does a high-wire dance on a high-tension wire, it is really too much. It is not so much an expressive liberty as a comic, tongue-in-cheek allusion to such conventional liberties that are sometimes permissible in film.

Even the exotic other is domesticated and contained. Thus, it ceases to be "other," ceases to be any real threat—or any real opportunity, for that matter—and becomes simply another part of the hyperreal landscape. After his breakup with Frannie, Hank meets Leila, a woman of vaguely European background, a model who seems also to have experience in circus performance. Leila *is* an image; the first time Hank sees her she is being set up as a live window display, a sexy and exotic Statue of Liberty, complete with sparklers. Frannie has her fling with Ray (Raul Julia), a conventional romantic Latin lover. Ray talks to Frannie about Bogart and *Casablanca*. Reverence for Bogart and *Casablanca* is another cliché; everyone from Godard to Woody Allen has by now paid homage to them. Together Frannie and Ray plan an escape from Las Vegas and all it represents. They almost carry out this plan, going so far as to actually board a plane to Bora Bora, an exotic, romantic island that *will* be different, that *will* be other, that *will* (they believe) be real. But, as in *Casablanca*, they do not in fact fly off together.

Of course, the island of Bora Bora is itself—for them and for most of us who have never been there—simply a simulacrum, a series of photos in a travel brochure, an image on a poster, or the totally artificial set representing an exotic locale that is part of a conventionalized dance piece embedded in the film. If Frannie *had* stayed on the plane the flight itself would probably have embodied all the irreality of air travel that Baudrillard describes in *America* (24), and Bora Bora, when they arrived, would have been transformed from the genuinely alien place it no doubt once was to a commercialized imitation of stereotypes of exotic isles, produced for the pleasure of tourists who want to experience something exotic, but only if it has been fully domesticated and represents no real threat. Bora Bora is no real escape but has been subsumed by the hyperreal.

Hank complains to Moe about "what's wrong with America," describing it as "tinsel." "It's phoney, bullshit, man, nothin's real." But of course, we've heard this all before, many times. Such complaints are themselves as conventional, standardized, and *unreal* as the very condition they address. The spontaneity of jazz is standardized, an exotic island provides no real contact with the *other*, being inspired by an inspiring movie is a fully conventionalized performance, and complaints about phoniness are as phony as anything else. There is no exit.

Perhaps the most beautifully executed cliché of the film is a musical number sung and danced by Frannie and Ray. It begins with Ray playing the piano on the stage of an empty club, singing for Frannie a song he wrote, a parodic tango containing the line, "Meet me tonight, it's raining Cuban cigars." Ray gets up to dance with Frannie as orchestral music begins, relieving him of the need to play. We quickly understand that this dance piece is a movie convention and we should not let its lack of literal realism stop us from suspending our disbelief. However, the fact that such full blown music and dance numbers have not previously been presented in the film does mark the scene and makes it harder to simply slip into it than it would have been if the convention had been established early on as one that was informing the structure of the film. Moreover, the excess of the piece, while rooted entirely in aspects of song and dance scenes we have seen many times, nevertheless serves to foreground its artificiality and conventionality.

Frannie and Ray embrace and lower themselves to the floor. When they rise the nightclub stage set has been transformed into a tropic isle, complete with a fountain, waterfall, flaming lanterns, stereotyped jungle bird sounds, and a stylized background depicting a cruise ship in a harbor. They are now, we assume, in Bora Bora, the island to which they have talked of escaping. Shortly thereafter, they run down a path, through a door, and out again onto the streets of Las Vegas, filled with dancers celebrating the Fourth of July. The dance piece, now including all those revelers, continues, constructed entirely of clichéd moves connoting passion, eroticism, and rhythmic abandon. As with the earlier shot of the jazz musician, there is irony in the utterly formulaic representation of actions that are supposed to be spontaneous and improvised. That which seemed to spring from the soul is depicted as something that has been practiced and learned. The "natural" is cultural.

On the street, the dance of Frannie and Ray is crosscut with shots of Hank, going to meet Leila, amid the lights and celebration. A large image of a woman's face in lights dissolves into Leila's face as she sings to him. Leila's song is developed visually into a montage of huge faces and lights and all sense of space, time, and narrative movement dissolves. The plot is, in effect, put on hold, and Hank's world—and the spectator's as well—becomes a Baudrillardian hyperreality cum Lacanian imaginary, as he is sung to by a large, sexily maternal Leila, addressing him as "Little Boy Blue." As Laura Mulvey argues in "Visual Pleasure and Narrative Cinema," narrative development, as well as one's normal sense of three-dimensional space, is threatened by the erotically charged image of a woman (309). Of course here there is parodic distance on this visual and musical montage in which all spatial and temporal coherence dissolves.

The dissolution of normal spatial and temporal references that occurs in this scene is simply an extreme instance of a tendency that is evident throughout the film. The many songs, written by Tom Waits and sung by

Waits and Crystal Gayle, have the effect of, if not stopping the action to the extent that the dance montage does, at least slowing it down dramatically. The songs are sultry and subtly parodic, at least in the context of the film, and they have the effect of making the film sometimes seem more like a series of music videos than a unified narrative.

The constant, elaborate, camera movement, the dramatic, sudden transitions, the slow dissolves, the superimpositions of one scene over another, the inserts of one scene in front of another, achieved through sophisticated electronic editing techniques, also disturb the film's representation of a coherent space and time. Often reflections in windows mix with people or objects that are behind the windows, so that a visual confusion, like that common in photorealist paintings, takes place. The confusion of space and time that occurs on the screen is mirrored by the spectator, who is decentered; rarely is there established a coherent position or organized set of positions that stabilize and make comprehensible the spectator's relation to a scene.

One from the Heart was, of course, bound to be a box office flop. The film, which cost about twenty-seven million dollars, grossed less than two million and resulted in the closing of Zoetrope's Hollywood studio (Chown, 152; Cowie, 147, 161). Most viewers missed the quotation marks and saw only bad performances, bad lines, bad acting, banal plot, and cinematic excess: fluff. Reading the film this way resulted in a special disappointment for Coppola fans who anticipated something more serious and substantial from the maker of large, epic statements about significant issues like crime, morality, and war: films like the *Godfather* films and *Apocalypse Now*.

However, *One from the Heart*, so brilliantly bad, *is* a statement. It is not so much a cliché as a film that is about clichés. And though there is humor in its parody, it is not really a lampoon. It is, in both its cinematic form and its stereotypical content, a brilliant depiction of the American hyperreal, presenting American life as itself the stuff of hyperreal representation. The decision to set the film in Las Vegas on the Fourth of July underlines this special connection between the hyperreal and America. In the travel office where she works, Frannie holds what at first appears to be a three-dimensional model of the Statue of Liberty, but when she moves it it turns out to be a flat cutout, a trompe l'oeil illusion of real, three-dimensional liberty.

Baudrillard describes America as the epitome of hyperreality, identifying even American people as simulations. "America is neither dream nor reality. It is a hyperreality. . . . Americans, for their part, have no sense of simulation. They are themselves simulation in its most developed state" (*America*, 28–29). America, including its people, he describes as a fiction, a hologram, and a film. "It is not the least of America's charms that even outside the movie theatres the whole country is cinematic." Describing the buildings of Los Angeles, but the American people as well, Baudrillard writes, "All around, the tinted glass facades of the buildings are like faces: frosted surfaces. It is as though there were no one inside the buildings, as if there were no one behind the faces. And there *really* is no one" (60).

The image of America and Americans that Baudrillard describes is precisely the one presented in Coppola's film. Frannie, Hank, Moe, Maggie, Leila, and Ray are characterless characters. There is no illusion of an essential subjectivity behind the flat characterizations that they are. Behind their faces "there *really* is no one." Thus, Coppola's film, fluffy as it is, does have content: the content of the film is the absence of content in American life. *One from the Heart* is an elegant cinematic representation of the hyperreal, a cinematic representation of the cinematization of life itself.

As in *The Stunt Man*, the characters in *One from the Heart* do not escape but remain contained within and defined by the hyperreal. Frannie does not go to Bora Bora but stays in Las Vegas: there is only Las Vegas, there is nowhere else, and even if she had gone to Bora Bora it would be like Las Vegas. She returns to Hank and, we assume, her job in the travel agency—which does not enable people really to travel but sends them on trips to a domesticated exotic that is no real escape at all, and no opportunity for discovery, either. The message of the film—or at least the solution accepted by its protagonists—is that since you can't escape from the world of movies and facades you may as well accept your confinement, enjoy the show, and take whatever simulacrum of love is available.

This message is similar to that of *The Stunt Man*. Frannie can no more escape the world of Las Vegas than Cameron can escape Cross's *Alice in Wonderland* world of film, and both eventually capitulate to and accept those worlds. However, *The Stunt Man* explicitly broaches problems like Vietnam, violence, and megalomaniacal control, whereas *One from the Heart* scrupulously avoids such issues, which would threaten to anchor the film in things that might *seem*, at least, real to someone. Unlike *The Stunt Man*, the hyperreal spectacle of *One from the Heart* is not controlled by any one person. There is no Eli Cross, no specific agent who is master-of-the-spectacle, no authority guilty of abusing his power. The hyperreal is not the result of an individual, group, or organization, but has its own life, its own energy. It is ubiquitous, the very landscape in which we live, and its source can no more be specified than the source of a natural landscape like a forest or a desert. Thus, *One from the Heart* seems not to be at odds with itself, as is *The Stunt Man*, which suggests serious references only to do violence to them in the end. If *One from the Heart* seems to be fluff, or even if it seems to be *about* fluff—taking fluff itself as its reference—then, at least, that's all it is or all it's about; it's not claiming to be or do anything more.

And yet this in itself implies, albeit indirectly, more serious issues, at least if we believe that the fluff of the film is a more or less accurate representation of the fluff of our lives. The superficiality and unreality of the whole thing, the flatness of the film's characters and their relationships, the avoidance of all life-and-death issues, might provoke thoughts of the emptiness and deadness of the hyperreal and its separation from any connection with what we believe or imagine once had something to do with life, death, joy, and suffering. And this separation is itself a kind of death, another kind of death, as Baudrillard describes it (*America*, 30–31).

Even Baudrillard, whose hyperbolic claims about the loss of reference in the hyperreal have caused him to be criticized by some—like Christopher Norris, who in *Uncritical Theory* uses Baudrillard as an exemplar of the irrational bankruptcy of the "postmodern"—does at times reveal a moral posture and, subtly and indirectly perhaps, a belief in reality and the referent. In *America* Baudrillard does recognize things like the slaughter of American Indians, the Vietnam War, poverty, and what he calls the "Fourth World"—a world that, unlike the Third World, has no political power because it is *not* represented at all. But in the hyperreal, none of these things exists, or at least they are in the process of ceasing to exist, because they are being progressively disenfranchised, excommunicated, denied representation. When they are not represented in the hyperreal, they do not exist, for all practical purposes. Describing the age of Reagan and Thatcher, Baudrillard writes,

Behind the appearance of socialization and participation [governments] are desocializing, disenfranchising, and ejecting. The social order is contracting to include only economic exchange, technology, the sophisticated and innovative; as it intensifies these sectors, entire zones are "disintensified," becoming reservations, and sometimes not even that: dumping grounds, wastelands, new deserts for the new poor, like the deserts you see forming around nuclear power stations or motorways. Nothing will be done to save them and perhaps nothing can be done, since enfranchisement, emancipation, and expansion have already taken place. There are therefore none of the elements here for a future revolution; what we see here are merely the inescapable results of an orgy of power. (113)

Clearly there is a moral attitude here, though it is an attitude of moral disgust and despair. And clearly the disenfranchised *do* exist—there *are* those who will not be saved, there *are*, in some sense or another, people behind the windows and faces of the disenfranchised, if not behind the facades of Americans—the Hanks and Frannies—who have adopted disappearance as their strategy. Behind Barbara Kruger's "reservoir of poses" there is someone posing. This, even though, in another sense, it is true that the disenfranchised are ceasing to exist. They are losing their existence in the hyperreal world, the multinational world of "communication-based societies," which increasingly represents them less and less, or if it represents them at all represents them as depthless facades and not as experiencing subjectivities. And since that world, a complex network of representation, production, and exchange, is the only world in which individuals can be recognized and achieve power and agency by *themselves* representing themselves as well as others, then those who are not part of that world are not part of *the* world. For those who are inside the borders, engaged in the network, those outside or not engaged increasingly do not exist at all.

Perhaps in *One from the Heart* behind the fluff is subtly implied the not so fluffy world that it does not represent. Perhaps the unrelenting flatness reminds us of the all but lost possibility of depth and reminds us that those who are left out are not cartoons but do, in fact, suffer. In any event, if we at least recognize the film as a representation, only slightly exaggerated, of the world we live in, then its flatness, the fact that there is no escape from it, and the utter emptiness of its "happy" ending should, at least, cause us some disturbance, some uneasiness, some gnawing dissatisfaction, even as we also delight in the roller coaster ride of disorienting pans, startling transitions, light, imagery, and visual excess.

The Player

Like *The Stunt Man*, Robert Altman's *The Player* (1992), based on the novel by Michael Tolkin, deals explicitly with the world of movie making, though more with the business of movies than with their actual production: the wheeling and dealing, the pitches, the schmoozing, and the human brutality. The "player" of the title refers both to someone who plays the game of film business successfully and to someone who plays a role in a film, and much of *The Player* proceeds like a series of embedded performances, some in front of, some behind, the camera. The kind of performance that is privileged in *The Player* is the "pitch," and the classical pitch is one that a writer presents to a studio executive in an attempt to sell him on a script or concept. During a pitch the writer is himself a performer and the pitch is a performance, almost a genre in its own right, with its own rules and conventions. It must be quick: you're lucky to have even a few minutes with a highly paid power broker so don't waste his time. It must be vivid: you have to capture his imagination. And it must be persuasive: the film will make money.

The pitch recurs throughout the film, even in scenes where one would not be expected. The protagonist, studio executive Griffin Mill (Tim Robbins), is being sent threatening mail by an unknown writer he has apparently snubbed. Griffin confides in his girlfriend, story editor Bonnie Sherow (Cynthia Stevenson), only indirectly, by fictionalizing his problem and describing it to her as if it is a movie treatment that has been pitched to him earlier in the day. In doing this, he himself enacts the pitch, questioning her about the story rather than directly asking for her opinion about his real situation. This scene suggests Griffin's reluctance to discuss his life with candor with anyone, even with someone with whom he is intimate. But it is also significant because it suggests that Griffin regards his real life as if it were a treatment for a movie, a perception that is later confirmed by the metacinematic conclusion to *The Player.*

The title of the film, as well as its subject matter, suggests that personality is a matter of playing roles, and it ambiguously refers to both the roles played in front of and those played behind the camera. This confusion of film roles and life roles is furthered by the casting. Besides the major parts in the film, performed by well-known actors, there are at least sixty-five performances by celebrities who play "themselves." These celebrities create an authentic seeming milieu for scenes in restaurants, lounges, and other gathering places. Usually their performances are small cameos, perhaps with throw away lines, as when Burt Reynolds calls Griffin Mill an "asshole" after greeting him in a trendy restaurant. But sometimes they are larger and more complex. Lily Tomlin, Scott Glenn, Julia Roberts, and Bruce Willis, for example, play themselves playing roles in scenes of movies that are being made by the studio represented in *The Player.*

The Player also includes constant allusions to famous films. Movie posters hanging on walls sometimes act as humorous or ironic comments on the main action. Or the allusions may be verbal references or descriptions contained in the dialogue. A reference to Billy Wilder's *Sunset Boulevard,* another dark film about Hollywood that also involves a writer who is murdered and incorporates celebrities playing themselves, provides a wry counterpoint to the action of *The Player.* The classic Italian neorealist film *The Bicycle Thief* is mentioned several times, and a clip of its conclusion is included. *The Bicycle Thief,* in its quest for authenticity of character and setting, in its use of nonprofessional actors, and in the modesty of its technical means of production functions as a foil for the film world represented in *The Player.* Orson Welles's *Touch of Evil* is also mentioned, and the initial tracking shot in *The Player* is, in part, a parody and upstaging of the famous first shot of that film. The various pitches, allusions, and film fragments contained in *The Player* combine to produce a structure a little like Calvino's *If on a winter's night a traveler*, an overall narrative with numerous incomplete narratives contained within it, all of them creating resonances and echoes among one another. They also create a milieu in which the real business of making movies becomes so implicated in the myriad fictions of existing and potential films that the two worlds become highly confused, for the viewer of as well as for the players (of both kinds) in *The Player*.

The complex mixing of levels of role playing also becomes confusing, especially when actors playing "themselves" interact with actors playing fictional roles. Burt Reynolds plays himself, but his remarks are a response to Griffin Mill, a fictional character, not Tim Robbins, who plays Mill. Of course even Reynolds, when he plays "himself" in a fictional film, is performing a fictional character, so the assymmetry is more apparent than real, but the nice distinction between Burt Reynolds and "Burt Reynolds" is easy to overlook. The resonances and allusions also are subtle and complex when Whoopi Goldberg, acting a lot like Whoopi Goldberg, but also a little like Peter Falk playing Columbo, plays Detective Avery, a hard-boiled cop and tough black female, who knows Griffin is guilty of murder but can't quite find the hard evidence she needs.

The result of all this confusion of roles is a slipperiness of personality, and this slipperiness is felt not only by the audience but also by the characters in the film. Lily Tomlin and Scott Glenn play "Lily Tomlin" and "Scott Glenn" playing characters in a scene, presented in the form of rushes being viewed by various studio people. The scene is a sleazy hotel room in a kind of contemporary film noir. When Glenn drops character and criticizes her performance, Tomlin, surprised by his shift out of character, asks, "Are you talking to me?" The humor results partly from the apparent absurdity of her question. Who *else* would he be talking to? They seem to be the only people in the room, or in the scene, at any rate. But in a sense there are more than two people present (even excluding the off-camera crew), since each of them is playing a role different from their off-camera identity. And so there is also the humor of her surprise that he would be talking to *her*, Lily Tomlin, rather than the character she has been playing. In a world of playing roles, the attempt to address a "real" person comes as a surprise, an unexpected breaking of the rules, even an indelicacy or breach of decorum.

Tomlin's last line in the scene, spoken as she peers wistfully toward the camera through a window that reflects a neon hotel sign, is, "Why would they think that I'd kill my own sister's husband? I was in love with him." The lurid atmosphere of the film noir scene provides a counterpoint to Griffin's own situation. Griffin, who is one of those watching the scene, has murdered a screenwriter and is falling in love with that writer's girlfriend. His position—like that of Tomlin's character—is precarious. We suspect that the Tomlin character may, in fact, be guilty; we know that Griffin is. There is a phone call for him. A reference in that call to *Sunset Boulevard* convinces him that it is his mysterious tormentor. Another complex resonance is set up, this one between Griffin's situation in *The Player* and the plot of another, "real," American film.

The first scene in the *The Player* is a major technical achievement, an elaborate and extended sequence shot that is in part a parody of the famous shot that begins *Touch of Evil.* Altman's shot, like Welles's, involves all kinds of movements and combinations of movement—tracking, panning, craning—recording various events that occur in different places in the movie lot. Welles's shot is explicitly alluded to in a conversation in this scene, when Walter (Fred Ward), the studio security guard and a serious film buff in his own right, mentions the Welles shot as being six and a half minutes long. When he is challenged on this he corrects himself, saying it is "three or four, anyway." This itself is another inside joke, since the Welles's shot is often mistakenly assumed to be longer than the three-minute length it actually is. But Altman's homage to and parody of Welles's shot surpasses not only its actual but also its mythical length. Altman's shot is a full eight minutes long.

The camera moves about the lot, recording various bits of action and conversation. It peers through windows, revealing several stories that are pitched to Griffin over the course of the shot. A group of Japanese VIPs, being given a tour of the lot, is assured that the studio intends to continue using Sony products. An accident occurs, involving a mail cart. Among the mail that is spilled is a threatening postcard, about to be delivered to Griffin.

Although *The Player*, as a whole, has a more linear and unified narrative than many of his other films, this first shot echoes a kind of signature modus operandi for Altman—establishing a certain setting and milieu and freely crosscutting among the various characters and plot threads in that setting. But here the movement from character to character, from situation to situation, is done entirely by moving the camera rather than cutting. In this long introductory take, a prelude to the rest of the film, camera movement acts as a kind of editing with the camera and juxtaposes in quasi-montage fashion various fragments of action and dialogue. Although *The Player* does come to focus on an individual—Griffin Mill—this beginning creates the sense of a contextual discourse, a combination of related, partial discourses, enacted by individuals who participate in the operations of a structure that is larger than any of them. That larger structure is the movie business itself, and the characters are masks, roles, "players" of small parts in the larger project that subsumes them all.

Early in the film Griffin identifies a writer, David Kahane (Vincent

D'Onofrio), whom he believes is the one who has been threatening him. He finds Kahane watching *The Bicycle Thief* in a small, out-of-the-way movie theater. The two go out for drinks, and Griffin tries to establish a truce with Kahane, promising him a fair reading of his script if he will stop the postcards. Kahane is uncooperative and instead of taking the opportunity, he goads Griffin. Outside, the two scuffle, and it is not Kahane but Griffin who reveals a murderous potential. Significantly, it is not the threats on Griffin's life that provoke the rage that results in Kahane's death but Kahane's goading Griffin about the vulnerability of his position in the studio.

Later, when Griffin continues receiving threatening messages, it becomes clear that he has killed the wrong man. But through luck, callousness, and a little help from Walter, he escapes prosecution. Callously, he abandons Bonnie and begins an affair with June Gudmundsdottir (Greta Scacchi), Kahane's beautiful Icelandic girlfriend.

There is a one year ellipsis in the narrative, during which Griffin is left alone by the harassing writer, marries June, and forms a truce with Larry Levy (Peter Gallagher), his former enemy, who even more than Griffin embodies the crassest and most cynical values of the film industry. Driving home from the studio, Griffin receives a call from Levy, who says he has a writer with him who has a pitch Griffin should hear. Griffin quickly recognizes the writer as his former tormentor and the pitch as the story of Kahane's murder and Griffin's life since the crime. The writer concludes, "He marries the dead writer's girl, and they live happily ever after." "Can you guarantee that ending?" Griffin asks, as he pulls up to his house and is greeted by June, who is obviously pregnant. "If the price is right, you got it," the writer replies. "If you can guarantee me that ending, you got a deal," Griffin says. Implicit in this exchange is blackmail, the negotiation of a payoff, and the guarantee of a happy ending, not only for the film but for Griffin's life. Griffin then asks the writer the name of the film and is told that it is called *The Player*.

Thus, the film's structure is self-engulfing; it is a story that contains a story that is itself. Griffin, who was an effective player in the corporate game of movie production, now is a character in a film. He is a character in the film we are watching, but he is also a character in a film alluded to inside that film, which is, presumably, the same film as the one we are watching.

In *The Player* the power of the commercial image wins against the possibility of authenticity of values or character, even to the point of getting away with murder. Griffin will lead a materially privileged life with a beautiful woman, whose previous lover he has killed. A moral standard against which the characters and action of the film are set is provided by Bonnie Sherow, the only sympathetic character in the film, and the film,

The Bicycle Thief. In the end, Bonnie is fired by Levy, and the principles of realism and social engagement, which were to be incorporated into a film called *Habeas Corpus*, are entirely abandoned.

If Bonnie represents the last vestiges of truth, authenticity, and integrity, June represents a free-floating loss of reference and an amoral acceptance of whatever happens. Griffin first encounters June when he is trying to locate Kahane. He drives to Kahane's address and calls him on his cellular phone. Since Kahane is not there—he is at the theater watching *The Bicycle Thief*—June answers. Griffin gets out of his car and watches her through a window as they talk. Their phone conversation is two-way, but the visual exchange is one-way—he sees her but she doesn't see him, and she doesn't know that she is being watched. Some shots include both of them, with her inside, him outside. Moreover, in the same kind of visual confusion that occurs in *The Stunt Man* and *One from the Heart,* some shots from the inside include him through the window along with her reflection in the same window.

In a later scene, after Kahane's death, June reverses the voyeuristic objectification implicit in the earlier scene. She takes photographs of Griffin, which she later incorporates into a painting. But Griffin takes the camera and turns it back on her, reasserting himself as controller of the gaze. This game of object and objectifier is fluid and, in its way, playful, as if neither of them is a subject that is real enough to be violated. With individuals so lacking in reality at the outset, it is difficult to regard objectification as a serious form of violence.

Many aspects of June's character suggest groundlessness and rootlessness. She is alien, or at least of alien origin, and seems to have no strong connections with anything besides her art. Through Kahane she knows people involved in the film industry but is apparently close to none of them, and she never goes to the movies. Although she is an artist, she is not interested in selling her art—which would require connecting with a wider social world—but works only for herself. Her works are never finished, always in progress. She does not not even seem close to Kahane, and his death arouses no evident grief in her. She says that she likes words and letters, but is not "crazy about complete sentences": propositions that sometimes seem to say things about the world. Thus, even in her relation to language she suggests rootlessness, absence of ground, the bracketing out of reference.

She and Griffin discuss whether or not one should have to pay for crimes one has committed. June says that the knowledge that one has committed a crime should be suffering enough and, "If you don't suffer, maybe it wasn't a crime after all. Anyway, what difference does it make? It has nothing to do with how things really are." And for June things really are a sequence of moments, of occasions, of situations, each of which she accepts without judgment and lets pass when the scene changes. It becomes increasingly likely that she surmises Griffin's role in Kahane's death; Griffin at one point all but tells her. But this changes nothing for her, either in relation to the passionate affair they begin or in relation to the idyllic life they eventually establish.

The loss of grounding in the world is also suggested by the fate of a film called *Habeas Corpus,* pitched to Griffin early in the film. Tom Oakley (Richard E. Grant), the writer, seems deeply committed to making a serious film about capital punishment. In the spirit of realism, it is to have an unhappy ending, an innocent woman executed for the murder of her husband. Moreover, "because the story is just too damn important to risk being overwhelmed by personality," Oakley insists that there are to be no stars in it, no Kevin Costner, Bruce Willis, or Julia Roberts.

After the year ellipsis late in the film there is a cut directly to the execution scene of *Habeas Corpus.* Subsequent shots clarify the fact that we are watching a studio preview of the recently completed film. In the audience are Bonnie, Levy, Oakley, and others. In the scene on the screen, Julia Roberts, playing the convicted woman, is strapped into a chair, gas is released, and she loses consciousness. But in a dramatic last minute rescue, Bruce Willis, playing a D.A. who is in love with her, runs down the corridor, fires a rifle into the door, and carries her out of the chamber. As she regains consciousness she asks, "What took you so long?" "Traffic was a bitch," he replies. These words are echoed later by June and Griffin, when she greets him at their home and the film ends.

Thus, *Habeas Corpus* sells out in all significant respects. Instead of utilizing little known performers who would not eclipse the seriousness of the statement through the aura of their stardom, it utilizes highly commercial actors who are certain box office draws. Instead of an unhappy ending that would force the audience to leave the theater dissatisfied with social realities and possibly stirred to action, it adds a tacked on happy ending, with a touch of silly humor, so that the audience can leave satisfied and passive.

Bonnie objects to Oakley, telling him that he has "sold out." When she asks, "What about the truth, reality?" Oakley replies, "What about the way the old ending tested in Canoga Park? Everybody hated it. We reshot it, now everybody loves it. *That's* reality." This writer, who a year earlier was uncompromising in his commitment to an aesthetics of realism and social engagement, now sees eye to eye with Levy, who values only profit. Levy's disdain for writers was established early in the film, when he suggested that they were unnecessary expenses and expendable. Oakley's conversion suggests that, while Levy has not yet gotten rid of writers, he has at least won them over to his way of thinking about movie values.

Levy fires Bonnie, who is the only unhappy one in the screening room, which is otherwise filled with self-satisfied individuals, congratulating themselves on a wonderful film. Rather than argue with her, rather than engage in a debate about what the appropriate values, aesthetics, and ethics of a powerful cultural institution should be, she is removed from the self-congratulatory discourse, which assumes without question, without even raising the issue, the values of profit and easy entertainment. Bonnie—like Baudrillard's Fourth World—is desocialized and disenfranchised, no longer a part of the world that speaks and can be spoken. She ceases to be. In the screening room the only ones who exist are those who have profited from the ideological conviction that success and happiness through profit and entertainment are correct values— and they are all successful, happy, and entertained. "Enfranchisement, emancipation, and expansion have already taken place," as Baudrillard says. In the last shot of Bonnie she is crying on some steps, powerless and nonexistent, as Griffin, who has refused to intervene on her behalf, drives off in his Land Rover to negotiate his peace with his previous tormentor and live his own "happily ever after" life. Not only does Bonnie not exist, David Kahane's death, like that of Burt in *The Stunt Man*, is forgotten, evidently the result of a random, unmemorable robbery and murder. History is the representation of history. What else could it be?

As in *The Stunt Man* and *One from the Heart* there is no escape from the hyperreal. Cameron accepts his place as a stunt man and actor in Cross's world of movies and illusions; his experience in Vietnam is repressed, as is Cross's megalomania. Frannie and Hank remain in Las Vegas; there is no Bora Bora, there is no *other*, no access to anything but Las Vegas, and rebellion and truth are themselves contained and domesticated, appropriated by that which they would oppose. And Bonnie Sherow is marginalized, deprived of all power, and the players who win are those who successfully play the game of constructing representations.

This is not to say that the judgments that these films suggest regarding the very similar situations they represent are the same. *The Stunt Man* attempts to repress its own contradictions; it raises serious issues only to act in the end as if they did not exist or had been securely resolved. *One from the Heart*, on the other hand, is the most deadpan. It absolutely immerses itself in the hyperreal and never leaves it, never mentions anything like war or death or seriously suggests that there might be a Bora Bora different from or more real than the clichéd dream of Hank and Frannie. Any *other* or any *real*—along with the ethical concerns that might come from an encounter with the other or the real—are matters of postulation and speculation for the audience. And *The Player* lays bare the contradiction between the represented and the unrepresented without resolving it. While the others celebrate, Bonnie is present, suffering, marginalized, and, no longer a player, visibly nonexistent. The three films suggest very different levels of critical consciousness, certainly; nevertheless, the worlds all three describe are similar, as are the outcomes of the struggles they represent.

In these films the subject is presented as radically constructed. Cameron is a stunt man and a performer; any memory of the soldier and fugitive he once was will be lost among the many other roles he will now perform. Hank and Frannie never exist as anything but masks or roles, and if they ever dreamed of existing in some other way, they, like Cameron, relinquish that dream in the end. Griffin, though his role in the movie game is different from Cameron's, is also a successful player, and his power is much greater. Controlling representation and making representations that are profitable for the studio and himself, he builds the life of a successful player that is as much a construction as the characters in *Habeas Corpus*, and any connection he may have had with the death of David Kahane is lost beneath revised readings of history. If we previously thought that growing up meant giving up impossible dreams so that we could live in the real world, in these films growing up is giving up on the real world so that we can live in the world of hyperreal dreams. Those who do not grow up are left crying on the steps, abandoned to a powerless "real" of non-representation, a real whose existence is ignored. In the end, they are not mentioned at all.

*   *   *

Creating coherent and comprehensible viewer relations to scenes is one of the primary purposes of classical film construction. Within the conventions of classical style, cuts and camera movement can cause shifts in the spectator's virtual position, but such shifts are subject to constraints that insure that comprehensibility is maintained, that individual shots are "sutured" into a single spatial and temporal whole, and that the illusion of a human perspective is maintained. Classical film texts, like classical texts of painting and literature, attempt to balance the impulse to present a complete, consistent, and total picture of the world and the impulse to present that picture as a human possibility. Thus, the viewing subject's sense of mastery and sense of his or her self as a localized consciousness existing in a coherent temporal and spatial field is reinforced.

Discussions of the role of cinema in subject construction have often likened the experience of viewing a film to Lacan's mirror stage, which instigates the imaginary order. A seminal article in this discussion was Jean-Louis Baudry's "Ideological Effects of the Basic Cinematographic Apparatus." Subsequently, Christian Metz, in *The Imaginary Signifier*,

drew on Baudry and extended and elaborated the application of psychoanalytic ideas, especially those of Lacan, to the cinema. Both Baudry and
Metz liken the photographic perspective of film to the perspective of
Quattrocento painting. "Fabricated on the model of the *camera obscura,*
[the camera] permits the construction of an image analogous to the perspective projections developed during the Italian Renaissance" (Baudry, 41). They also argue that spectators not only identify with characters
in films, but, more significantly, with the camera itself. "[T]he spectator
identifies less with what is represented, the spectacle itself, than what
stages the spectacle" (Baudry, 45). Metz emphasizes the need to apply
psychoanalysis to specifically cinematic signifiers—those involving the
camera, camera movement, and editing. The photographic image, like
Renaissance painting, implies, according to the laws of perspective, a
clear viewer position. This fixing of the viewer—and both Baudry and
Metz would argue that it is an ideological fixing, an implied Althusserian
"hailing" of the subject—is precisely the kind of fixing that occurs in
paintings like Perugino's *Giving the Keys to St. Peter.*

Of course in film, unlike painting, there is movement, or at least the
illusion of movement. Metz compares movements of the camera to common movements of the human head and body.

All of us have experienced our own look, even outside the so-called *salles obscures*
[=cinemas], as a kind of searchlight turning on the axis of our own necks (like a
pan) and shifting when we shift (a tracking shot now): as a cone of light (without
the microscopic dust scattered through it and streaking it in the cinema) whose
vicariousness draws successive and variable slices of obscurity from nothingness
wherever and whenever it comes to rest. (49–50)

And yet there is in the film medium the potential to transgress such
restraints and transcend the merely human point of view. The camera's
mobility and the ease by which editing permits leaps in time and space is
seductive, encouraging the creation of cinematic structures that present
impossible and inhuman transitions, angles, and movements. In 1922
Dziga Vertov described the film camera as follows:

. . . I am eye. I am a mechanical eye.

I, a machine, am showing you a world, the likes of which only I can see.

I free myself today and forever from human immobility, I approach and draw
away from objects, I crawl under them, I move alongside the mouth of a running
horse, I cut into a crowd at full speed, I run in front of running soldiers, I turn
on my back, I rise with an airplane, I fall and soar together with falling and rising
bodies. . . .

My road is towards the creation of a fresh perception of the world. Thus I
decipher in a new way the world unknown to you. . . .

A mechanical eye—that's the movie camera. It refuses to use the human eye,
as if the latter were a crib-sheet; it is attracted and repelled by motion, feeling

through the chaos of observed events for a roadway for its own mobility and modulation; it experiments, extending time, dissecting movement, or on the contrary absorbing into itself the time, swallowing years and thus diagramming some processes unattainable to the normal eye. (86–87)

Metz describes this expansive aspect of film and the spectator's identification with the camera as the "all-perceiving subject" (45–49), and Baudry writes,

The movability of the camera seems to fulfill the most favorable conditions for the manifestation of the "transcendental subject." There is both fantasmatization of an objective reality (images, sounds, colors) and of an objective reality which, limiting its powers of constraint, seems equally to augment the possibilities or power of the subject. (43)

But classical film conventions have imposed constraints on this potential so that, while the human eye may be freed by the camera and the editing table, the illusion of a humanly possible point of view is, if not always strictly maintained, at least not violated with impunity.[1]

Not only are classical camera movements restrained so that something like real visual experience can be approximated (turning the head, walking), classical editing conventions are similarly designed to maintain the illusion of human possibility. In film criticism the term "suture" has come to refer to the organization of shots in a scene such that they complement each other and, together, create the illusion of a complete, self-contained, self-sufficient space. This spatial representation is seemingly unauthored, as if the film simply reflects a scene that is there. Discussions of "suture" have often focused on shot/reverse shot patterning, in which the camera adopts the approximate position of the characters in a scene. That which is lacking in one shot and which might provoke in the viewer an uneasy awareness of the shot's being controlled by an off-camera "absent one" is compensated by a second shot, which provides closure and suggests that the point of view of the first shot was that of a character in the scene. Because the camera's point of view is identified with the characters in a scene, its control by someone off-camera, who really structures the shots and their arrangement, is obscured. A visual discourse so organized encourages the viewer to forget that controlling "absent one." The viewer who psychologically submits to the system becomes a passive consumer of images and the ideology they suggest, implicitly or explicitly, rather than an active, critical reader of films. The "absent one" is repressed in order to encourage the misunderstanding that the film is an ideologically neutral, transparent reflection of a world rather than an ideologically determined construction of a world.[2]

In ways that are obvious, conventions like the 180 degree rule, shot/

reverse shot patterning, reasonably frequent use of establishing shots, and editing on movement have as their goal maintaining continuity across the cut, maintaining the viewer's sense of coherence in spite of the shift in his or her virtual position, and reinforcing the viewer's sense of mastery of the spatial organization of a scene. The viewer's position may undergo an impossible instantaneous shift, but the disruptive potential of the cut is attenuated by the 180 degree rule, which limits the viewer's movement and assures coherence. Editing on movement, conjoined with the 180 degree rule, makes the cut unobtrusive and nearly "invisible." Establishing shots further clarify spatial relationships and confirm the viewer's sense of mastery. The unobtrusiveness of style in classical film, its incredible success at creating an illusion of transparency, is an impressive achievement, especially when one considers the fact that the cut is, on the face of it, a fairly obvious thing, a clear disjunction in the spatial coherence of the film that would seem to have an inevitably disruptive effect on the illusion.

Films like *The Stunt Man, One from the Heart,* and *The Player* frequently use editing and camera movement in ways that transgress classical constraints and thus subvert the centering and totalizing effect classical editing and camera movement have for the viewer. The prologue sequence of *The Stunt Man* and the introductory sequence shot in *The Player* suggest the partial and fragmentary nature of individual experience and the fact that such experience is part of a network of causes and coincidences whose larger organization, if there is one, eludes all individuals. The transitions and camera movements in *One from the Heart* clearly are flagrantly transgressive of any kind of normal human movement. Sometimes those movements may convey a godlike sense of power and freedom, zooming from inside one apartment, across the city, into another. But such movements also may be disorienting for the viewer, confusing rather than clarifying spatial relationships.

Of course, many films that are now regarded as "classics" themselves anticipate this subversion of the classical system as well as the unity and coherence of the subject that the classical system supports. Kaja Silverman argues that Alfred Hitchcock's *Psycho* (1960) foregrounds the classical system of suture, even as it uses it to ensnare the viewing subject. Shot/reverse shot patterning is distorted in such a way as to force our awareness of the camera, whose point of view we share; impossible points of view are sometimes presented; and the viewing subject at times abruptly shifts position, alternating between that of victim and that of victimizer, frustrating the viewer's desire for a simple identification with a particular character (206–215). Raymond Bellour argues that in Hitchcock's *The Birds* (1963) there is no unified spectator position, and the viewer of the film shifts identification between characters who are objects of the gaze and those who voyeuristically do the gazing (Lapsley and Westlake, 152–55). The use of elaborate and complicated tracking and panning in films by Welles and Alain Resnais are antecedents to the elaborate movements in *One from the Heart* and, as in that film, disorient the viewer and subvert the illusion of a clear spectator position. Stephen Heath argues that Welles's *Touch of Evil* (1958), to which *The Player* pays explicit homage even as it tries to upstage it, cannot contain its own contradictions and fails to resolve satisfactorily its narrative and confirm the power of its protagonist or the coherence of the viewer (Lapsley and Westlake, 149–152). Ingmar Bergman's *Persona* (1966) is a powerful challenge to the unitary subject, both that of the personality or personalities represented and, through violations of classical conventions of shooting and editing, the subject who views the film (Gaggi, 97–114). Luis Buñuel, in *That Obscure Object of Desire* (1977), reveals the origins of desire not to be in the desirability of the object of desire itself but in a fundamental lack or absence in the subject that is desiring. Of course, the director who is probably most significant in his subversion of classical conventions and the classical subject is Jean-Luc Godard, who challenges the subject on the level of content, but whose use of the jump cut, whose violations of the 180 degree rule and the 30 degree rule, and whose Brechtian dissonance among the visual, verbal, and musical aspects of his films produce a dislocation of and challenge to the viewing subject as well.

Chapter 4
Hyperrealities and Hypertexts

The Loss of a Primary Axis

Fredric Jameson, in *Postmodernism, or, The Cultural Logic of Late Capitalism*, discusses the organization of various contemporary art forms—painting, photography, architecture, film, video, and literature—as formal analogies of postmodern hyperspace, a disjointed and incoherent space in which the individual becomes disoriented and loses his or her sense of clear physical placement in a whole that is comprehensible. Jameson discusses, as an example, John Portman's Bonaventure Hotel in Los Angeles. The Bonaventure has three entrances, none of which is designed in such a way as to connote a traditional hotel entrance and none of which leads directly into the lobby. The interior space of the structure is large, complex, and intuitively incomprehensible. Hanging streamers in the lobby (once one finds it) disturb the visitor's ability to comprehend the organization of space, and the "absolute symmetry" of the four residential towers that surround the lobby is actually confusing; pure symmetry tends to make different axes and their culminations indistinguishable from one another. So confusing is the organization of the hotel that, in spite of its popularity with both locals and tourists, businesses located in the various balconies do poorly. There is simply too much difficulty finding a shop one is looking for or returning to a shop one has happened upon. The rotating cocktail lounge above transforms the city into a spectacle, like a film, and not a real place at all (39–44). Baudrillard, discussing the same hotel, notes that when sitting in the lounge one might at first think that it is the city, rather than the spectator, that is moving (*America*, 59).

This architectural disturbance of the subject's sense of being clearly positioned in a comprehensible space is similar to related formal strategies that might be employed in other art forms. A painting that has more than one vanishing point splits the subject who views it; and yet it might appear to represent a single, continuous space, in spite of its inconsistency. A narrative structure can move from incident to incident, from one set of characters to another, with little sense of overall organization, and yet continuities and recurrences preclude the conclusion that the story is completely disorganized. A camera can move in complex, labyrinthine ways that disorient the viewer, or a series of close-ups can juxtapose different objects and events, suggesting relationships that are unclear and confusing to the viewer, who naturally assumes there is a reason for the organization of images.

For Jameson, this kind of structure is an analogue of the decentered, high-tech, multinational world in which we live.

> [T]his latest mutation in space—postmodern hyperspace—has finally succeeded in transcending the capacities of the individual human body to locate itself, to organize its immediate surroundings perceptually, and cognitively to map its position in a mappable external world. . . . [T]his alarming disjunction point between the body and its built environment . . . can itself stand as the symbol and analogue of that even sharper dilemma which is the incapacity of our minds, at least at present, to map the great global multinational and decentered communicational network in which we find ourselves caught as individual subjects. (44)

For Jameson this postmodern organization—of space, of communication, of language, and of images—is an expression of the "cultural logic of late capitalism." For him it is a special problem because it all but eliminates the possibility of achieving critical distance. Postmodern hyperspace is so ubiquitous that it cannot be escaped; one is always in it, disoriented by its organization and by the "logic of the simulacrum." One cannot find a place from which one might be able to evaluate or analyze, from which one might engage in an "old-fashioned ideological critique" that would make political judgment and effective action possible (44–46).

> [D]istance in general (including "critical distance" in particular) has very precisely been abolished in the new space of postmodernism. We are submerged in its henceforth filled and suffused volumes to the point where our now postmodern bodies are bereft of spatial coordinates and practically (let alone theoretically) incapable of distantiation. (48–49)

Jameson advocates a double attitude toward postmodern forms. On one hand those forms are mystifications and distractions that disguise reality and divert us from it. On the other hand, they can be "read as new forms of realism" that are valid reflections of the world of multinational capitalism (49–50). In their latter aspect they hold out the hope that they may point toward a new political art that will be capable of representing this confusing and disorienting new world, that will provide us with a cognitive map enabling us to gain a critical perspective on that world.

[T]he new political art (if it is possible at all) will have to hold to the truth of postmodernism, that is to say, to its fundamental object—the world space of multinational capital—at the same time at which it achieves a breakthrough to some as yet unimaginable new mode of representing this last, in which we may again begin to grasp our positioning as individual and collective subjects and regain a capacity to act and struggle which is at present neutralized by our spatial as well as our social confusion. (54)

Thus, Jameson maintains some hope for the emergence of a critical consciousness capable of comprehending the world and acting effectively to change it. And the forms that serve multinational capitalism may in fact serve this emergent critical consciousness as well. They are symptoms that reveal at the same time that they mystify—just as a dream simultaneously expresses a truth and keeps it at bay, just as a symbol simultaneously conceals and reveals.

But it is a slim hope. In Jameson's postmodern hyperspace, similar to Baudrillard's even more despairing vision of the hyperreal, the subject is reduced radically, rendered incapable of mastering the world. Simulacra—divorced from all connection with the referent—dominate our landscape and replace representations, which might have been judged on the basis of how accurately they reflect political and social truth. The profusion of simulacra and the absence of reference produce a sense of groundlessness. The subject cannot orient itself inside this space. Clear coordinates are lost or ambiguous, so that the position of the subject is always unclear, and dominant axes, which might clarify the direction of the subject's movement, do not exist. The subject moves from point to point along various channels, from node to node through various links. There may be plenty of choices available, but the subject acts without knowing where it is and without sufficient basis for determining where it *should* or might *want* to go. As in painting, film, and literary texts, the dispersal and decentering of the subject in relation to a physical or conceptual space exterior to that subject is reflected in a dispersal and decentering of the Cartesian locus of subjectivity itself.

Jorge Luis Borges, in his story "The Library of Babel" (which is really more an elaboration of a metaphor than a story), imagines a library that is much like the postmodern hyperspace that Jameson describes. The library is an infinite network of hexagonal galleries that contain all possible books:

the minutely detailed history of the future, the archangels' autobiographies, the faithful catalogue of the Library, thousands and thousands of false catalogues, the demonstration of the fallacy of those catalogues, the demonstration of the fallacy of the true catalogue, the Gnostic gospel of Basilides, the commentary on that gospel, the commentary on the commentary on that gospel, the true story of your death, the translation of every book in all languages, the interpolations of every book in all books. (54)

In this library there is no center, or, rather, any position, any gallery, becomes a provisional center for the person occupying it. As in other descriptions of postmodern hyperspace, the complexity of its network and the proliferation of simulacra make gaining critical distance—devising or finding a map or guide to its overall structure—nearly impossible. Although the logic of Borges's library insists that somewhere such a map or guide, a "total book" clarifying the organization of the library itself, does exist, the probability of ever finding it is, for all practical purposes, zero. Moreover, the same logic that insists that such a guide exists also insists on the existence of thousands of imperfect facsimiles, nearly indistinguishable from the correct original.

Hypertext

Borges's library, with its absence of a primary axis and its infinitely networked galleries, is an appropriate metaphor for hypertextual systems. Landow, in *Hypertext,* discusses textual networks, such as those utilizing Intermedia, a hypertext system developed at Brown University. If one imagines a book as a series of segments of text ("lexias," to use Barthes's term) joined by links, a conventional text establishes a clear axis of development. Links between segments of text are implied simply by virtue of the juxtaposition of those segments on the page or from one page to the next, and a straightforward reading involves moving from lexia to lexia, in the order in which they appear in the book. Thus, a conventional book has a clear axis of development, from beginning through middle to end.

It is, of course, possible for a reader, especially a more "writerly" kind of reader (to adopt again Barthes's terminology), to depart from the main axis of the book by looking up words in a dictionary, researching allusions contained in the text, checking footnotes, seeking out critical commentary, researching aspects of historical and biographical context, or noticing relationships among various noncontiguous elements of the text—images, symbols, analogous events, and so forth. For an active, writerly reader reading a text is not really a linear experience. Such a reader, through memory or research or by flipping back and forth among a book's pages, follows links that lead away from the original text to new texts and creates new links among nonsequential elements within the text. Electronic hypertextual networks (like Intermedia) facilitate and encourage this kind of branching. One can move to a footnote and then to the actual source of that footnote, or to the source of an allusion, or from one section of the text to another noncontiguous section quickly and simply, by means of a keystroke or two.

On one hand, this may seem to be simply a quick and convenient way of researching extra-textual aspects of a work, thus avoiding trips to the library, groping through stacks, photocopying articles, taking notes, and so forth, as well as an easy way of seeking and finding formal and thematic connections within a text. But, significantly, in this process of making standard scholarly investigation and critical analysis more efficient, something else happens. The ease by which one follows links away from the text to other texts and the ease of following alternate paths within the text weaken the privilege of the original text as well as the sense of there being a single dominant axis that directs the reader from beginning through middle to end.

In a fully developed hypertextual system, texts to which one moves are also networked to their own references and allusions. In the end, what results is a complex, interconnected network of nodes and links. The reader enters at any node and chooses any path through and about the network. Because there is no possibility of ever reading the entire hypertext (it is far too vast), a pragmatic consequence is that the temporal as well as the textual beginning and end of the reading experience is determined solely by the reader. One *can*, of course, read a primary text—a novel or a poem, for example—as it was originally created and simply use the hypertext version as a convenient way of checking sources, allusions, and biographical and historical context. But it is not difficult to imagine that over time the effect of hypertext will be to subvert the very sense of a primary text with a defined beginning, a dominant axis of movement, and a clear end. What has begun as a way of facilitating a richer reading experience of conventional texts in the end will radically alter our whole notion of what a text is—and what reading is, as well. In the most utopian scenario, all texts will be linked hypertextually, so that readers will be able to travel through world literature in diverse ways according to complex and labyrinthine paths chosen only by themselves. Michael Heim characterizes this utopian scenario:

The optical character reader will scan and digitize hard-copy printed texts; the entire tradition of books will be converted into information on disk files that can be accessed instantly by computers. By connecting a small computer to a phone, a professional will be able to read "books" whose footnotes can be expanded into further "books" which in turn open out onto a vast sea of data bases systematizing all of human cognition. (11)

In this discussion the word "hypertext" will be used to refer to specific textual networks organized around a work or theme, like the *In Memoriam* project, developed at Brown University. In this sense, any organization of segments of text electronically linked in a network in such a way that the reader has freedom of movement within that network will be called hypertext. But the term will also be used to refer to the more utopian notion of such a network expanded outward to access other systems and even a large, indeterminate portion of the textuality of the world.

When, in the near future, hypertextual systems—especially those that integrate multiple works—become our dominant textual vehicle, both the way we read and what we understand literature to be will be altered. Books, stories, poems, essays, or articles may no longer be conceived of as primary units, more or less complete and self-sufficient statements of one kind or another. Instead there will simply be a textual network that one enters, through which one moves, and from which one exits, after pursuing whatever purposes one has or learning whatever one is trying to learn. As the system grows and as individuals become more habituated to working with hypertext, the sense of centrality of certain primary texts within the network will be weakened. The distinction between text and context will dissolve and intertextuality will cease to be regarded as such because there will be, in fact, only one text, one intertext, one hypertext. "Hypertext . . . emphasizes that the marginal has as much to offer as does the central, in part because hypertext [redefines] the central by refusing to grant centrality to anything, to any lexia, for more than the time a gaze rests upon it" (Landow, 69–70).

This kind of system has radical implications for the subject. In the most utopian scenario the subject is empowered in a way never before possible. In hypertext there is no primary axis, no clear road in or out, no coordinates that have priority over any other coordinates—except as the reader determines. Thus lacking an authority or guide, the reader is thrust back onto his or her self. There may be instructions clarifying how to move from one place to another, but there is no source of values or priorities that tell the reader which direction or path he or she *should* choose.

From this perspective, the development of hypertext suggests an empowerment of the reader—at least those readers who have access to it. In another way, as well, the empowerment of the reader is a potential of hypertextuality. In hypertext, as Landow and others describe it, readers can append their own comments and responses, add new nodes or lexias, to any parts of the text that they are interested in, and they can create new links among the various lexias. Thus, the distinction between reader and writer is attenuated, perhaps even dissolved entirely. The text is no longer a one-way communication system in which information and ideas proceed only from author to reader, but a communication system in which all participants can contribute to and affect the content and direction of the conversation.

Landow sees far-reaching implications and possibilities for hypertext in education. Working with Intermedia, he has created networks for use in his literature classes. The *In Memoriam* Web, for example, is a hypertextual system built around Tennyson's poem, and the Soyinka Web is built around the work of the Nigerian poet Wole Soyinka. For the *In Memoriam* project, Landow, in conjunction with a graduate seminar, created a hypertextual system that included Tennyson's poem, variant readings from manuscripts of that poem, published critical commentary, relevant passages of other literary works, and commentary by participants in the seminar. Students added new links to the network and hundreds of new documents, both verbal and graphic, relating to aspects of Victorian science, history, and culture. Assignments were themselves appended to sections of the poem and became part of the web.

Students reading *In Memoriam* on Intermedia face a Macintosh style screen, one portion of which contains a segment of the text. At any point in the text they can branch out in different directions, accessing information about Tennyson's life, the historical context of the poem, Victorian science, and so forth. Moreover, image categories—death, wind, poetry, and flowers, for example—permit movement throughout the text among related but noncontiguous passages (Landow, 39, 141–149). Of course, to describe such passages as "noncontiguous" assumes the primacy of the original, printed text, because only in that form might any two passages necessarily be noncontiguous. In hypertext, any two passages that can be linked are potentially contiguous in any reading experience.

All this suggests an empowerment. Hypertext is a mode of textuality that encourages writerly, active reading rather than passive consumption of what has been produced by a conventionally authorial author. Landow sees hypertext as a technological embodiment of the insights of poststructural theory, which valorizes modern and postmodern texts that are anti-classical and "writerly," in contrast to classic realist texts that are less demanding and encourage passivity. Barthes writes,

Why is the writerly our value? Because the goal of literary work (of literature as work) is to make the reader no longer a consumer, but a producer of the text. Our [classic] literature is characterized by the pitiless divorce which the literary institution maintains between the producer of the text and its user, between its owner and its customer, between its author and its reader. This reader is thereby plunged into a kind of idleness—he is intransitive. . . . We call any readerly text a classic text. (*S/Z*, 4)

However, in spite of the reader's seeming control and empowerment, the structure of movement in and about a hypertextual system suggests a decentering analogous to the kind of decentering that can occur in other kinds of visual and verbal texts. There is no center of the text, no vanishing point, no primary axis, no clear unitary authorial voice that, like a vanishing point, implies a clear subject to which the text speaks. Heim writes,

The new publishing resembles more the modern megapolis, which is often described as a concrete jungle, a maze of activities and hidden byways, with no apparent center or guiding steeple. This is the architectural equivalent of the absence of the philosophical and religious absolute. (221)

And although the reader's ability to make choices *seems* to indicate control and empowerment, that empowerment may be specious. The complexity of the web and the possibility of having to make decisions without sufficient information regarding where any choice may lead can result in a disorientation that precludes meaningful freedom. Terence Harpold writes,

the user will not only forfeit a workable vision of the density and direction of the threads, but she will also . . . lose her place as participant (reader, author) in the hypertextual narratives. As the turns become more frequent and the digressions more vigorous, the user risks becoming *lost* in the docuverse. (172)

Thus, the complexity of hypertext and the inability of the subject to conceptualize a vision of the whole "has a subversive effect on the navigating subject" (Harpold, 173). This disorientation is analogous to the disorientation of the subject in the postmodern space described by Jameson and the inability of the subject to construct a conceptual map of the whole that would make effective action possible.

Also, according to Heim, in an electronic network the distinction between truth and falsehood gets all but obliterated. Heim describes a dissolution of that distinction that is similar to the loss of reference that occurs with the simulacrum, as described by Jameson and Baudrillard.

The overabundance of the electronic network of symbols is equivalent to an annihilating emptiness where restless curiosity swallows up the sharpness of truth in a sea of information overload. In this symbol pollution, everything without exception gets symbolized—which nullifies the act of symbolization as a unique event. In the general symbolic noise, and fortified by the power of the computer, the most stupid formulation reaches the same level as the most intelligent: the transfer and production of symbols goes on and on. (238)

Heim argues that word processing "provides a metaphor for the eclipse of all absolutes" (212), and he gives examples in which people have treated computer representations of truth as something less permanent than the truth they believed to reside in the written word. He quotes Donald Regan, President Ronald Reagan's secretary of the treasury, who, when questioned about a tax proposal, said, "It was written on a word processor. That means it can be changed" (212). And an epigraph to one of Heim's chapters is a quote of Pamela McCorduck's description of a decision by Jewish rabbis, who determined that the prohibition against destroying or erasing the written name of God did not apply to word processing, which they decided was not really writing. "[E]lectronic text is impermanent, flimsy, malleable, contingent. Where is Truth in impermanence, flimsiness, malleability, and contingency?" (Heim, 192; McCorduck, 51).

The Author

The subject of the author, most significantly, is challenged by hypertext. One of the strengths of hypertextual systems is their encouragement of collaboration in the creation of knowledge and their capacity for a free, rapid, and unimpeded dissemination of that knowledge. As a result, notions of intellectual property and authorship, which are very much tied to the fixity and permanence of the book as an object for which an individual can take responsibility and credit, are challenged. The speed and ease of comment and response in hypertext makes it difficult to keep track of the specific contributions of various writer/readers.

But the challenge to individual authorship is not only the result of pragmatic difficulties, it is also psychological, an attitude or state of mind that tends to be encouraged by hypertext. Walter J. Ong argues that "[p]rint creates a new sense of the private ownership of words" and that "resentment at plagiarism" develops with writing (131). Hypertext, in contrast, reinforces a sense of learning more as a communal than an individual endeavor. It creates situations in which individual contributions are likely to get lost within the conversation as a whole, and it creates new kinds of communities emancipated from physical, geographical, or political boundaries.

Exchange of ideas and information in hypertext is something more like the way problems are dealt with in "live" conversations than in printed books. When an understanding or solution emerges from a casual conversation or an informal meeting it may be difficult or impossible to determine how much each participant contributed to the result. Even if a specific individual made a proposal that was finally accepted, others very likely contributed by helping focus discussion, eliminating bad possibilities, making suggestions that helped lead discussion toward the solution, encouraging promising suggestions, or making any number of subtle contributions. Hypertext—like a conversation—encourages a value system that emphasizes the solving of problems and the growth of learning by and for the good of the community as a whole, rather than one that insists that individuals always be recognized and rewarded for the exact part that they have played in that communal endeavor.

Individuals accustomed to an ethical system based on the book regard any infringement on their authorial rights or any use of a published text, without appropriate permission, as a moral and legal wrong. Refusing to share knowledge and establishing restrictions on the dissemination of knowledge are legitimate prerogatives of the author or copyright owner; or, if such restrictions are viewed as inappropriate, they are regarded as much lesser evils than plagiarism or unauthorized use of information not one's own. In contrast, individuals who have become accustomed to hypertextual exchange tend to regard any impediment to free exchange as a serious wrong. The free development and dissemination of knowledge is more important than always giving precise credit where credit is due. Richard A. Lanham says that "[e]lectronic information seems to resist ownership" (19), and Landow argues that "from the point of view of the author of hypertext, for whom collaboration and sharing are of the essence of 'writing,' restrictions on the availability of text, like prohibitions against copying or linking, appear absurd, indeed immoral, constraints" (198).

Obviously this new attitude and new potential creates all sorts of problems. Most of us work in systems that recognize—or try to recognize—the value of individuals *as* individuals and attempt to reward them accordingly, and it is unlikely that we will relinquish our need for confirmation of our individual value quickly or easily. Therefore, it seems inevitable that notions of authorship and intellectual property will be maintained, even as hypertextual systems, which mitigate against such notions, become more important. Nevertheless, it is possible to imagine, perhaps only dimly, a day when those ideas will be abandoned because our entire understanding of who we are and what we should be doing and why we should be doing it will have shifted.

Landow argues, in effect, that hypertext de-naturalizes our ideas about authorship, authorial property, and texts as objects, and forces us to notice that those ideas are products of a specific historical period with a specific kind of technology.

This technology—that of the printed book and its close relations, which include the typed or printed page—engenders certain notions of authorial property, authorial uniqueness, and a physically isolated text that hypertext makes untenable. The evidence of hypertext, in other words, historicizes many of our most commonplace assumptions, thereby forcing them to descend from the ethereality of abstraction and appear as corollaries to a particular technology rooted in specific times and places. (33)

And Heim writes,

As the model of the integrated private self of the author fades, the rights of the author as a persistent self-identity also become more evanescent, more difficult to define. If the work of the author no longer carries with it definite physical properties as a unique original, as a book in a definite form, then the author's rights too grow more tenuous, more indistinct. (221)

Described this way, hypertext and electronic networking seem to respond to the call for an alteration of the role of the "author" that Foucault made. For Foucault the "author-function" acts as an ideological constraint on the reading of texts, and he argues for a loosening of that authorial hold, which "impedes the free circulation, the free manipulation, the free composition, decomposition, and recomposition of fiction" ("What Is an Author?" 158). Viewing the author-function as historically contingent, he is able to envision a time when it might be different.

Although, since the eighteenth century, the author has played the role of the regulator of the fictive, a role quite characteristic of our era of industrial and bourgeois society, of individualism and private property, still, given the historical modifications that are taking place, it does not seem necessary that the author-function remain constant in form, complexity, and even in existence. (159–160)

Although Foucault is talking about fiction in particular, his ideas could easily be taken to apply to other forms of textual ownership. As writers like Landow and Heim describe it, experience in working in hypertext can provoke a Foucauldian realization that notions like authorship and intellectual property, as natural and self-evident and just as they seem to be, are constructs that are historically specific. In different historical situations there might be different understandings of the proper relationship of an individual to his or her discourse and the discourse of others.

Nevertheless, Landow argues that authorship and intellectual property will have to be maintained in some modified or qualified way even within hypertextual exchange. In spite of his earlier statement that hypertext makes notions like authorial property and authorial uniqueness "untenable," in the end he argues that such concepts and the rights related to them are necessary to motivate authors, "for without such protection authors receive little encouragement to publish their work" (198). One might argue that inquiry, discussion, and exchange might be their own rewards and that some individuals might actually engage in them in spite of the absence of monetary reward. No doubt this will sound naive to some, but anyone who has, in recent years, participated in electronic discussion groups knows that many scholars spend hours (sometimes too many hours) engaged in intellectual exchange with little hope that it will bring them tenure or salary increases. Nevertheless, Landow's domestication of the subversive potential of hypertext is necessary, at least for the time being, so that the medium might be more palatable to administrators who need to evaluate individuals and to scholars who want to be evaluated themselves on the basis of objective, verifiable evidence of the value of individual contributions.

In any event, there is little doubt that for pragmatic reasons and in order to minimize the disruptive effects of this new medium of communication and intellectual exchange, ownership and attribution will be maintained as possibilities within electronic communications systems for the indefinite future at least. And, for that indefinite future, hypertext and printed texts will exist alongside one another in some complementary way. Landow argues for copyright laws that protect the rights of authors to profit from their work but at the same time are not so strict as to "restrict the flow of information that can benefit large numbers of people" (198).

Hypertext demands new classes or conceptions of copyright that protect the rights of the author while permitting others to link to that author's text. Hypertext, in other words, requires a new balancing of rights belonging to those entities we can describe variously as primary versus secondary authors, authors versus reader-authors, or authors versus linkers. Although no one should have the right to modify or appropriate another's text any more than one does now, hypertext reader-authors should be able to link their own texts or those by a third party to a text created by someone else, and they should also be able to copyright their own link sets should they wish to do so. A crucial component in the coming financial and legal reconception of authorship involves developing schemes for equitable royalties or some other form of payment to authors. (198)

Theodor Holm Nelson has devised an elaborate system for recognizing and compensating individual authors within hypertextual systems. Nelson, a pioneer of computerized networks, claims to have been the first to use the word "hypertext" (Nelson, 0/2).[1] For over two decades he has been working on a utopian system, which he calls Xanadu. Nelson argues that Xanadu, or something like it, will become "the standard publishing and archival medium of the future" (2/47). Xanadu operates as a utility that provides instantaneous access to nearly unlimited electronic documents (including traditional documents entered electronically into the network). Subscribers pay fees based on usage, as with other utilities.

Documents in Xanadu are classified as private or published. If private, access is limited to authors themselves and other designated individuals. If published, owners (whether the owners are authors, editors, or conventional publishers) earn royalties every time a user accesses their work. The original work is inviolate in that it can always be retrieved in its original form and only the owner can change it. However, owners of published documents relinquish all right to control who can access their work; all individuals subscribing to Xanadu and paying the required fee, based on the amount of time they use the system, are automatically granted the right to use whatever they access in any way they choose. They are free to quote any published text, create links to their own comments or to other texts, print texts, and use them in any way, without restraint, impediment, or censorship of any kind.

In Nelson's system authorship and the rights of authorship are maintained, and the author or owner of a document is entitled to a standard royalty, determined by the actual use of the document by readers. But the use and exchange of ideas is completely unimpeded—except, of course (and perhaps not insignificantly), by financial constraints on those who need to access the system. The decision to enter the system is a decision to open up one's writing to a community and to receive reasonable compensation in return. One might argue that this is not fundamentally different from the way publishing and copywright work today. But, in fact, as in descriptions of hypertext by Landow, there is an important shift in emphasis from individual proprietary rights to those of a community to access learning. In Xanadu, once a work is entered into the network, individual written permissions from specific authors or publishers, constraints based on "fair use," limitations on the length of text that might be quoted, or restrictions on appropriating and re-presenting a text in an altered form, are unnecessary. The work is embedded in the network, and anyone who can access it is free to use it in any way he or she chooses. Any author who finds this arrangement unsatisfactory, according to Nelson, "had better withhold his or her stuff from this system" (2/48). Of course, if some system like Xanadu were the major means by which ideas were exchanged, such a decision might be tantamount to nonparticipation and silence.

Authorial rights and intellectual property are technical and legal problems; they do not, directly, affect the sense of subjectivity that is implied or reinforced by the engagement with a certain kind of textual vehicle. Nevertheless, to the extent that laws and conventions presuppose and confirm certain values and understandings, modifications in copyright law along the lines that Landow imagines or the relinquishing of authorial rights that Nelson envisions reinforce a somewhat different notion of the subject and the subject's relationship to society. Although the notion of individual authorship is not abandoned, the right of a community to have access to ideas that have "originated" in such individuals is given greater emphasis. What is implied is that ideas, unlike other "products," are not things that one can choose or not choose to sell. The community has a right to have access to the ideas of the individual, and an author has a responsibility to make his or her ideas available, to permit them to be discussed, debated, and developed. The responsibility of an individual to his or her community is emphasized, and the rights of individuals, which still include reasonable recognition and reward, must accommodate that greater responsibility.

Thus, subtly, the notion that learning and the development of knowledge are the results of an ongoing conversation is reinforced and with it the corollary that they are not such individual things as we may have believed. Though ownership of and access to texts are legal and pragmatic matters, there is, even in this qualified and admittedly domesticated representation of the impact of electronic communication systems on the subject, a diminished valorization of the individual and a greater emphasis on the community. If individual authorship is an ineluctable consequence of the printed text, collaboration in print can be achieved only through a conscious decision, an act of will. Conversely, if collaboration is an ineluctable tendency of electronic networks, then individual authorship can be maintained within such systems only through a conscious effort to resist that tendency.

Psychic Life Redefined

Certainly, in subtler and more immediate ways, working with electronic textuality modifies our feeling of subjectivity. Traditional texts, both visual and verbal, address a localized spectator or reader—implied by logical vanishing points or by narrating voices that seem directed toward an individual reader. A conventional book creates the illusion that at the moment of its being read a single author addresses a single reader. In electronic networks no single author addresses any single reader, or, if one does, their exchange emerges from and immediately reenters a broader context of multiple speakers and listeners. There is a polyphony of voices, and the authority of each of them is continually qualified by their mutually commenting on one another. An active, writerly reader interrogates a conventional text and does not passively consume it, but interrogation is built into electronic conversations.

Electronic networks create a horizonless conceptual space that speaks almost to itself. Texts that are closed, coherent, and focused, whether visual or verbal, tend to elicit mirroring subjects that recognize—or misrecognize—themselves as separate, unified, and centered. Autonomous texts reflect and are reflected by subjects that conceive of themselves as autonomous. Conversely, the conceptual dispersal of textuality that occurs in hypertext may be reflected by a decentered subject that engages that decentered textuality. The lack of a clearly delineated autonomous text in hypertextual systems may be reflected by a subject that is less autonomous. Landow, believing that the challenge to the subject posed by hypertext is precisely the one anticipated by Barthes, Derrida, Foucault, and Lyotard, writes that "the unboundedness of the new textuality disperses the author" (74). And Heim argues that "[a]s the authoritativeness of text diminishes, so too does the recognition of the private self of the creative author" (221).

In electronic networks, space—where one is and where the text is—becomes increasingly irrelevant. The text is "everywhere and nowhere" (Heim, 22) and "psychic life is redefined" (Heim, 164). Psychically, one extends outward into that indeterminate space, and even the body, as a physically localized entity, becomes less relevant, not only because one is freed (or obligated) to work in different places (office, home, beach), but also because of an intuitive effect of engaging the medium. Just as, when using any tool, one can come to feel the machine as a part of one-self, to intuitively sense it as an extension of one's body, in electronic networks one enters a postmodern body that extends the organic body, as well as the psyche, outward. And, because it is a tool of communication and exchange, one joins with others who are engaging it, so that the whole becomes a complex cybernetic human and machine intelligence. "We are [all] cyborgs," Donna Haraway argues (66), and no doubt there never was such a cyborg as the Internet. It achieves almost a life of its own, different from, though dependent on, the life of the individuals who use it and become part of it.

Thus, apart from the legal and pragmatic problems relating to copyright and authorship, there is a phenomenological weakening and de-centering of the localized subject that occurs when one engages an electronic network. But there is a paradoxical extension and an enlargement of the subject, as well. Engaging hypertext creates an extended, communal subject that is both an enlargement and a weakening of that former, centered subject.

Heim argues that changes in the way we symbolize the world produce changes in the psyche. Characterizing the thinking of the pre-Socratic philosopher Anaximander in a way wholly compatible with poststructuralist thought, he writes,

Language, then, does not describe a pregiven, fixed world. Language instead is a world, a limited order out of total chaos. The world is continually emergent in words; reality is the world we bespeak. . . . For Anaximander, language, or *logos*, is the emergence of identity out of the chaos of an infinite matrix of possibilities. (30)

Similarly, textual technology is not simply a tool but the mode by which we engage the world and produce a sense of selfhood. Basing his ideas on the work of Ong and Eric Havelock, Heim describes "the theory of transformative technologies," which identifies major shifts in textual technology as occurring with the emergence of chirographic—or hand-writing—culture from one that was predominantly oral, the development of typographic culture with the invention of the printing press, and the development of word-processing and electronically networked textuality that is emerging at the present time. (When Heim discusses "word processing" he normally does so with the assumption that anyone's word processing is hypertextually linked to a larger network of texts and links.) Each of these shifts produced changes in the psyche: changes in the way we structure our thinking, the way we feel ourselves to be, and the way we engage and interact with the world and others. Ong writes,

> Since at least the time of Hegel, awareness has been growing that human consciousness evolves. . . . Modern studies in the shift from orality to literacy and the sequels of literacy, print and electronic processing of verbalization make more and more apparent some of the ways this evolution has depended on writing. (178)

Heim, drawing on Ong, argues that "each historical shift in the symbolization of reality brings with it a restructuring of the psyche" and that the "entire human personality is configured anew with every shift in the dominant medium for preserving thought" (59), and he extends Ong's insights more fully into digital writing and hypertext.

According to Heim and Ong, literary culture is characterized by a more complex, sequential, and hierarchical style of thought than the highly patterned and repetitive thinking of preliterate, oral cultures. Enumerations and aggregations characterize oral thinking, but more complex syntactical and organizational arrangements are possible when thought can be stabilized by writing (Heim, 110–111; Ong, 37–39).

Heim describes the psychic life associated with the book as characterized by a contemplative and meditative attitude. There is the belief that such an attitude, promoted by writing and reading, is a means of personal transcendence, of providing access to higher truths of God or nature. Moreover, the stability of the book encourages a view of ideas as fixed and permanent, and this Platonic sense of the permanence of ideas is reflected in the mind itself, whose flux is stabilized and focused as a result. "Through learning to focus on ideas, the mind itself grows more steady" (Heim, 183). Finally, the book fosters a sense of mental privacy, in which the individual mind is felt to be a locus where ideas originate. Thus, the book encourages a disciplined and orderly mental attitude that valorizes personal, individual contemplation as a means of gaining access to ideas that are regarded as transcendent truths.

Digital writing changes this psychic framework. It recaptures some of the immediacy—the apparent near-identity of thought and symbolization—that characterized oral culture.[2] Formulaic aspects of writing are easily routinized by algorithmic procedures, and as a result personal expression is de-emphasized. Word processing, more fluid than writing on paper, embodies a sense of thought as an "ideational flow" (Heim, 152), as a continual process that is not necessarily centered around static and transcendental ideas. The sense of a contemplative permanence is supplanted by a dynamic, volatile "superabundance of possibilities" (211). Indeed, this abundance of possibilities threatens to preclude one's sense of having a consistent vision and, in fact, "may lead to the disappearance of the authentic and determinate human voice or personal presence behind symbolized words" (212). Again, in a manner consistent with poststructural perspectives (though he does not invoke poststructural thinkers), Heim writes, "It becomes possible to treat the entire verbal life of the human race as one continuous, anonymous code without essential reference to a human presence behind it, which neither feels it must answer to anyone nor necessarily awaits an answer from anyone" (213).

Linking with networks makes writing less private and more public. It is more collaborative, and there is greater integration with a community; the individual self is less separate and isolated, and individual authorship is threatened (Heim, 191). There is the sense that linking electronically with a larger community may itself create "a new kind of collective intelligence" (217) and even the hint that this collective, interactive intelligence may become an entity in its own right and individuals will act as parts of that larger entity, losing some of their existential priority in the process.

Enhancing individuals' sense of community certainly has its positive side, encouraging cooperation where conflict might have been predominant. But a negative possibility is that with the erosion of the private self comes a loss of privacy, both because the private self loses existential priority and because it is the nature of networks to be public and accessible. There is the "ever-present possibility of digital writing being intercepted or in some way recovered" (Heim, 222).[3]

Thus, hypertext involves a paradoxical relationship to the subject. In the most obvious respect, it suggests the potential for empowerment; but that potential for empowerment coexists with a psychological decentering that results from engagement with electronic networks. Individuals can access a horizonless textual space, forge their own paths and links within it, and contribute to it just as they might contribute to a nonvirtual conversation. But in that space there are no clear axes or established directions, no vanishing points to help the subject position his or her self. The subject, physically seated in front of a networked computer and monitor, is in effect "everywhere and nowhere," conceptually occupying a virtual space that cannot be grasped the way streets, rooms, and natural landscapes can be grasped. The *cogito* is both dispersed and enlarged, not by a challenge of philosophy or theory, but by the subject's experience in a decentered network that threatens to eclipse the "individual" subject that understands itself as physically embodied and clearly localized in space and time. The groundless, shifting subject articulated by poststructural theory and represented in postmodern art and literature is actualized in the virtual space of hypertext.

Bonnie Mitchell, who has been involved in a number of collaborative art projects created on the Internet, writes, as her contribution to a piece she organized,

Living in the electrons of cyberspace, we have no gender, we have no race, we are neither old nor young, intelligent nor naive, we have only an e-mail address to identify us. Our writing style and smileys reveal our virtual personalities. We are not alone. Yet we sit in physical isolation. Our machines satisfy our quest for social acknowledgment. We speak with our fingers and the machine replies. . . . Nonphysical intimacy. Security and privacy. Suppressed expression. Electrically altered ego. We have no need for faces. Don't show me yours. We have no need for bodies. They deteriorate anyway. We have no need for voice. We speak through thought. We have no need for any of these things. We have fingers, words, and images. We have an Internet connection. We have our virtual selves.[4]

Utopia and Dystopia

In spite of qualifications and warnings, many writers, like Landow, display an irrepressible enthusiasm for the new technology, emphasizing its democratizing potential and its pedagogical possibilities. Landow explicitly states the optimistic position: "I contend that the history of information technology from writing to hypertext reveals an increasing democratization or dissemination of power" (174), and one of McCorduck's books is entitled *The Universal Machine: Confessions of a Technological Optimist.* Landow (120–161), McCorduck (225–233), Lanham (98–153), and Michael Joyce ("Siren Shapes") see great potential for hypertext in education, and McCorduck sees it as even helpful to international cooperation, arguing that computer assisted negotiations in the international arena encourage "a deep and powerful human capacity to cooperate, to fashion a whole greater than the sum of its parts" (178).

Certainly, on the face of it, electronic networks do seem to have this potential for democracy and cooperative exchange. Jay David Bolter sees contemporary culture as organized as a network rather than a hierarchy; traditional institutions no longer have the authority they once had, and individuals form voluntary, nonhierarchical affiliations instead. "The network has replaced the hierarchy" (Bolter, 232). Although this network organization of society is not entirely a function of technology, it is facilitated by the computer (238).

Even at the present time, anyone who has a computer, communications software, a modem, and a telephone line can access hundreds of sources of information of all kinds, including many full text publications—entire articles, complete journals, and literary works. *Project Gutenberg*, for example, makes available on-line the full texts of *Moby Dick*, the King James Bible, *Paradise Lost, The Scarlet Letter,* the *Oedipus* trilogy, the complete works of Shakespeare, and many other works of the Western canon. Users can download these items, search texts for specific words and images, and navigate the texts in various ways. The *Electronic Poetry Center* is a World Wide Web site that acts as a resource for production of and research into contemporary poetry, both print and electronic. It archives full text poems, provides access to home pages of individual poets, has its own electronic journal, provides access to other electronic journals and other Internet pages, and stores audio interviews of poets that readers can retrieve. All texts can be downloaded and used for personal and educational purposes without constraint, but cannot be reproduced and sold for profit. By participating in any of the thousands of electronic discussion groups now available, scholars can engage in debate and exchange with colleagues they have never seen and may never meet face to face. For those interested in critical studies it will soon be possible to access hypertextual systems that will open up a large portion of world literature and cultural criticism. This is a seductive scenario.

However, clearly the utopian scenario is not a *fait accompli,* and there is a dystopian scenario as well, one very different from the nonhierarchical egalitarian society described by Landau, McCorduck, Lanham, and Bolter. Electronic networking has grown much faster than the capacity of anyone to control its rules and structure, and therein lies its strength—as well as its messiness. Lacking a hierarchical system of authority and control, it seems to function in a way that is quite egalitarian, at least for those individuals who have access to it. But already there have been attempts to control hypertext, to limit the kinds of materials that can be transmitted. The most publicized such cases involve pornography, but if, in that context, systems are devised that successfully control what can or cannot be sent, certainly a broad range of other kinds of material might be affected as well. Thus, all the old issues relating to free speech as opposed to legitimate restraints on speech are raised in hypertext, but with an even greater urgency. Because it is new, because of its incredible power and the threat it poses to restraint of any kind, and because of its promise as a medium that might emancipate, it is easy to see how individuals would line up on one side or the other, those desiring to let it continue to develop in an unrestrained fashion or those wishing to impose larger social and legal controls on it.[5] The most dystopian scenario is described by William Gibson in his 1984 classic cyberpunk novel *Neuromancer*, in which multinational corporations control a well-protected virtual hyperreality that excludes rather than includes, and freelance cybernetic hackers work as hired pirates who, at great risk to their lives and minds, enter that space to steal information.

Strictly speaking, of course, the kind of total hypertext imagined by Heim—one that contained all of world literature (literature defined in the most inclusive sense)—is logically and pragmatically impossible. Will the hypertext contain instructions for using the hypertext? No doubt, on some level it will. But the instructions for getting to those instructions? A system that attempts to be total needs to contain itself and in doing so produces paradoxes and infinite regresses. Borges's imaginary Library of Babel, which would contain not only all books but also catalogs, catalogs of catalogs, and a compendium of the entire library, is a logical paradox and a pragmatic impossibility.

Stuart Moulthrop writes of hypertext, "The text gestures toward openness—what options can you imagine?—but then it forecloses: some options are available but not others, and someone clearly has done the defining" ("You Say You Want a Revolution?" 21).[6] And William Paulson notes the implications of the pragmatic constraints on what can be included in hypertext.

[I]n the humanities, the contemporary textual base pales in comparison with the textual archive of the past, which can be made machine-readable only at considerable cost and after decisions have been made about what to include and exclude—decisions that would certainly raise the stakes of already heated arguments over canons. A substantial portion of the written past would be left behind—preserved in libraries, of course, but accessible only in a manner that could come to seem archaic or inefficient. (295)

Perhaps at some point the potential for expanding the canon utilizing hypertext will be so great as to make such objections appear to be purely academic. But it is important to note that there is a logical and pragmatic limit on hypertext. Because hypertextual totality is an impossibility, decisions will always have to be made regarding what is included and accessible and what is not. Thus, issues regarding the "canon" will still be relevant, and some one or ones will, in one way or another, be empowered to make those decisions.

For a *text* to be excluded from hypertext is likely to be even more crippling than its being excluded from the "canon" as presently constituted. The ease and speed of navigating among texts embedded in hypertextual networks has as its flip side a tendency to ignore texts that are not included, as if they did not exist at all. If one is in the habit of getting all the information one needs conveniently from a terminal in one's home or office, one will be less likely to go to a library or archive in order to seek out some text that isn't available on the network. As Paulson notes, accessing texts not included in hypertext—by going to the library—"could come to seem archaic or inefficient" (295). And Landow writes, "When . . . some connections require no more effort than does continuing to read the same text, *un*connected texts are experienced as lying much farther off and availability and accessibility become very different matters" (187). Just as individuals who lack access to the network may cease to be persons, texts not included in the network may also cease to exist.

If hypertext is to have the emancipating and broadly empowering potential that is envisioned, several conditions must obtain. It must, for example, be accessible to large numbers of people and be inexpensive and "friendly" enough to be available to anyone who wants or needs to engage it. One can imagine the most utopian hypertextual system possible, having all the empowering effects on its users that writers like Landow and McCorduck imagine, but with restricted access. The restrictions might be economic, involving fees, or access could be limited to those with political or professional qualifications—those who held certain positions or were members of certain organizations. If this were to happen, individuals unable to participate in the system would be susceptible to the danger Baudrillard described in *America*. They would be unspoken and mute. Those who were able to engage the network would be empowered, free, and emancipated. Those who could not engage it would not exist.

Moulthrop, who has written about hypertext and written interactive fiction as well, generally sides with the optimists regarding the future of hypertext, but his optimism is not unqualified. He points out that the potential of hypertext for providing easy access to information and open discussion, indifferent to social, economic, and political power, is completely dependent upon sophisticated and expensive technology that can only be provided by large corporate agencies, often as not affiliated with the defense establishment. And if those large and powerful agencies that produce the hardware and software of hypertext decide that "truly interactive information networks do not make wise investments" (42), certainly they will find the means to impose constraints on those networks. "Directly or indirectly, most development of hardware and software depends on heavily capitalized multinational companies that do a thriving business with the defense establishment. This affiliation clearly influences the development of new media" (49). Moreover, the intellectual community itself has an interest in continuing the "existing institutions of intellectual authority: the printed word, the book, the library, the university, the publishing house" (53). The democratizing and utopian potential of hypertext may, indeed, be resisted by forces most in a position to limit democracy and egalitarianism.

It is not difficult to imagine a future in which there is a polarization of society based on wealth and the ability of individuals to access information. With money one will be able to buy access to information, and access to information will be able to produce wealth, but those with neither will have a difficult time altering their station in life. Society will be divided into informational haves and have-nots. The informationally privileged will protect themselves behind gates, fences, and alarm systems, and will seat themselves at computer terminals, safely experiencing a virtual reality and virtual mobility within their chosen electronic neighborhoods. They will seldom venture into the "real" streets, which will be ruled by the marginalized and the disenfranchised, who will act on the basis of more dangerous, nonvirtual forces and impulses.

Moreover, if this dystopian scenario is not to be the future, hypertext must remain interactive, not only in its exploratory capacity but also in its constructive capacity.[7] That is, users should be able to navigate it according to choices that they make, and they also should have the power to affect it by adding text of their own or creating new links that might later be used by others.

It is the interactive aspect of electronic networking that makes it different from other media with which it is often associated—television (as it has thus far existed) in particular. Commercial TV is a one-way communication system. It is not—or is not yet—interactive to any significant degree, though certainly interactive video—teleconferencing and interactive marketing, for example—are becoming more widespread. Indeed, the entire communications and information industry is undergoing a revolution, and enhanced interactivity is a major component of that revolution. Nevertheless, up to this point television has involved a clear discrimination between the technology of reception and that of transmission; receivers do not function as transmitters, and transmitters do not receive messages from those to whom they send signals. This is in contrast to the telephone, which combines receiver and transmitter in a single unit. A computer engaging an electronic network by means of a telephone or communication line combines the interactiveness of the telephone with television's potential for mass participation. The networked personal computer functions as both transmitter and receiver; anyone with access to such equipment can listen and speak, read and write, as he or she chooses.

Thus, although they are often discussed in the same breath, there is a big difference between the hyperreality that Baudrillard has described, rooted so much in observations of the effects of television and mass media, and the hypertextuality of electronic networks. Both involve a world that is constructed, one that is in some way "virtual." Heim writes of electronic networks that "digital phenomenon is one facet of a totally controlled environment, an environment where what we experience is what we have created" (85). But, in the hyperreal, that constructed world is imposed on the masses by a relatively small number of powerful controllers of the media. In hypertext there is at least the possibility of a democratic world created by the interaction of all participants. It is precisely this difference between the two, between the hyperreal and the hypertextual, that may justify some optimism in relation to the growth of hypertext, that suggests that it may be more difficult—though certainly not impossible—to control hypertextuality and use it as a vehicle for restricting and directing rather than opening up and freeing possibility.

Indeed, the hyperreal exists in relation to hypertext as the imaginary exists in relation to the symbolic. Baudrillard writes, "The mirror phase has given way to the video phase" (*America*, 37), but Joyce writes, as if as a rejoinder, "[H]ypertext is the word's revenge on TV" ("Siren Shapes," 14). If television induces an attitude of passive receptivity in a viewer visually enthralled and powerless to affect the enthralling medium, hypertext invites a more active engagement through symbolic constitution in a semiotic network. If one enters the symbolic when one is inscribed in language by being represented by a pronoun or a proper name, one enters the hypertextual symbolic when one gets a network address, a log-on ID, and a password, which enable one to become listener and speaker, reader and author. The signs of video are illusionistic—iconic and analogue, cinematic and videographic; the signs of hypertext are conventional—symbolic and digital, dominated by verbal or alphanumeric inscriptions or schematic visual icons. Hypertext may, indeed, supplant MTV, which, for all its efforts to create spectacular visual effects and shocking content, has, for the most part, become highly conventionalized and uninteresting. Authentic interaction, on the other hand, always holds open the possibility of inventiveness and surprise. Just as the linguistic symbolic involves constitution within a structure of signifiers the whole of which is abstract and invisible, so the hypertextual symbolic involves constitution within and by a perceptually absent but conceptually present network of relationships, a kind of *langue* of the Internet.

Thus, at a time when controlling forces, when Madison Avenue, MTV, and reactionary political groups, seem to have a stranglehold on culture and ideology, the emergence of electronic networking seems fortuituous. In its present, somewhat chaotic and anarchistic form, it may afford the first opportunity since the 1960s for culture to be produced from the bottom up rather than imposed from the top down. Of course, as in the sixties, it is precisely this threat that motivates the attempts to co-opt, appropriate, and domesticate the oppositional potential.

Finally, the choices available in hypertext—the texts included and the links among them—must be significant. Hypertext, huge as it may be, cannot be total, cannot contain all texts ever produced by humans. Therefore, those texts that are made available must be meaningful. In television it is the proliferation of irrelevant choices that produces a specious freedom that obscures increasingly powerful constraints on imaginable possibilities. Ninety cable channels might broadcast shows that entertain but none of which contain serious social or political analysis. Thus, viewers are provided with an illusion of freedom that is really equivalent to a grocery aisle filled with different brands of laundry detergent. They can point to all kinds of objectively real choices that provide evidence for an unprecedented freedom they seem to possess, at the same time that their lives are increasingly constrained ideologically by sophisticated commercials and entertainment shows that construct consumer subjects. Incapable of conceiving things or themselves differently, convinced that the choices they are presented with are the most anyone can reasonably expect, viewers are impotent to affect things that touch them in important ways.

Discussions of interactive video often have focused on similar trivial or pseudo choices, choices that may, at best, be conveniences but that do not fundamentally enlarge people's lives. We may provide feedback to networks regarding preferences for shows, provide information to mass marketers regarding the products they distribute, shop through the TV, or express opinions to pollsters about political candidates. If hypertext also comes to be dominated by the interactive equivalents of sitcoms or home shopping, not much will really be gained and the interaction will be meaningless. What is worse is that, because it will present itself as an enlargement of choices but limit those choices to the trivial, it will really be a means of control disguising itself as freedom.

But for the moment, electronic networking is a vast and expanding system, permitting relatively free movement and intellectual exchange. Its effect on the world outside it, however—that nontextual reality, Baudrillard's Fourth World, the world that is not spoken and does not speak—is uncertain. The interactivity of hypertext may be confirming and empowering for those who can engage it, but unless it contains links to the world outside hypertext, or at least cracks or openings that permit the socially, politically, and textually excluded to affect it—even though that effect is likely to be a disruptive one—hypertext will simply be a virtual neighborhood—and a safe and privileged one at that—coexisting with other nonvirtual neighborhoods that are not so nice.

Hypertextual Narratives

Not only has hypertext been used as a scholarly and educational tool, as in networks like the *In Memoriam* Web and Perseus 1.0, an elaborate, multimedia program for studying Greek art, literature, language, mythology, and history, utilizing CD-ROM and video disk technologies, it has also been used for the creation of interactive literature: stories, novels, and poems that require readers to make choices as they navigate a text. To some extent, this kind of story has been forecast by modern and postmodern literature, which has often been ambiguous, open, and demanding for the reader. In an obvious way it was anticipated in novels like John Fowles's *The French Lieutenant's Woman*, which contains two different endings and "permits" the reader to choose the one that he or she prefers. And Calvino's *If on a winter's night a traveler* forecasts the labyrinthine movements of a reader through a complex hypertextual system. Bolter, who notes a convergence between the concerns of modern fiction and the technological possibilities of the computer, writes, "Fiction, at least modern fiction, is by nature open to experiment, and being open and open-ended is precisely the quality that the computer lends to all writing" (121).

But in true hypertextual literature there is a more literal control by the reader than is possible in books, where the order of reading is to a great extent determined by a pre-established sequence of paragraphs and pages. True, an active reader might flip back and forth among the pages of a book, checking details and identifying relationships among noncontiguous parts, but the tendency will be to read the text in the order encouraged by its physical structure. When reading a printed text, the reader always knows at least what page he or she is on and what page comes next. But when a reader gets lost in a hypertextual labyrinth of nodes and links, that reader really is without bearings.

Hypertextual fiction is hypertext in the same sense as that described earlier—a variety of nodes or lexias are connected by various links, creating a web or network that the reader navigates in diverse ways. Some fictions provide a map of the network, which can aid the reader in determining which paths to choose. Some do not, so that the reader must make choices based on limited information; choices among brief titles of sections may determine the direction of the text, or choices among selected key words in a lexia will link to other lexias related to those words. When there is no map provided, the reader must explore the text the way one explores a labyrinth, slowly building a mental map of the structure, or at least of a portion of it. Often the reader's path loops back to paths already traveled, but the newer context may suggest different meanings. A description may seem at first to be related to a certain character; but when the same description is encountered in a later context the reader may realize that it might also apply to a different character and reading it this new way alters the interpretation of the story. Sometimes (as in a maze) the reader may backtrack in order to try another path, perhaps frustrated because he or she is unable to answer a question or resolve some mystery evoked by the narrative. Although there are a finite number of lexias, the reader may never be sure whether or not they all have been read. One may find oneself looping back to familiar lexias and become convinced that one has read everything; then, suddenly, a turn previously ignored may reveal an entire section of the narrative—the background of a character, for example—that hadn't been previously encountered.

Thus, the narrative is not a clearly delineated path but a textual space available for exploration. The reader's role is enhanced not only because the reader bears the responsibility for navigating the network but also because lexias, which can be organized in different ways, are often ambiguous; their meaning changes when their context—the other lexias surrounding them—changes. The narrative will probably not provide any clear classical closure, though whether or not it seems to may itself be determined by reader choices. In the end the reader decides when the story is over, when he or she has had enough. If some lexias have been missed there is less a sense that the reader has failed—has lacked the patience to complete a demanding task—and more the sense that the reader has simply made a determination that is, after all, his or hers to make.

Michael Joyce's "Afternoon, a story" (1987) has become, at least at this very early stage in the development of the genre, a hypertextual classic. Like much of the hypertextual literature available at the present time, it is published by Eastgate Systems in Cambridge, Massachusetts, and it utilizes a program called Storyspace in its writing. Storyspace (which is not necessary for reading the story) enables writers to create units of text (or illustrations or sounds or even moving images) and link them in diverse ways so that a reader, with the aid of a computer, can read the story as a hypertext.

"Afternoon" is a construction of 539 textual segments with 951 links among them. The most linear way of moving through the story normally results from simply hitting the return key after one has read the lexia on screen at the moment. Hitting the return key is more or less like turning the pages of a book. However, one can take different paths through the text by clicking on a "browse" icon and then choosing from one or more options (indicated by brief titles) for moving to other lexias. It is also possible to click on certain words in the text on screen, words that "yield," and link to other lexias, related to those words in some way.

Sometimes questions in the text invite "yes" or "no" responses from the reader, which result in movement along links to different parts of the story. And although hitting the return key usually produces the most "linear" movement through the story, this is not always the case. Sometimes making a certain choice under the "browse" option produces more coherence. Moreover, at times the reader reaches an impasse, the end of a path, and it is impossible to proceed further with the return key. At such points, if one wishes to continue, one must choose another way of proceeding—using the "browse" option, clicking on words that yield, or backtracking through the text and then choosing "browse" or clicking on words that yield.

Although there is much ambiguity in "Afternoon," largely because its hypertextual structure permits diverse readings, certain aspects of the story seem reasonably clear. There are four major characters: Peter, Wert, Nausicaa, and Lolly. Peter, who really wants to write poetry, works for Wert, who has gotten wealthy in insurance related businesses. Wert's company utilizes a program called WUNDERWRITER, which analyzes "situational variables and client information" in order to determine risks for insurance companies. Wert, a calculating, manipulative individual interested in power and control, believes that everything in the world can be quantified and digitized. He is interested in (possibly already is) sleeping with Lisa, Peter's estranged wife, perhaps more as a challenge to Peter than as a result of an attraction to the woman herself. Peter himself is having an affair with Nausicaa, who also works in Wert's office. Nausicaa is an ex-drug addict and ex-prostitute, as well as a client of Lolly, Wert's wife, a psychotherapist originally from the Old South.

Like many conventional stories, "Afternoon" presents us with a brief series of events in "present time"—Peter's witnessing the aftermath of an accident that may have involved, possibly killed, Lisa and their son, and his panicked attempts to find out if they were, in fact, the victims. Like many conventional stories, flashbacks reveal the complexities of the characters' backgrounds and relationships. Sometimes this background emerges in a coherent fashion; often it is disjointed and confusing.

The point of view usually is Peter's, though some sections assume that of other of the major characters. Other texts are collaged or quoted in the main text—bits of writings by Robert Creeley, Anaïs Nin, and Adrienne Rich, and a statement by the artist Josef Albers, for example. There are also numerous allusions to famous films, such as Antonioni's *Red Desert* and *Blow-Up*, B-movies like *The Daughter of Frankenstein*, as well as a fragment of Julio Cortazar's story "Blow-Up," on which Antonioni's film is based.

One becomes involved in "Afternoon" in much the same way one becomes involved in conventional stories, except that navigating one's way through it is more demanding and confusing. Sometimes lexias get linked in ways that don't make sense or, if they do, it may be a strange sense that they make (as when lexias involving different characters get oddly juxtaposed). The story involves a fairly standard kind of mystery and suspense, what Barthes called the "hermeneutic code," an enigma that is established, "distinguished, suggested, formulated, held in suspense, and finally disclosed" (*S/Z*, 19), except that the last aspect—the clear disclosure or resolution of the mystery—does not seem to be present. Did the accident involve Lisa and their son and were they killed, or is this fear simply a horrible negative fantasy of Peter? What really did or did not happen is never resolved, at least in this reader's reading. But readings differ. One reader, writing about "Floppy Fiction," views Peter as "mourning his son's recent death" (Zimmer, 36). On the other hand, Bolter (who, along with Joyce, was one of the developers of the Storyspace program), mentions the "automobile accident which *may* have killed Peter's former wife and his son" (125, italics mine).

Because of the variety of ways in which the story's lexias can be collaged together by different readers, it is difficult—and perhaps inappropriate—to try to define an unambiguously correct reading of such a work, even on the literal level of character and action. Acknowledging this variety of readings, Bolter says, "There is no single story of which each reading is a version, because each reading determines the story as it goes. We could say that there is no story at all; there are only readings" (124). He argues that the reader of "Afternoon" engages in a struggle for meaning analogous to that of the characters in the story. Just as Peter engages in frantic calls to try to find out about his wife and son, so the reader struggles with the electronic text to resolve the same question (126).

"Afternoon," which often incorporates a postmodern self-referentiality, commenting on its own processes, is suspicious of closure, and one of its lexias describes this suspicion and also provides a good description of what the reader experiences in progressing through the text:

Closure is, as in any fiction, a suspect quality, although here it is made manifest. When the story no longer progresses, or when it cycles, or when you tire of the paths, the experience of reading it ends. Even so, there are likely to be more opportunities than you think there are at first. A word which doesn't yield the first time you read a section may take you elsewhere if you choose it when you encounter the section again, and sometimes what seems like a loop, like memory, heads off again in another direction.

Because of the degree of indeterminacy in "Afternoon," reading it becomes an exercise in constructing a fictional world, in engaging in an interrogation with materials—textual segments viewed on a computer screen—that undeniably exist but do not in themselves point inevitably toward a fixed order or meaning. One is never sure to what extent the sense that one makes of the story is the story's own sense or the reader's construction. Thus, experiencing the story may actualize, may make more explicit, the kind of activity one normally engages in when one builds a picture of, contructs an understanding of, the world.

This sense of the reader's activity in constructing the story is heightened by the electronic medium, which, besides creating different possibilities for navigating the story, dematerializes the story as an object, makes much more elusive its existence as a physical thing. Although the textual segments undeniably exist in some sense or another, the nature of their "reality" is problematic. Is their reality the image on the screen? Or is it the information in the computer's memory, which is simply made visible on the monitor? Or is the story the information on a disk, subsequently read by the computer and held in its memory? And how should one conceptualize the actuality of the paths among the different segments? One can imagine the story as a large diagram consisting of boxes of text with lines connecting them in various ways. But where exactly are those lines, when what they "really" are are digitized instructions for moving from one area of information to another, and the electronic organization of that information does not look at all like an imaginable diagram of texts and links? In fact, that electronic organization of information "looks" like nothing whatsoever. The reader may imagine various pictures of the story, its structure and organization, but it is obvious that none of those pictures will comport with what is really there. Of course, one might argue that what is really there is information, and that information electronically stored isn't fundamentally different from information stored with ink and paper. This may be true, but the electronic medium brings home in a very obvious way the fact that the reader, in imagining a shape and substance to the story, is not simply studying something that is there but is actively involved in constructing it.

If "Afternoon" is the best known example of hypertextual fiction, Stuart Moulthrop's *Victory Garden* (1991) is certainly the most ambitious work thus far attempted in the emerging genre, a work that, according to Robert Coover, "exceeds all other known examples of the form in complexity, sophistication, narrative richness and formal exploration" ("Hyperfiction," 11). Most of the action of *Victory Garden* takes place at a Southern University in 1991, at the outset of the Gulf War. *Victory Garden* is, in part, a conventional academic novel, set in campus bars and hangouts, apartments, classrooms, and bedrooms. Parties, affairs, campus politics, protests, struggles over curricular reform, wacky professors, uptight administrators, and neurotic students are all set against a backdrop of the war, which is presented largely as a hyperreal event. Moulthrop has incorporated into the novel much of the television coverage of the war, as reported by well-known anchors like Tom Brokaw, Dan Rather, and Peter Jennings, as well as by others like Bernard Shaw and Peter Arnett, who were trapped in (but still reporting from) the Al Rashid Hotel in Baghdad. Televisions are often on in the novel, either the center of attention themselves, or intruding on, interfering with, other activities. Always the reality of the war, the problematical nature of the "real" behind the media representation of it, is an issue.

The central event in the novel is the death of Emily Runbird, a graduate student in cultural anthropology. Emily has had an ongoing relationship with a professor, Boris Urquhart, and a more recent affair with another graduate student, Victor Gardner (whose name suggests that he has a special place in the novel). She is called to active duty in the gulf and, although she is supposed to be safe, sorting mail away from the action, she is killed by a missile. Her passing is represented—or *not* represented (death being at least one possibility of the real that stands outside of any representation of it)—by an image that simulates a crack in the reader's monitor. When the reader hits the return button, the next screen is entirely black.

Clearly the gap between, the *aporia of*, the real and the hyperreal is a central issue of the novel. From one entrance into it, the novel begins with a scene in which Veronica Runbird, Emily's sister, watches reports of the Gulf War with Dorothea Agnew, a professor of rhetoric, and both have difficulty accepting the war's reality.

[Veronica] kept telling herself it was only a movie. . . . She was seeing a report on military intelligence delivered by a bearded tough guy named "Wolf Blitzer." What did it mean? Had there been a coup de tube by the World Wrestling Federation? Would the cameras cut now to Atlanta to show Hulk Hogan at the anchor desk?

Veronica imagines the production of the war as "some kind of warmup for the Superbowl" and compares it to Orson Welles's 1938 *War of the Worlds* radio show. In wondering about the possibility of resistance, she echoes Baudrillard's and Jameson's recognition of the difficulty of politics in the postmodern world: "If there's going to be resistance, there has to be something to kick against," she says. The impulse to resist or protest can only manifest itself in relation to something more or less tangible that one wishes to resist or protest, but the ubiquitous, highly produced coverage of the Gulf War made it seem more like a video production than a real war. Thea recognizes that they live in the "Mondo Video." "What would it mean to resist?" she asks. In spite of their recognition that the war had to be real, that somewhere people, including at least one individual very close to both of them, were having their lives disrupted, violated, and terminated, it is nevertheless difficult "to get away from war as Event, war as Program."[8]

The Gulf War was the first fully *produced* war, if not in its military aspects (war, even with "smart" weapons and "surgical" strikes, tending to produce results that cannot be entirely predicted and controlled), at least in its reporting. Certainly all wars have involved ideological and propagandistic manipulation of the way in which they have been represented. But the war in Vietnam demonstrated the subversive potential of the media to challenge the authorized versions of the truth of the war. The disturbing and uncontrollable events on the battlefield were disturbingly, uncontrollably, and messily brought into people's homes. Reporters and photographers willing to take the risk were free to hop on planes and choppers and go where they pleased, documenting everything they witnessed. Later American actions, and especially the Gulf War, can be seen as attempts to recoup the control of reality and representation that was traumatically lost in Vietnam. The assembling of massive manpower, firepower, and technological sophistication insured the fact that the war could have only one outcome. But also significant was the struggle to control the representation of the war. For people at home, in spite of the apparent massive coverage, the flow of information was rigorously controlled and the war became, as Veronica and Thea observe, a hyperreal event, a production, a kind of nationalistic entertainment.

In Vietnam most of the images used in reporting the war were filmed. The need to transport, process, and edit film stock, before it was actually televised, foregrounded the constructed nature of the media's representation of the war and marked the gap between the real and the represented. Critical awareness, not only of the war itself but of the fact that the war was known only through its reporting, was heightened. In the Gulf War the "real time" nature of much of the coverage enhanced the illusion that viewers were receiving the unmediated truth, that the media operated as "speech" rather than "writing." A metaphysics of presence in relation to the war was encouraged, even as the "truth" of the war— the truth as it was known to those who experienced it through the media—became a much more fully and successfully constructed truth than that of Vietnam.

The perception of the Gulf War presented in *Victory Garden* converges with views Baudrillard himself expressed in several articles written at the time of the war. Like the characters in Moulthrop's hypertextual novel, Baudrillard described the war as a hyperreal event rather than a "real" reality, as a media production rather than a war. Baudrillard first argued that the war would not take place because the site of struggle was no longer the battlefield but the media. "Our strategic site is the television screen, from which we are daily bombarded, and in front of which we also serve as a bargaining counter. . . . [T]oday, television and news have become the ground itself" ("The Reality Gulf," 25). When the war *did*, in fact, take place Baudrillard did not retreat but steadfastly maintained what on the surface seemed to be an outrageous position, that, all evidence to the contrary, the war had *not* taken place. Baudrillard's articles on the nonreality of the Gulf War provoke a moral and intellectual outrage in critics like Christopher Norris, who take Baudrillard as the epitome of the bankruptcy of postmodernism, someone who regards ontological and ethical truth as irretrievably lost behind the hyperreality of media simulacra (Norris, 11–15, 192–196).

And yet Baudrillard's point may not really be quite so outrageous, intellectually or morally, as it at first appears. Baudrillard does, of course, recognize the existence of the "facts" of the war, outside of its hyperreal representation, and Norris acknowledges that he does (192). In a later interview, Baudrillard states, referring to his Gulf War articles,

> my articles in *Libération* on the Gulf War also tried to say that politically that war didn't happen. It is also a statement of impotence in the face of the total political debility on both sides. . . . But above all, what is really happening on the ground there, in Iraq, it's so vile. It's enough to drive you either into depression or into a rage! It arouses feelings you can neither describe nor transpose. What can a writer say about this heap of cowardice and stupidity? While the situation presented itself in abstract terms of war or no war, it was an exciting problem. But now we are in the real. If I fall into the real, I experience the same anger as the others, even if they've taken plenty of time to react, all these kind souls. ("This Beer," 181)

As in other of Baudrillard's statements, there is here a recognition of the real and a moral response, even if it is one of moral outrage and impotence. What bothers critics like Norris is Baudrillard's insistence on the inaccessibility of the facts of the real, which if known would enable one to make some judgment of the truth or falsehood of their media representations (Norris, 193–195). But such claims of inaccessibility are belied by statements like the one above, which recognize facts that are, presumably, known. Clearly, Baudrillard's description of the hyperreal must be taken in the context of such statements, which acknowledge the real and express a moral response.

But there is another aspect to Baudrillard's point, which relates to what he elsewhere refers to as the "precession of simulacra"—the argument that simulacra, "models," themselves take precedence over facts, that facts, which do indeed exist, may serve the model rather than the other way around (*Simulacra*, 32). Looked at this way, it is not difficult to believe that the Gulf War *was* primarily a media event and that the "reality" of the war—the war involving weapons, destruction, and death—did not occur in order to determine which army would occupy what territory or which government would eventually rule, but was a "staging," an unfortunately necessary production carried out to serve the representation of the war in the media. If this is the case, things become confusing. The media may, after all, have presented some partial, qualified truth about the war, but that truth was itself constructed for the sake of the media. There is nothing entirely new about this, of course. Leni Riefenstahl claimed that her 1935 film *Triumph of the Will* was not Nazi propaganda but an objective documentation of the 1934 rally in Nuremberg. However, as Susan Sontag has pointed out, that rally itself was really a production created for the sake of Riefenstahl's cameras (Sontag, 36). Morally, of course, the Gulf War becomes all the more outrageous if one believes that the real purpose of the death and destruction was to contribute to the creation of the most convincing of all possible spectacles of death and destruction.

Victory Garden, similarly, presents the Gulf War as a sophisticated media production. At the same time there is, behind the hyperreal production, an unmediated reality, one that is not represented, that is inaccessible to representation. In *Victory Garden* the war is represented only as it appears on television, and its reality outside of media representation is suggested by a cracked screen and a black screen, the former indicating a crisis of representation and the latter, its ultimate inadequacy. Clearly such strategies, utilized in the hypertextual medium of *Victory Garden*, are analogous to devices suggesting a similar impasse of representation in other media: the cracked mirror in Kruger's *You Are Not Yourself* and the blank space in the text, where Addie indicates herself, in Faulkner's *As I Lay Dying*.

Victory Garden uses the Storyspace program and is set up the same way as "Afternoon," with different entrances into the story as well as different possibilities for navigating within it. As in "Afternoon," the return key usually provides the most linear way of progressing. Occasionally this is not the case, however, and hitting the return key leads to a digression. In such cases, if one wishes to follow the main action, one must experiment with various "browse" options in order to discover which one keeps to the subject.

Sometimes a dead end is reached—as happens both literally and figuratively with the black screen that suggests Emily's death. Then the reader *must* browse or backtrack. One browse option leads to a symbol of infinity, and that symbol is followed (when the return key is hit) by the word "peace." At that point the reader can neither move forward with the return key *nor* branch elsewhere with the browse option, but must backtrack and branch out from an earlier screen. The text is a maze and navigating it is like making one's way through a "Garden of Forking Paths," to use the title of the Borges story that is itself an important influence on *Victory Garden*.

In another instance, a kind of postmodern joke is produced when one screen, titled "Name That Fear," challenges the reader to "Name the Horror, go ahead and name it"; when the return key is hit the reader moves to a new screen titled "This Is It." Below that title the screen is blank. Hitting the return key then produces only a loop between the screens. The reader can only escape from the loop by using "browse," which links to a screen identifying "a basic narrative problem, representing the unrepresentable."

Victory Garden has a total of 993 textual segments connected by 2,804 links. Unlike "Afternoon," it does provide a schematic map of its overall organization. That map has thirty-nine sections, each of which represents a different "area" of the narrative structure. The map can be used as a way of deciding where one wishes to enter the novel. By clicking on a particular area, one determines where one enters. The map is also useful after one has explored a significant amount of the novel and wishes to identify parts one may have missed and may wish to investigate.

The subject in *Victory Garden* is challenged in a number of ways. Jude Busch, for example, is an undergraduate student who seduces Victor after Emily is killed. In doing so, she dresses herself as Emily, wearing a blond wig and arranging her room so as to heighten the illusion. She sets up a mirror, which she observes as she and Victor make love. "She wanted to join with both of them [Victor and Emily], he who was with her and she who wasn't, the present and the represented." Although her goal seems to be to connect and unify sign and referent, mask and self, present and past, in fact her masquerade, her intentional construction of herself as a simulacrum, heightens her disunity and fragmentation. She is doubled in complex ways. Not only does she play the role of Emily, she observes herself as Emily in the mirror. On one level she is inside her disguise, different from it but controlling it. On another level, in the mirror, the dissociation is more radical; she is not watching herself make love to Victor, but voyeuristically observing Victor and Emily make love.

So everything she did that night came in twos, superimposed. She felt a doubled presence—her own body here and now with its needs and desires, the body of the other, lost in that past, retained only in story and memory. She felt doubled motives—every touch both a passionate overture and a deliberate deception.

Jude might, indeed, be the woman in Yeats's poem, "The Mask," who refuses to reveal to her lover the "real" woman behind the mask she wears. In response to his insistence that she show him that woman, she reminds him that

> "It was the mask engaged your mind,
> And after set your heart to beat,
> Not what's behind. . . .
> What matter, so there is but fire
> In you, in me?"

As in Yeats's poem, the artificiality of Jude's strategy does not weaken its effectiveness, at least for Victor. In fact, in spite of her doubling and fragmentation, there is a moment at which dichotomies are transcended. Fire is kindled and a heart set beating: at the moment of climax—that other kind of "dying" that like death itself exceeds representation—Victor hears Jude *as* Emily.

Boris Urquhart, Victor's thesis adviser, who has been having an affair with Emily for some time, suffers a nervous breakdown in the course of the novel. He is a science professor, involved in defense related research, but he is also interested in the humanities and has been teaching courses like "Postmodern Delusions" and "Interactive Aesthetics"—both titles of which are, of course, relevant to the electronic novel we are actually reading. Urquhart's reading has caused him to think "about the effacement of the subject, about the self as a scene of inscription." Included in his reading is the work of Borges, one of Moulthrop's favorite precursors of hypertextual writing. Urquhart's readings of Borges and postmodernism, aggravated by stress over Emily's duty in the Gulf as well as his conflict with the university provost over proposed changes in the university's humanities requirement, provoke a confrontation with his own multiplicity that makes the ideas he encounters in his reading all too real. In a letter to Emily, Urquhart writes, referring to himself by his initial, "something's the matter with U. . . . He feels distributed, disseminated, broadcast." Not only does the "U" of his initial pun on the second-person reader of the story (evoking Calvino's second-person protagonist in *If on a winter's night a traveler*), the use of the term "broadcast" suggests psychoanalytic fragmentation, poststructural challenges to the integrity of the subject, and a Warholian multiplication of the subject's image in a postmodern world of mass media replication.

There are many references and allusions to Borges's works in *Victory Garden*, especially to "The Garden of Forking Paths," which is discussed in one of Urquhart's seminars.[9] Moulthrop acknowledges his debt to Borges in his introduction to the novel. The "U" used by Urquhart to refer to himself evokes not only the second-person reader of the story but, in the context of other Borgesian allusions, Yu Tsun, the Chinese protagonist of "The Garden of Forking Paths." A symptom of Urquhart's breakdown is his experiencing a "swarming sensation," the same ailment as that experienced by Yu Tsun as the moment at which he had to com-mit a desperate murder approached and as his perspective on time and reality had been altered by an encounter with a challenging philosophy expounded by an ancestor of his. The connection between Urquhart and Yu Tsun is further reinforced by the fact that Urquhart is at one point pursued by an FBI agent named Madden, the same name as that of the British agent who pursues Yu Tsun in Borges's story. An allusion to another Borges story results when, in his madness, Urquhart assumes the identity of a mad prophet named Uqbar. "Uqbar" is the name of a fictitious, nonexistent country, a hoax creation of some mysterious, yet obviously sophisticated and highly organized conspiracy in Borges's "Tlön, Uqbar, Orbis Tertius."

There are other allusions and references to Borges. At times passages from Borges are quoted directly and embedded into the story, like parts of a collage. In "The Garden of Forking Paths" Yu Tsun's German contact is Viktor Runeberg, whose name relates to both Victor Gardner and to Emily Runbird, whom Victor loves. The title of Moulthrop's novel, *Victory Garden*, resonates with both the name Viktor Runeberg and the title of the Borges's story in which Runeberg figures significantly. These various resonances between Moulthrop's characters and those of Borges reinforce a sense of character as shifting. Moulthrop's characters—Urquhart, Victor, Emily, and Madden—are not simple transplants of Borges's characters, but there is a sense that they somehow are connected with the characters of the Argentine writer, that the various identities modulate and metamorphose one into the other, cross paths or "fork" in some way or another.

Most significantly, of course, the hypertextual structure of *Victory Garden* is a structure of "forking paths," like that of the novel written by Yu Tsun's ancestor Ts'ui Pên. Ts'ui Pên's novel, described in Borges's story, is constructed as a labyrinth and is intended to reflect a notion of the universe in which diverse times, diverse futures, coexist, crossing in some places, converging, diverging, sometimes coalescing, and sometimes remaining separate for centuries. Interestingly, the labyrinthine structure of Ts'ui Pên's novel corresponds to the structure of Moulthrop's novel, but not to that of the Borges story in which it is described.

Urquhart's enemy, Stephen A. Tate, the university provost, is also quite crazy in his own way. His own interest in the multiplicity of the subject is suggested by the annual campus party he hosts. Not only is it a masquerade, thus encouraging individuals to assume alternative identities, the theme of the party at the time of the novel, the "Hero with Ten Thousand Faces" (alluding to Joseph Campbell's study *The Hero with a Thousand Faces*), further emphasizes the multiplicity of the subject. Tate has a plan to create a virtual economy, a vast simulacrum embracing all aspects of economic activity, a gigantic competitive structure with hundreds of millions of players—or are they workers?—who would in fact derive their livelihood from subsidies paid out according to their performance in the game. A game involving technologies, philosophies, belief systems.

It might be argued—as Jameson and Baudrillard in effect do—that this is *already* the simulation game played in contemporary economics, politics, and war, that the divorce between signs and referents is so complete that economic, political, and military winners and losers result from a game of signs that has very little to do with economic, political, and military reality.

Victor Gardner himself, as much as any other character, challenges the notion of an essential subject. The reader comes to know very little about Victor, and this is ironic, considering the fact that the correspondence of his name and the title of the novel suggests that he has a special place in the novel as a whole. There may be some relationship between the relative absence of Victor in *Victory Garden* and the complete absence of Viktor Runeberg in "The Garden of Forking Paths." Runeberg is mentioned but makes no appearance in Borges's story. Indeed, he may even be dead. But it is the discovery that he has been captured or murdered that provokes a desperate plan on the part of Yu Tsun and instigates the action of the story.

Moulthrop's Victor is not quite as invisible as Borges's Viktor. We do know a few details about him—the fact that he is skeptical about the value of graduate school, that he loves Emily, and that his affair with her resulted in her only orgasm. But apart from such details, Victor, more than any other major character in the novel, is something of a blank, a blank that nevertheless is somehow central to the novel. In fact, if we fully identify Victor with the novel as a whole, it might be argued that the decentered structure of the novel itself represents or is analogous to Victor himself. If the novel is the portrait of a person—as the correspondence between the title and the name of the character may imply—then we have an image of the individual as multiple, ambiguous, and decentered.

"Dreamtime" (1992), also by Stuart Moulthrop, is a section of *Chaos*, a larger work in progress, and in some respects it breaks with conventional fiction even more than do "Afternoon" and *Victory Garden*. The mechanism for moving through "Dreamtime" seems, at least at first, to provide no privileged, more or less linear choice, as hitting the return key did for "Afternoon" and *Victory Garden*. Moreover, "Dreamtime" is regularly interspersed with visuals—drawings and patterns that dissolve one into the other, icons that move about the screen—as well as sounds—words and phrases primarily, that punctuate one's reading, especially in the beginning as one enters the story and during the transitions as one moves from one lexia to another. Thus, "Dreamtime" is as much "hypermedia" as "hypertext," incorporating dynamic visual and auditory components, in counterpoint to the written verbal text.

The lexias of "Dreamtime" are enclosed in windows inserted over graphics. Some of them take the form of e-mail messages, with addressers and addressees indicated at the top. The date and time of these e-mail simulacra are the *actual* date and time of the reader's reading the text (assuming the clock and calendar of the reader's computer are set correctly). This coincidence of real and fictional time confuses reality and representation and contributes to the illusion that the reader is reading real electronic messages. After reading a particular lexia, the reader clicks the mouse or trackball and four transitional symbols appear in the corners of the screen. Usually (though not when the lexia takes the form of an e-mail message) the names of the four symbols are also enclosed in a box at the bottom of the screen, followed by brief titles indicating the lexias to which each will lead. A moving icon rapidly travels around the screen, sometimes clockwise, sometimes counterclockwise, sometimes changing direction, touching each of the corner symbols as it passes. The reader clicks when the moving icon touches or comes close to the transitional symbol he or she wishes to choose. After a brief transition of visuals and sounds, the next lexia appears.

Moving through the text in this way produces an extremely disjointed, nonlinear series of lexias. The lexias represent small segments of dreams by two or three dreamers—Aloysius McIntosh, Moira da Szem, and possibly a third, "higher" dream consciousness, whose dream fragments consist of the e-mail lexias. Some of the lexias are poetic, some are pop-surreal, often they are satirical or apocalyptic. In "Dreamtime" there seems to be no privileged axis of movement. The reader, following the instructions in a "ReadMe" file, chooses one of the four transitional symbols, with little indication of where any of them will lead and no indication of which is likely to produce the most straightforward, coherent, or linear narrative choice. The titles that appear at the bottom of the screen are really not much help in trying to make an intelligent or informed decision.

Proceeding this way, the reader skips almost randomly from one fragment of a dream to another. Only by accident might the reader discover that by using the arrow keys he or she can move through the dreams of each dreamer, one at a time. Moving through the text using the arrow keys—while still producing a rather disjointed and collage-like structure—at least provides the reader with continuity within the various dream episodes. Moving this way, those episodes are parts of a dream sequence of first one, then another, dreamer.

Still, the narrative that emerges in "Dreamtime" is less coherent than that of "Afternoon" or *Victory Garden*, partly because it is a representation of *dreams*, which one expects to be disjointed and incoherent, but also because the story is a "component" of a larger work. *Chaos* (unavailable at the time of this writing) is "about a party attended by mystics, robot designers, ghostwriters, and assorted geniuses and misfits." [10] By clicking on certain icons, the reader of *Chaos* chooses which characters attending the party he or she wishes to investigate (Zimmer, 34). In "Dreamtime" those choices are limited to "the dream activity of two persons, Aloysius McIntosh and Moira da Szem, as well as a third, unspecified consciousness" (Moulthrop, "Dreamtime"). One of the e-mail lexias from "Dreamtime" reads, "A man is saying This Stack Called Dreamtime Represents The Dream Activity Of At Least Two Characters In Chaos, Aloysius McIntosh And Moira da Szem, Who Fall Asleep And Dream At Some Point In The Evening."

Clearly these two names, "Aloysius McIntosh" and "Moira da Szem," are intended, at least on one level, to suggest the two main systems that previously dominated the personal computer market, Apple's Macintosh and the MS-DOS operating systems. Perhaps the third dreamer represents some new, emerging system that will mediate and enable compatibility between the two. It is unlikely that that is *all* that is being suggested, however. The dream of McIntosh contains a significant amount of water imagery—rain, melting polar caps, floods—while the dream of da Szem includes a significant amount of fire imagery—a house fire, nuclear missiles, the heat of the sun, the light of stars, the "heat" of sex. Both dream sequences have an apocalyptic tone and involve disasters of various types. McIntosh's dream includes episodes that involve terrorism on plane flights, catastrophes at sea, or disasters that take place in cyberspace itself. Da Szem's sequence culminates in a scene that synthesizes a sexual climax with an end-of-the-world nuclear annihilation.

Allusions are frequent in both dream sequences, both to high and popular culture—T. S. Eliot and James Joyce (both of whose allusive and collage-like structures are often seen as antecedents to hypertextual literature), commercials, TV shows, and Tarzan movies. Allusions and in-jokes are also common in the e-mail simulacra, especially in the names of the senders, who include (sometimes through obvious puns) Marshall McLuhan, Timothy Leary, John Lennon, Gilles Deleuze, Felix Guattari, and Umberto Eco. One message is addressed to Peter@WONDER-WRITE.DATACOM.COM, an in-joke alluding to the character Peter from Michael Joyce's "Afternoon." The dream structure and the popular imagery combine to produce a satirical pop-surrealism, aimed at American consumerism and the middle class (complete with shopping malls and childbirth classes), as well as militarism (the vision of an apocalypse that involves an erotic and thanatotic sexual consummation and nuclear annihilation).

Besides the fire-water imagery, with its occult connotations, the various icons and symbols suggest something arcane and mystical. The transitional symbols have mysterious sounding names—Plex, Mu, Flo, Mort, Trans, Spire, Arc, or Opt, for example—and visually they resemble the schematic images or signs one might find in some arcane text. The text of "Dreamtime" is itself structured around the idea of dreams, which often have been interpreted as having arcane significance, and references to drugs and major figures in the drug culture of the sixties, with all their occult and metaphysical mythology, occur in the text.

Thus, the fire-water dialectic of Aloysius McIntosh and Moira da Szem (with the suggestion of a possible synthesis in the "third, unspecified consciousness") is clearly meant to evoke some other kind of contrast. The fact that the "third, unspecified consciousness" is represented through e-mail messages suggests that the other consciousness that synthesizes the dialectic is to be associated with technology and computers. One of the auditory messages included in the story is a sentence, created by collaging separately recorded words and phrases together, the way an electronic time or weather report might be constructed: "In fact / consciousness / is just a / complex / simulation." Those verbal segments seem to be individually recorded fragments, stated by two or three different voices. Our tendency to regard the unitary conscious subject as something absolute or privileged, something natural rather than cultural, is challenged. Individual subjectivities, as we normally conceive them, have thoughts that are continuous and, in one way or another, coherent. The fact that here a single continuous and coherent thought is presented as if emanating from several different "entities"—suggested by the different voices that construct the thought—effectively dissociates the normal identification of thought with unified individuals.

If the conscious subject is, in fact, a construction, then, of course, there is no essential difference between human consciousness and technological simulations of consciousness. Although "Dreamtime" certainly suggests this demystified notion of consciousness, it also conflates the idea of hypertext as a larger consciousness, created by linking diverse texts and diverse individuals, with the idea of a collective consciousness suggested by the mythical "dreamtime" evoked in some tribal and aboriginal cultures.

* * *

There is a kind of hypertextual art and literature that goes beyond the kind of works discussed thus far. Such works involve on-line artistic and literary collaboration. The amount of text and the interactive possibilities that can be contained on a floppy disk or even on a CD-ROM are extremely large, but not infinite. Stories like "Afternoon," "Dreamtime," and *Victory Garden* have a kind of frame—the inherent limit on the amount of information that can be contained on the disk. And although a story on a disk can be navigated in various ways, the disk itself—not entirely unlike a book—has a kind of discreteness, separation, and permanence. It is not part of the "rules" of works like those so far discussed that the reader alter the contents of the disk, apart from marking certain spots where previous readings have been left off, so that such places can be located when he or she resumes reading. Similarly, although there is a degree of indeterminacy resulting from the reader's activity, the number of possibilities—though very large—is still logically limited. Finally, in spite of the fact that the reader's role is greater than what is characteristic of traditional writing, there is still a clear primary author of the work.

However, when art and literature move out onto the net, when verbal, visual, auditory, and kinetic texts are created and become part of an evolving virtual electronic collage—as is now possible on the Internet and World Wide Web—the constraints of a disk or CD-ROM are not a factor, the possibilities become limitless and completely unpredictable, and the sense of a primary author can be lost completely. The Internet is limitless in size and its parts tend toward integration and the blurring of boundaries rather than toward articulation and separation. When art is generated collaboratively on-line, there is neither an original, although there may be an *instigating*, text or image, nor, necessarily, a final product to define the "work."

Verbal and visual artists are now actively exploring collaborative creativity in cyberspace. Robert Coover, for example, has taught workshops in hypertextual fiction at Brown. His students have produced both individually authored works as well as collaborative works. Coover describes such an on-line collaboration:

[W]e in the workshop have also played freely and often quite anarchically in a group fiction space called "Hotel." Here, writers are free to check in, to open up new rooms, new corridors, new intrigues, to unlink texts or create new links, to intrude upon or subvert the texts of others, to alter plot trajectories, manipulate time and space, to engage in dialogue through invented characters, then kill off one another's characters or even to sabotage the hotel's plumbing. . . . This space of essentially anonymous text fragments remains on line and each new set of workshop students is invited to check in there and continue the story of the Hypertext Hotel. ("The End of Books," 23)

Bonnie Mitchell, quoted earlier, has organized the creation of various works that involve contributions by herself, her students at Syracuse University, as well as other individuals, all working collaboratively on the Internet. In works like "International Internet Chain Art Project" and "Digital Journey," she and her students create visual or verbal "starter images" or "theme pages" and circulate them among other individuals nationally and internationally. Each participant alters, adds to, or comments on whatever he or she receives. Under such circumstances, surprise—as well as disappointment—is always possible. Although contributions are matters of conscious decisions individuals make—except when technical problems result in "corruption"—those who create an image or text cannot predict or control what will happen to it.[11] Once someone initiates a text, it moves through cyberspace, returning to its original creators having been altered into something totally different and unintended, part of a perpetually ongoing project, a perpetual passage of information. The process has the characteristics of play, whether that play is directed toward the world outside the net or directed self-consciously only toward itself. Working in this collaborative interactive way, the notion of individual authorship and individual genius is for all practical purposes lost.

Epilogue: After the Subject

But, as the title of a recent collection of essays devoted to the problem asks, "Who comes after the subject?" [1] The subject cannot be easily dispensed with, as David Carroll has pointed out, and dispensing with it entirely may not be such a desirable thing. Strictly speaking, of course, no one is "dispensing with" the subject, but rather deconstructing and reconstructing our understanding of what it is, revising the way we view it. Rather than regard it as an ontological, Cartesian *a priori*, we might view it as a social, linguistic construction. Derrida says,

> I have never said that the subject should be dispensed with. Only that it should be deconstructed. To deconstruct the subject does not mean to deny its existence. . . . To acknowledge this does not mean, however, that the subject is what it *says* it is. The subject is not some meta-linguistic substance or identity, some pure *cogito* of self-presence; it is always inscribed in language. My work does not, therefore, destroy the subject; it simply tries to resituate it. ("Deconstruction and the Other," 125)

But if the subject is a construction, what could be the basis for according it a value that is in any way different from the value one might ascribe to any other construction—a building, an automobile, or a computer, all of which we might construct or destroy as needed, without necessarily feeling that an ethical or moral issue is involved, or at least without feeling the same *kind* of ethical or moral imperatives traditionally associated with our treatment of human beings? And yet, inevitably, we do feel that human individuals, deconstructed, decentered, misrecognized as they may be, are nevertheless different from nonsentient objects and because of this difference demand moral consideration. We become uneasy when confronted with an attitude that seems to threaten that special status.

This threat is something that conservative spokespersons have latched onto and used as a means of attacking contemporary criticism and theory. But nervousness in the face of this challenge to the subject is not limited to spokespersons of the right. Christopher Norris, one of the major writers on and defenders of Derrida and deconstruction, writes,

> Merely to use concepts such as conscience, good faith, responsibility, or ethical judgment in the presence of right-thinking orthodox post-structuralists is to find

oneself treated with pitying fondness as a relic of that old "Enlightenment" discourse. For if—as their argument standardly goes—the autonomous subject has now been dispersed into a range of plural, polymorphous "subject-positions" inscribed within language or existing solely as figments of this or that constitutive discourse, then of course there is no question of those values surviving as anything but a species of chronic self-delusion, a form of "imaginary" specular investment whose claims have long since been deconstructed through the insights of psychoanalysis, structural linguistics, Foucauldian discourse-theory, etc. (30)

Norris recognizes the threat to the subject represented by poststructural and postmodern theory, and in this passage he implies sympathy for supposed outmoded enlightenment and humanistic values. At the same time, he wishes to distance Derrida and deconstruction from this abdication of truth and the subject, as if deconstruction itself must not be confused with poststructuralism or postmodernism. However, it is significant that Derrida himself recognizes that there *is* a problem reconciling a deconstructed subject with an ethics and politics that might justify democracy and provide insurance against fascism.

[C]an one take into account the necessity of the existential analytic and what it shatters in the subject and turn towards an ethics, a politics (are these words still appropriate?), indeed an "other" democracy (would it still be a democracy?), in any case towards another type of responsibility that safeguards against what a moment ago I very quickly called the "worst" [form of national socialism]? (" 'Eating Well,' " 104)

Mikkel Borch-Jacobsen asks, "[I]n the end, *on behalf of what* should we reject totalitarianism? In the name of what notion of 'subject' and 'politics,' if it can truly no longer be that of the Individual against the State, nor that of the Rights of the Human-Subject?" ("The Freudian Subject," 72).[2]

Elizabeth A. Wheeler, writing in the electronic journal *Postmodern Culture*, takes the position that postmodern thinkers like Lyotard and Baudrillard, who problematize reference and the subject, provide rationalizations for the crassest and most brutal actions against the marginalized and disenfranchised segments of our society. After all, if the "subject" is entirely constructed and lacks any essential ontological foundation, then why worry about it? Or why worry about it any more than one would worry about any other construction, which might be destroyed and reconstructed as was convenient. Borch-Jacobsen says that "the totalitarian Chief more easily imposes the fiction or figure of his absolute subjectivity because he knows fully well that it *is* a myth and that what he has before him is a mass of nonsubjects" ("The Freudian Subject," 70). And Wheeler, characterizing the brutality and insensitivity of urban planners in their willingness to uproot the poor and homeless, writes, "[T]he death of a homeless 'subject' creates a vacuum that can be filled by a 'subject' with a better credit rating" (23). If the subject is a radially constructed thing, how does one deal with the suffering that obviously does exist?

Anyone who has ever tried to get around Los Angeles without a car knows how real it is, how mired in "space and dimensions," how cruel to the poor. In promoting the unreality of Los Angeles, Baudrillard does the cops' dirty work. . . . The myth of Los Angeles as a fabulous unreality justifies the quiet elimination of its less-than-fabulous, all-too-real aspects. . . . [W]ithout the intellectual tool of unmasking, there is no suffering to uncover. (Wheeler, 12–13)[3]

Wheeler is criticizing the apparent amorality of Baudrillard's description of the world as composed of hyperreal surfaces, of people as windows with nothing behind them. Taking Baudrillard at face value, she argues that views like his permit an amorality in relation to the poor, a discounting of their needs in order to construct an attractive postmodern urban surface. "The critic learns to look the other way when he hears the bulldozers coming" (24).

Wheeler's response, unfashionable as it may be from the standpoint of contemporary critical theory, is to "invoke the category of experience" (29). Unless we view people as, in some sense, experiencing subjectivities, then it is impossible to discuss suffering—or joy or happiness, for that matter—in a way that is meaningful, and there is really no basis for asserting that any ethical or moral imperatives need to be considered in deciding what behavior or policies we should adopt in relation to people. Unless, in some sense or another, experiencing subjectivities exist—whether as people, animals, or (possibly even) hypertextual networks, whether as unified loci of consciousness or as dispersed, heterogeneous, shifting multiplicities that nevertheless experience themselves and the world—there really is no reason to have a morality or ethics at all. There simply "is no suffering to uncover." Noting the political implications of the denial of the subject, Wheeler refers to "the irony that, just as previously-silenced, darker-skinned, non-Western, female subjects begin to make themselves heard, the white European male declares 'the death of the subject' " (45). For Wheeler maintaining some notion of the subject is necessary in order to combat oppression against minorities, women, gays, and the homeless.

Nina Eugenia Serebrennikov, in her introductory remarks to the session "Agency in Art History" at the 1995 conference of the College Art Association, identifies 1992—the year of the inaugural session of the Oxford Amnesty Lectures—as a watershed year in the relationship between theory and politics, specifically in relation to the problem of ethical and political action in the face of the deconstruction of the subject. Serebrennikov quotes from the letter of invitation, which asked speakers "to consider the consequences of deconstruction of the self for the liberal tradition. Does the self as construed by the liberal tradition still exist? If not, whose human rights are we defending?" (Johnson, 2) Serebrennikov believes that at the present time

an air of urgency is palpable. A need is intimated to somehow reassert, however provisionally, some renewed presence in the face of the constructionist position that humans carry within themselves nothing more than that which is complicit with one or another restraining discourse.[4]

Participants in the CAA session attempted to mark out or identify some small space in which there might reside the possibility of agency within the constraints of social construction. They tried to "examine containing systems for the unstable or vulnerable point at which, however marginally, agency might be said to assert itself" (Serebrennikov), to identify "semiotic slippage" and play "the instability of signs to advantage" (Barzman). Speakers also challenged the rigid distinction between construction and agency, passivity and activity, emphasizing complexity and ambiguity rather than rigid binary opposition. "Agency can be partial and it can be reactive" (Serebrennikov). A couple of them focused on artists' assumption of different names and roles (Barzman and Diggory), and they imagined subjectivity as fluid, as capable of assuming diverse roles that, though not identified with a unified subject, were not mere masks with a lifeless absence behind.

Attacks on postmodernism and poststructuralism have been increasingly common, choreographed in part by the conservative political establishment, part of a continuing attack on intellectuals, artists, and the academy itself.[5] Those attacks have involved oversimplification of the complexity of problems and issues as well as of the ideas of critics and artists who attempt to address those problems and issues. But statements like Wheeler's, statements by Derrida, statements by Norris (even as he tries to dissociate Derrida from the bankrupt "postmodernism" he, Norris, attacks), and the focus of the 1992 Oxford Amnesty Lectures suggest that all such challenges do not come from the political and social right or from a regressive contingent in academia, suggest that there *is* a difficulty in dealing with compelling moral and political issues from a postmodern and poststructuralist perspective.

As a result of both kinds of attacks—those from foes and friends alike—there have been a number of clarifications and elaborations by those who have been involved in critical theory of the last twenty-five years. Norris, in *Uncritical Theory*, attempts to divorce deconstruction from postmodernism and sets Derrida against Baudrillard. Rather than associate the term "postmodern" with a constellation of diverse lines of thought that problematize, in different ways and to different degrees, reality and reference—an approach that would place Derrida and Baudrillard together in the postmodern camp, in spite of their differences—Norris emphasizes their differences in order to set Derrida apart from Baudrillard, postmodernism, and poststructuralism generally. He emphasizes Derrida's continuation of the Enlightenment project of using reason to apprehend the world and to criticize itself in order to assure the rigor of its endeavor. Focusing on Baudrillard's statements on the Gulf War, Norris casts Baudrillard as the villain who abandons this project, regarding reality outside of representational practice as nonexistent or inaccessible. In Norris's scenario, Baudrillard is the most extreme instance of an unconscionable postmodern relativization of truth, a belief that reference is absolutely lost behind various practices of language and representation.

Derrida's challenge (as Norris describes it) is less extreme than Baudrillard's, problematizing but not dispensing with the Enlightenment project. Derrida's critique of reason is itself done in the spirit of that Enlightenment project, with the goal of assuring its happy outcome, and not done to overthrow or entirely dispense with it. Postmodern thinkers like Baudrillard play into the hands of right-wing revisionist historians, but when Derrida's ideas are used to justify the same kind of relativism, it is because he has been misinterpreted and oversimplified, according to Norris.

One cannot help but applaud *Uncritical Theory* in that it is a powerful and necessary assertion of some kind of moral posture in the face of atrocious human events and conditions and a recognition that postmodern and poststructural thinkers have been used—justifiably or unjustifiably—to rationalize ignoring contemporary social and political realities as they affect real people in real situations. However, it is difficult to accept Norris's dissociation of Derrida from the postmodern and poststructuralist camp that has been so used or misused. Certainly one might, as Norris admits, find in Derrida passages that *seem* to confirm the reading of his texts as arguing for the radical relativism of truth that Norris associates with the word "postmodern," passages in which Derrida's position seems nearly indistinguishable from Baudrillard's. In fact, Norris himself quotes numerous such passages. True, he also quotes other passages that suggest that Derrida is *not* abandoning the quest for truth and reality, so that the two kinds of statements do have to be reconciled. Obviously Norris takes those passages that support Derrida's connection with the Enlightenment project as the more accurate expressions of his real beliefs. But one could do the same selective reading of Baudrillard, taking some passages as hyperbole and some as stating what he really means, some as implying that a radical loss of reference has occurred and others as implying that there is, after all, a real world that exists outside of representational practice that is done violence by that practice (e.g., his references in *America* to American Indians, Vietnam, poverty, and the Fourth World). In fact, deconstruction is one extremely important manifestation of postmodern theory, and aspects of it have been assimilated by and incorporated into all sorts of other theoretical positions that do not define themselves as "deconstruction." Any attempt to dissociate deconstruction from the postmodern and the postructural must be regarded as disingenuous.

The problem of the subject and representation becomes especially urgent when the object of representation involves matters that are ethically compelling, topics that *need* to be discussed, that can't be ignored. For a poststructuralist, such situations bring home the conflict between the moral imperative to speak and the conviction that speech is never adequate to its task, that it does violence because it distances and distorts the truth while producing the illusion that it provides access to it.

Jean-François Lyotard, for example, grapples with this problem in *Heidegger and "the jews."* Probably no topic provokes this dilemma more powerfully than the Holocaust. One does not have to be a poststructuralist to be disturbed by the conflict between the compelling need to represent, to keep in memory, the Holocaust, and the impossibility of doing so—the fact that all representations, all understandings seem inevitably to fall short of a historical truth that is ungraspable, a truth that produces in the end only a sense that one does not and cannot understand. Thus, grappling with the Holocaust becomes an exemplary problem and a challenge to poststructuralists. It brings home issues related to representation and politics in a compelling way that requires attention and allows no easy solutions. Lyotard attempts to engage the problem of representing the Holocaust and at the same time being faithful to postmodern insights.

For Lyotard "the jews" (uncapitalized, in quotation marks, and distinguished from real "Jews"), along with the Shoah, represent ungraspable referents, inaccessible to representation, subversive and dangerous, alien and nomadic, referents that representation attempts to contain, domesticate, and control. Because the Holocaust cannot be represented, the attempt to comprehend it, to hold it in memory, is an absurdity: the attempt to represent it assures its inevitable loss. The struggle to come to grips with the Holocaust distances it, distorts it, simplifies it, and domesticates it. Because, at the same time, it must never be forgotten, we are caught between the two evils of forgetting and misrepresentation (which is itself a kind of forgetting).

Thus, we must content ourselves not with remembering it, but with remembering that it should but cannot be remembered, with representing the fact that it cannot be represented. For Lyotard the "sublime" is that which suggests the excess that transgresses all representation. "What art can do is bear witness not to the sublime, but to this aporia of art and to its pain. It does not say the unsayable, but says that it cannot say it" (*Heidegger,* 47). Lyotard deals with Jews as a category in the same way that the French feminists deal with the category "woman." They are categories that exceed all categories, that challenge all definitions, that are not really categories, in fact. Nevertheless, for pragmatic and political reasons one may, inevitably, have to speak of "women" and "Jews" as provisional categories. There may be no essential "woman" or "Jew," but once women or Jews are spoken of as a class, there are, in fact, practical and political consequences for those identified as women or Jews.[6]

Lyotard's book may be a significant attempt to deal with a most serious issue, or it may be a poststructural tour de force, a sophisticated sleight of hand in which he demonstrates that he, who earlier wrote that a *"self* does not amount to much" (*Postmodern Condition,* 15) and who is sometimes set alongside Baudrillard as exemplifying the excesses of postmodernism, *can* deal with the most compelling moral issues and can do so on his own terms. In either case, the problem of representing (in some highly qualified and subtle manner) the unrepresentable is a theme and challenge he shares with other postmodern writers. Like others, he describes the difficult dance of representation around and about a radically elusive subject.

To deny a unitary subject or to argue that the subject is decentered or inaccessible to representation is not quite to deny entirely that "it" in some way exists. Lacan's "hommelette," characterized by "prematurity," "dehiscence," "primordial discord," "uneasiness," and "motor uncoordination" (4), may be a mess, but it is a mess that responds to the imaginary and symbolic invitation to (mis)recognize itself as something other than a mess. And for Althusser, the "hailing" of the individual by ideology is a hailing of something that can respond with self-(mis)recognition and accept its ideological constitution. When Althusser writes, "*all ideology hails or interpellates concrete individuals as concrete subjects,* by the functioning of the category of the subject" (162), or "religious ideology is indeed addressed to individuals, in order to 'transform them into subjects'" (166), the word "individual" hedges and is not defined, for what is this individual that is hailed and responds to that hailing and is therefore transformed, subjected? His footnoting of the word, anticipating this question, does not really help: "Although we know that the individual is always already a subject, we go on using this term, convenient because of the contrasting effect it produces" (166 n.

19). The suggestion is that the subject as we know it is always already a subject, that there never was a time when the subject, the human subject, was not constituted ideologically as a subject. But, of course, there might have been something before the subject that was not quite what we would call a subject but which was nevertheless a condition of the subject's emergence.

Derrida, in an interview dealing with the question of the subject, argues that the major poststructuralists do not, in fact, dispense with or "liquidate" the subject. "For these three discourses (Lacan, Althusser, Foucault) and for some of the thinkers they privilege (Freud, Marx, Nietzsche) the subject can be re-interpreted, restored, re-inscribed, it certainly isn't 'liquidated' " (" 'Eating Well,' " 97). And when he earlier argued that "[m]ost often, in the very form of meaning, in all its modifications, consciousness offers itself to thought only as self-presence, as the perception of self in presence" (*Margins*, 16), it is the slightly hedging "most often" that leaves the door open, perhaps just a crack, to the possibility of an unselfconscious, not quite human as we understand human, experiencing proto-subject—the stuff of animals and pre-linguistic humans, disunified, multiple, uncoordinated—which responds to the symbolic and ideological call.

When Derrida distinguishes between a Heideggerian, phenomenological, "human" relation to the self and a "*nonhuman* relation to self, incapable of the phenomenological *as such*" (" 'Eating Well,' " 105), he recognizes the possibility of a relation to self outside of human language, though not necessarily outside of *différance* (116). Moreover, he clearly accords value to this "nonhuman" relation to self, even the nonhuman relation to self that animals might experience. He says that while he is not calling for "a support group for vegetarianism, ecologism, or for the societies for the protection of animals," such activities are nevertheless ones he "might also want to do," and he tellingly adds that those activities "would lead us to the center of the subject" (112). Exploring the nonhuman relation to the self, even that of animals, would shed light on the subject—the human relation to the self—in a way that exploring the human relation to the self alone might not be capable of.

Only by attributing to animals some form of subjectivity or proto-subjectivity or relation to self can we feel any responsibility toward them. Derrida argues, in fact, that the "subject," as it has been spoken, excludes not only animals but women and children as well. The classical subject is associated with phallocentric and logocentric power, and the deconstruction of that subject is a moral imperative for Derrida. He explicitly recognizes the value of the marginalized who have not been included in this classical "fraternal" subject, as well as our responsibility to an "origin" that is not yet a "subject."

The origin of the call that comes from nowhere, an origin in any case that is not yet a divine or human "subject," institutes a responsibility that is to be found at the root of all ulterior responsibilities (moral, juridical, political), and of every categorical imperative. To say of this responsiblity, and even of this friendship, that it is not "human," no more than it is "divine," does not simply come down to saying that it is inhuman. . . . Something of this call of the other must remain nonreappropriable, nonsubjectivable, and in a certain way nonidentifiable, a sheer supposition, so as to remain *other*, a *singular* call to response or to responsibility. ("'Eating Well,'" 110–111)

It is this origin, which must remain "a sheer supposition," that is, in fact, the basis of all responsibility, "moral, juridical, political." Only by acknowledging such an origin—even if that acknowledgment must be based on a supposition—can we even begin to talk about responsibility. Derrida's insistent use of words like "nonsubjectivable" and "nonidentifiable" is his attempt to insure that this origin not be domesticated by defining it in terms that might make it comprehensible but which would do violence to it. In effect, we must respect that origin enough to refuse to speak it, even as we allow it to have its effect, leave its trace, on us. In this sense all origin is excluded from reference and bound to be characterized by an apparent lack: Addie's "not-Anse" and the blank she uses to (not) represent herself; Lyotard's "jews" who always elude the struggle to represent them and who can only be represented with violence; Baudrillard's Fourth World that lies outside the system of hyperreal representation; the character Bonnie Sherow, in *The Player*, who does not play and thereby relinquishes her right to exist. On the other hand, the "subject" that has been constructed, the subject that excludes, that does violence to that origin, *can* be deconstructed, and Derrida argues that rigorously deconstructing it—coming to terms with its phallocentric, logocentric, and, indeed, its carnivorous aspects—is a moral responsibility that must be undertaken before anything like a "subject" can be responsibly spoken again ("'Eating Well,'" 108–114).

In fact, one might argue that there is a moral imperative implicit not only in Derrida but in most of the postmodern and poststructuralist discussions that are often seen as abdicating the possibility of a moral position. But because they challenge, deconstruct, or problematize conventional understandings—like those of the unitary subject or of "truth" as traditionally understood—understandings that seem essential to maintaining any kind of ethics or epistemology, they are often taken as advocating an amoral or nihilistic position. Nevertheless, in nearly all such discussions there is some thing, being, group, or truth that is done violence by representation and the symbolic, by being repressed, marginalized, denied representation, or misrepresented. And it is understood that that thing, being, or group that is violated must have value. The pre-linguistic and pre-imaginary infant and the nonverbal animal have an existence or value different from clay or stone, even though they may not be subjects, quite, yet, and even if we acknowledge that a subject is "always already" constituted as a subject. In both Lacan and Jameson there is a real that exists, even if it is outside of and inaccessible to representation. And even Lyotard describes a sublime that exceeds representation, and Baudrillard refers to the Fourth World that is excluded from the hyperreal.

Julia Kristeva's notion of the "semiotic" is an attempt to identify a fundamental, pre-symbolic condition of the subject that continually informs, challenges, and demands reconstitution of the symbolic subject. The semiotic is a "fundamental stage—or region—in the process of the subject, a stage that is hidden by the arrival of signification, in other words, by the *symbolic*" (*Revolution*, 40). Although it is pre-linguistic, it is already involved in a semiotic process. Kristeva associates it with the Freudian drives and Freud's *primary process*. In the semiotic,

Discrete quantities of energy move through the body of the subject who is not yet constituted as such and, in the course of his development, they are arranged according to the various constraints imposed on this body—always already involved in a semiotic process—by family and social structures. (25)

If the symbolic is associated with the father and society at large, the semiotic is associated with the mother. And although Kristeva describes the semiotic sometimes as a "stage," it is not merely a stage, but an ongoing mode of the individual. For Kristeva there is no irrevocable breach between the semiotic and the symbolic, but rather a perpetual, inevitable interaction between them. That interaction produces a subject in flux, a symbolic subject that perpetually adjusts and redefines itself in response to ungovernable energies that always lie beyond it. Music is a medium that is "constructed exclusively on the basis of the semiotic" (*Revolution*, 24), on the energies, blockages, tensions, and rhythms of the semiotic, resulting from the energies of the body in pre-linguistic relationship to the world and other people. But all discourse involves some degree of interaction between the semiotic and the symbolic. In this sense, poetic language is normal and no linguistic practice is purely symbolic. Of course, in literature the incursion of the semiotic into the symbolic, an incursion that is an inevitable aspect of the subject's condition, is most explicit (82). In poetic language the semiotic makes these incursions, even engages in a "dismantling of the symbolic" (64), without destroying the possibility of meaning. "No text, no matter how 'musicalized,' is devoid of meaning or signification; on the contrary, musicalization pluralizes meanings" (65).

If it is not possible to represent that which cannot be represented, it is, nevertheless, possible to let that which eludes representation have its effect on representation, leave its trace. Tracks in the snow may not constitute a picture of an animal, but they indicate that something has passed, and one might wish to adjust one's own movements in response to them. A cry of pain or joy or Derrida's "call that comes from nowhere" may not prove the existence of a fixed self, but they do suggest something that needs to be taken into account when we plan urban projects, social programs, or wars.

If representation threatens to do violence to that which it seeks to contain, the unrepresented stands as a perpetual threat and challenge to representation. But, as Kristeva argues, without symbolic representation there would be no society at all, and psychosis would result. Therefore, the only hope is not the victory of representation over the real or the destruction of representation by the real, but a dialectic between the two, in which the representation of the subject is dynamic and not static, fluid and not fixed, perpetually informed and challenged by that which it cannot contain. One can assume diverse subject positions or diverse subject representations, not because all positions and definitions are equal or arbitrary, but because the subject is never adequate to that which it struggles to represent. "[What] remodels the symbolic order is always the influx of the semiotic" (Kristeva, *Revolution*, 62). Only through a capacity to shift and redefine the subject on the basis of energies that can never quite be pinned down can there be produced a dynamic and constructive subject that is neither absolutely repressive nor absolutely vulnerable.

*   *   *

The construction of subjects can take extremely diverse forms. The subject can be constructed as a temporal and spatial position, an abstract point defined geometrically and optically by a perspective grid, a locus that gathers light and organizes it into a coherent perceptual representation of a world of space and time and presents itself as a stable center of being. This visual, imaginary locus can be reinforced and reconstituted by an other subject that addresses it linguistically, that hails it and inscribes it in a social network. The apparently coherent linguistic and conceptual realm occupied by both addresser and addressee and all other subjects so constituted is laid over the imaginary field of perception, without replacing or destroying it, and the subject is inscribed in another realm of consolidation, constitution, and subjection. But this classical subject can be fractured and fragmented by a polyphony of voices, multiple addressers that speak to it confusingly and in their multiplicity decenter the subject they address. The you who is hailed is no longer a unity but a plurality. And visually, vanishing points can multiply, fragmenting the viewer as well as the viewed. In film the subject is emancipated through the mobility of the camera and the power of editing, but the same forces that cinematically enlarge and empower it have the potential to decenter and disperse it, shattering the fragile sutures that construct it as a unity and coherence. The subject of hypertext decenters itself even more radically, flows into an expanding network that disperses outward toward an indeterminate horizon. In its playful multiplicity, its assumption of diverse provisional masks, none of which can quite contain it, the subject continues to play the risky interactive game of agency and construction, of constituting and being constituted.

Notes

Chapter 1: The Subject's Eye

1. J. Douglas Canfield, in *Word as Bond in English Literature from the Middle Ages to the Restoration*, discusses the disintegration of the medieval code of the word, as evident in numerous literary works that can be seen as responses of one kind or another to that disintegration. The code of the word attempts to bind individuals in feudal alliances and marriages and to keep at bay men's potential for violence. However, in the bourgeois world the feudal tradition of word as bond becomes insufficient. Nevertheless, words—written words—remain important; it is good business to convince people that one's word is good. "Contracts and covenants continue to be important, but words have become insufficient bonds: we have become a society dominated by lawyers, loopholes, and litigiousness" (313).

2. Panofsky's identification of the subject was based largely on inventory and other historical descriptions of the painting—or a painting much like it ("Jan van Eyck's 'Arnolfini' Portrait," 194–196). Peter H. Schabacker argues, however, that the couple represented in the painting cannot be Arnolfini and Cenami. Those two were of equal social status, and the position of the hands in the painting (bridegroom holding bride's right hand in his left) was the gesture utilized in *morganatic* marriages—marriages of men to women of lesser social standing. Panofsky explains this discrepancy on the basis of poetic license—van Eyck wanted to avoid the cumbersome contraposto that would result from a joining of right hand to right hand, the appropriate gesture for a ceremony involving individuals of equal rank. But Schabacker argues that van Eyck was far too literal an artist to engage in this kind of liberty (Schabacker, 375–398). Julius Held takes issue with Schabacker, arguing that the raising of the groom's right hand—which would have been impossible if right hands were joined—is a more significant gesture than the joining of the hands, and this further explains the necessity of taking some liberty in the representation of the joined hands. Moreover, the same liberty was taken in representations on English matrimonial slabs. Finally, there is no evidence of morganatic marriages taking place in the Netherlands at the time and also, so far as Held knows, no depictions of morganatic marriages (Held, 56–57). One might add that although van Eyck is, indeed, a very "literal" artist regarding visual detail, he is not really so literal in the situations and setting he represents. Craig Harbison makes the point that van Eyck's churches are not actual churches, in spite of the wealth of architectural detail. Thus, according to Harbison, van Eyck's paintings are "ultimately . . . not faithfully descriptive at all" ("Realism and Symbolism in Early Flemish Painting," 589, 591).

3. Compare the relationship between the verbal and the visual here with that relationship in the work of René Magritte, van Eyck's countryman of half a millennium later. Magritte's painting *The Treachery of Images* (*La Trahison des Images*, often referred to as *This Is Not a Pipe*, 1928–29), similar in that it juxtaposes visual

and verbal elements, is not designed to suture the gap between sign and referent or between visual and verbal signs, but to provoke a questioning of all such relationships. In an extended meditation on this and other modern paintings, Michel Foucault discusses various aspects of the relationship between verbal and visual representation. Foucault takes as his point of departure the idea of the calligram—an image constructed out of words, a poem that is shaped to form a visual image of its subject. The calligram, through the congruence and redundancy of the visual and the verbal, attempts to ensnare and hold the referent, the real thing it claims to represent. "Pursuing its quarry by two paths," Foucault writes, "the calligram sets a most perfect trap. By its double function, it guarantees capture, as neither discourse alone nor a pure drawing could do" (*This Is Not a Pipe*, 22). As much, of course, could be said for the strategy utilized in the *Arnolfini* portrait. Magritte's painting, on the other hand, unravels the calligram, separates its verbal and visual components, and frees up, makes ambiguous, the relationship between the verbal, the visual, and their possible referents.

4. For Peirce an icon is a "sign" that in some respect resembles the "object" to which it refers (102, 104–107).

5. Clearly the distinction between the "motivated" and "arbitrary" is more complex and ambiguous than presented here. The fact that a dog is chosen as a symbol of fidelity is not completely arbitrary, and, as visual art theorists such as E. H. Gombrich and Nelson Goodman have pointed out, the techniques of illusionistic painting are more involved in conventions and codes than a casual glance might indicate. Even Saussure, whose recognition of the "arbitrary" nature of the linguistic sign is often emphasized, realized that it is not so simple and that in language there is a perpetual evolutionary movement between arbitrariness and motivation, in both directions. Nevertheless, certain representational modes more readily create an *impression* of resemblance and transparency than other modes; certain configurations of paint, manipulated according to the conventions of illusionistic painting, are more easily seen as resembling their objects than written or spoken words, for example (Gombrich, passim; Goodman, 1–19; Saussure, 133–134).

6. David L. Carleton calls this "elliptical" perspective. He argues that there is a mathematical system behind the space in this and other of van Eyck's paintings, even though that space does not conform to the rules for "correct" optical perspective. The illusionistic space resulting from van Eyck's split vanishing points or, at least, vanishing "areas" emulates that created by a convex mirror such as the very one hanging on the wall inside the *Arnolfini* painting (118–124). Others have argued that van Eyck's perspective is not as methodical as Carleton believes, that imprecision in his drawings and selectivity in the orthogonals he examines result in his exaggeration of the mathematical consistency of van Eyck's interiors. Van Eyck's perspective is empirical and intuitive and is affected by expressive concerns as much as a desire for realism (Ward, 680–686; Collier, 691).

7. Jonathan Culler provides a useful, brief summary of some of the key points in feminist deconstructions of Freud's description of the anatomical basis of gender construction in *On Deconstruction*, 167–175. Culler draws on Luce Irigaray, Sarah Kofman, Juliet Mitchell, Shoshana Felman, Hélène Cixous, and Julia Kristeva. Selections by Cixous, Irigaray, and others, included in Elaine Marks and Isabelle de Courtivron's *New French Feminisms*, are also helpful.

8. Silverman is drawing on Michele Montrelay, "Inquiry into Femininity," *m/f*, no. 1 (1978): 83–101.

Chapter 2: The Subject of Discourse

1. The framing levels of *Heart of Darkness* have been much discussed. L. J. Morrissey provides a straightforward discussion and analysis of those narrative levels in "The Tellers in *Heart of Darkness*: Conrad's Chinese Boxes."

2. This, of course, is not to imply that Conrad himself was not racist or that racism is not evident in *Heart of Darkness*. Conrad's racism is evident in his fiction as well as his nonfictional writing. See Chinua Achebe, "An Image of Africa: Racism in Conrad's *Heart of Darkness*." In spite of this racism, however, *Heart of Darkness* clearly subverts the ideology of colonialism and clarifies the hypocrisy of its supposedly altruistic justification.

3. Nevertheless, there have been numerous attempts to identify a coherent, overarching narrative voice in *As I Lay Dying*. M. E. Bradford, for example, views Addie as the ultimate narrator, as if she is a troubled ghost who cannot rest until she is buried in her hometown cemetery. Daniel Ferrer sees Darl as the ultimate source of the monologues, emphasizing his "delirious raving" and the apparent compatibility between his voice and the "authorial" voice (33). Ann Lecercle-Sweet argues that the novel transcends such "rather narrow anchorages" as those provided by Bradford and Ferrer (n. 5, 47–48). However, in spite of her close analysis of the polyphony of voices in the novel and of its cleavages, disjunctions, ruptures, and interferences, Lecercle-Sweet privileges too much the authorial *Grundsprache*, arguing that in the end it seizes power and is able to win in its conflict with the divisive voices of the individual characters (60). I would argue that the authorial voice that periodically manifests itself is too occasional and sporadic to provide a useful and stabilizing anchor, a reliable *Grundsprache*, for the reader.

4. Derrida, of course, uses his neologism *différance*, which conflates "differ" and "defer," to indicate this originary scission. See, for example, "Différance" in *Margins of Philosophy*, 8–9 and passim.

5. See, for example, my discussion of Warhol's parodic strategy, in *Modern/Postmodern*, 57–59 and 66–68.

6. Mariolina Salvatori ("Italo Calvino's *If on a winter's night a traveler*: Writer's Authority, Reader's Autonomy") argues that Calvino's text does, in fact, on one level, entrap and "frame" the reader by, for example, setting up expectations of *lack* of closure and then confirming those expectations by *not* providing closure. In Calvino's novel, the reader's apparent autonomy is itself a "programmed response" and "we may have to admit that once more we have been framed" (203). "I think it would be possible . . . to suggest that Calvino's text is mocking its readers into the realization that though writers might celebrate the creativity and free play of the reader, they ultimately expect of *their* readers the response they have themselves envisioned. In fact, the whole text frames the reader's response to such an extent that, it could be argued, the more active the reader, the greater the possibility of his being framed" (210). On another level, however, she argues that the reader who learns from the text will genuinely interrogate himself, his presuppositions, and issues of authority and autonomy in writing and reading.

7. For Donna Haraway the cyborg is a central metaphor for boundary crossings and fusions of all kinds—human-animal, organism-machine, physical-nonphysical. Cyborgs are constructed, nonessentialist, "illegitimate offspring of militarism and patriarchal capitalism, not to mention state socialism," offspring that may turn out to be "exceedingly unfaithful to their origins," provided oppositional

groups and individuals do not succumb to technophobia and are able to appropriate the cyborg, along with all it stands for. Cyborgs are in opposition to purity and essence, which constrain identity and limit the possibilities for political alliances. They are destabilizing monsters, inclusive and able to construct ad hoc, impure, partial identities and alliances. Haraway's "cyborg myth is about transgressed boundaries, potent fusions, and dangerous possibilities which progressive people might explore as one part of needed political work" (65–72).

Chapter 3: The Moving Subject

1. Stephen Heath notes that classical film does not absolutely limit camera movements and angles to the humanly possible and can, in fact, tolerate departures from the strictly human point of view. Classical film can tolerate certain excesses—excesses done in the name of "style," for example—provided shots are contained and controlled by an overall coherent narrative movement. It is this subordination of shots to an overriding narrative, not a narrowly construed visual credibility and transparency, that regulates a mobile (not a static) viewer position in film. Still, Heath acknowledges that "it remains no less true . . . that movement represents a potentially radical disturbance of the smooth stability of the scenographic vision (hence the need for a systematic organization to contain it)" (Heath, 49).

2. Some key articles on suture are included in *Screen*, 18, no. 4 (1977–78) ("Dossier on Suture," containing articles by Jacques-Alain Miller, Jean-Pierre Oudart, and Stephen Heath) and in Bill Nichols's *Movies and Methods: An Anthology* (articles by Daniel Dayan and William Rothman). See also Kaja Silverman's chapter on suture in *The Subject of Semiotics*.

Chapter 4: Hyperrealities and Hypertexts

1. References to Nelson's *Literary Machines* are to chapters and pages, separated by a slash.

2. Heim's description of the "immediacy" of word processing and its connection with the immediacy of oral communication suggests a valorization of "speech" over "writing" that would certainly be challenged by Derrida, for whom all language involves a *différance* that problematizes reference and for whom writing—at least an arche-writing—precedes speech itself ("Linguistics and Grammatology," in *Of Grammatology*). Heim is describing a psychological effect and Derrida is speaking philosophically.

3. An e-mail note, dated September 23, 1993, from the acting general counsel of the University of South Florida to the multiple recipients of the list USF-News, warns that Florida public records law regards e-mail messages as public records available for scrutiny upon request. In order to comply with the law the university is maintaining magnetic tape copies of e-mail messages for one year.

4. Mitchell discussed her work in the session "The Computer and the Visual Arts: A Revolution in Progress," at the Eighty-third Annual Conference of the College Art Association, San Antonio, Texas, January 25–28, 1995. The session was chaired by Anne Morgan Spalter. References to this conference are drawn from personal notes and from tapes of sessions, produced and sold by Audio

Archives International, La Crescenta, California. This quotation is transcribed from the Audio Archives tape of the session.

5. A number of recent legal, legislative, and economic battles relate to the issue of freedom and control in electronic networks. Here are just a few examples:

In July 1994 Robert and Carleen Thomas, who operated "Amateur Action" BBS, a members only bulletin board system, out of Milpitas, California, were convicted by a Memphis jury of sending pornography across state lines. The materials sent would not have violated community standards in California, but they did so in Memphis. The case raised many issues, including what the definition of a "community" ought to be in an age of electronic communications. Because the Supreme Court, in 1974, required that community standards determine what obscenity is, in this instance the standards of a community, defined geographically and politically (Memphis), were allowed to dictate the standards that would apply to individuals anywhere who wished to participate in the BBS. Because it is impossible to control who will request the materials of a BBS, those who create bulletin board systems will have to conform to the laws of all communities (narrowly defined) where their materials might be received. This case, which is being appealed, makes it clear that restricting the definition of community to a geographical or political entity is inappropriate. Individuals who conduct a large part of their personal or professional activities on electronic networks might be members of communities for which geography is irrelevant. Even before electronic networks, one often thought of scholars, scientists, artists, or members of religious denominations as "communities" not geographically defined. The electronic network is, in fact, a "place" where many diverse communities coexist, often having little knowledge of or interest in one another. Various materials relating to the Thomas case are included in the electronic journal/newsletter *Computer Underground Digest* 6, no. 69 (July 31, 1994). The brief for the appeal is included in *Computer Underground Digest* 7, no. 31 (April 9, 1995).

The possibility of new, more restrictive pricing policies for Internet usage is another issue that concerns many users of the net. In 1994 the National Science Foundation awarded contracts to four telephone companies, who would operate four Internet "Network Access Points," and there was concern that new pricing methods would follow. Some worry that if usage-based pricing systems replace fixed rates for Internet connections, the free, democratic flow of information that currently exists might become more restricted. This issue was discussed in *TAP-INFO* (May 7, 1994), an Internet distribution list of the Taxpayer Assets Project, founded by Ralph Nader.

In early 1995 the U.S. Senate proposed the "Communications Decency Act of 1995" (Senate Bill 314), which would subject electronic communications, even supposedly "private" communications, to government censorship. A later amendment, the Exon/Gorton Amendment, altered the act to apply to users only, rather than providers (networks run by colleges and universities, as well as servers like CompuServe, America Online, and Prodigy), who sent messages deemed obscene or indecent. Even in its amended form, certain forms of private communication—a lusty love note sent between spouses—might be regarded as illegal, and literary works, legally sold in bookstores, might be illegal if transmitted on-line. Various Internet communities, as well as the ACLU, lobbied against the act, in both its original and amended forms. [*Computer Underground Digest* 7, no. 13 (February 15, 1995), 7, no. 24 (March 26, 1995).] Nevertheless, the act was added to the Telecommunications Act of 1996, which passed overwhelmingly in both houses and was signed by the president in February 1996. Ironically (or perhaps not so ironically), a bill designed to increase the freedom of phone and cable companies to compete with each other and which is touted as a way of increasing choices among consumers, may in important ways reduce the freedom of those who use those services. We will have more choice about which communication service we subscribe to, but less about what we can communicate. Court challenges, of course, may reduce the ability of the act to censor content and reduce freedom of speech (Kantor, Lemonick, Levy).

6. The numbers in parenthetical citations referring to Moulthrop's "You Say You Want a Revolution?," which appeared in the electronic journal *Postmodern Culture*, refer to paragraphs (which are numbered in the journal) rather than to pages.

7. Joyce describes the distinction between exploratory and constructive hypertexts in "Siren Shapes: Exploratory and Constructive Hypertexts."

8. In this respect the O. J. Simpson trial was similar. In spite of all of one's efforts not to forget the horror and brutality of the crime involved, one inevitably became caught up in the trial as a media event, a contest or sport, a competition of intelligence and rhetoric between opposed teams of lawyers and prosecutors, with judge, jurors, and witnesses playing ancillary roles. Thus, a second violence was added to the first. That second violence resulted when the representation of utterly serious events became a form of entertainment, profit, and quick fame, trivializing those events and distancing further their reality.

9. One of Moulthrop's earlier works was a hypertextual version of "The Garden of Forking Paths." Moulthrop describes his rendering of the Borges story in "Reading from the Map: Metonymy and Metaphor in the Fiction of 'Forking Paths,' " in Delany and Landow, *Hypermedia and Literary Studies.*

10. It is worth noting that at least part of "Dreamtime" is drawn from a section of *Victory Garden.* The text of the water dream sequence of Aloysius McIntosh is taken from a section entitled "Dreamtime" in the novel. Of course the "Dreamtime" section of *Victory Garden* has none of the audiovisual pyrotechnics that enliven the "Dreamtime" that is to be part of *Chaos.*

11. Discussed in the session "The Computer and the Visual Arts: A Revolution in Progress," at the Eighty-third Annual Conference of the College Art Association. See n. 4.

Notes to Epilogue

1. Cadava, Connor, and Nancy, eds., *Who Comes After the Subject?*

2. This quote should not be taken to imply that Borch-Jacobsen favors any kind of reinstatement of the subject as classically understood, though his challenge to the subject forces him to grapple with the problem of politics without a subject. Borch-Jacobsen's challenge is, in its own way, as rigorous as any. He argues, in his book *The Freudian Subject* and in his essay "The Freudian Subject, from Politics to Ethics," that Freud's challenge to the subject was incomplete and that Freud tended merely to redefine the "subject" as the unconscious or the id. Borch-Jacobsen argues for a more radical abandonment of the subject. For him, in no sense does the individual—conscious or unconscious, ego or id, whatever—have any foundational claim to existence. Rather, the collective, the relationship with others (without ego or subject) is primary, and the individual subject emerges only as an illusion, the result of a hypnosis. Describing what he regards as the

"failure of individual psychology," Borch-Jacobsen writes, "From this point on, no individual, no individual psychology is available to support, uphold, or subtend group psychology. Group psychology, in the form of hypnosis, invades everything, up to and including the relation of the ego to its ideal. There is no more ego, now, except when it is permeated by another, primordially intimated and broached in its very intimacy—in short, suggested" (*The Freudian Subject*, 233–234). And, "In the beginning, then, was the band . . . the bond (rather than the group). From the beginnings (they are lost in the depths of time, and they will thus always have been numerous, plural), *That* bound men, enjoined them and adjoined them beyond themselves. . . . *That*—who is It? No one at all. The bond, being older than the subjects that it enjoins and adjoins, is not one of them—it is detached from them, unbound from them" (236).

3. The numbers in parenthetical citations referring to Wheeler's "Bulldozing the Subject," which appeared in the electronic journal *Postmodern Culture*, refer to paragraphs (which are numbered in the journal) rather than to pages.

4. Participants included, besides Serebrennikov, Karen-edis Barzman (whose paper was read in absentia), Todd P. Olson, Meir Joel Wigoder, Terence Diggory, and Steven Z. Levine.

5. Jon Wiener, writing in *The Nation*, describes an example of this choreographed attack. Early in the Reagan era a right-wing foundation, the Olin Foundation, "set up and funded a network of conservative student newspapers, the flagship of which was the virulently racist *Dartmouth Review*, where [Dinesh] D'Souza first demonstrated his talents as editor in chief." After graduating Dartmouth, D'Souza was rewarded with a position in the Reagan White House, where he was given the title "Domestic Policy Analyst." He was then employed by the American Enterprise Institute, where, supported by a grant from the Olin Foundation, he wrote, *Illiberal Education*, an attack on "political correctness" on campus, including affirmative action and curricular reform (Wiener, "What Happened at Harvard," 386–388). Perhaps the most visible politicization of culture during the Reagan-Bush years were the attacks on and attempts to control the National Endowment for the Arts, attacks that focused on the funding of certain controversial artists and activities, grants that represented a tiny portion of a budget that has predominantly supported noncontroversial, mainstream cultural activity. Since the 1994 election the threats to NEA, as well as to the National Endowment for Humanities and the Corporation for Public Broadcasting, have intensified dramatically.

6. See, for example, Julia Kristeva, "Woman Can Never Be Defined," in Marks and de Courtivron, *New French Feminisms.*

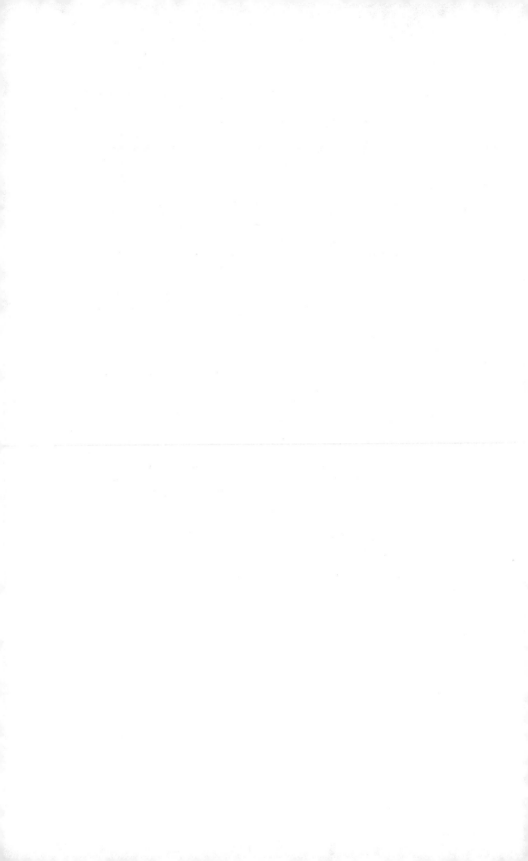

References

Achebe, Chinua. "An Image of Africa: Racism in Conrad's *Heart of Darkness.*" In *Joseph Conrad, Heart of Darkness: A Norton Critical Edition,* ed. Robert Kimbrough. New York: Norton, 1988. First published in *Massachusetts Review* 18 (1977): 782–794.

Acker, Kathy. *Empire of the Senseless.* New York: Grove Weidenfeld, 1988.

Althusser, Louis. *Lenin and Philosophy and Other Essays.* Trans. Ben Brewster. London: New Left Books, 1971.

Altman, Robert, dir. *The Player* (film). Written by Michael Tolkin. Cinematography by Jean Lepine. Avenue Pictures, in association with Spelling Entertainment, released by Fine Line Features, 1992.

Badley, Linda C. "Calvino *engagé*: Reading as Resistance in *If on a Winter's Night a Traveler.*" *Perspectives on Contemporary Literature* 10 (1984): 102–111.

Baldass, Ludwig. *Jan van Eyck.* New York: Phaidon, 1952.

Barthes, Roland. *The Pleasure of the Text.* Trans. Richard Miller. New York: Hill and Wang, 1975.

———. *S/Z.* Trans. Richard Miller. New York: Hill and Wang, 1974.

Baudrillard, Jean. *America.* Trans. Chris Turner (Material Word). London and New York: Verso, 1988.

———. "The Reality Gulf." *Guardian,* January 11, 1991, p. 25. This article originally appeared as "La Guerre du Golfe n'aura pas lieu," in *Libération,* January 4, 1991, p. 5.

———. *Selected Writings.* Ed. and intro. Mark Poster. Stanford, Calif.: Stanford University Press, 1988.

———. *Simulacra and Simulations.* Trans. Paul Foss, Paul Patton, and Philip Beitchman. New York: Sémiotext(e), 1983.

———. "This Beer Isn't a Beer, Interview with Anne Laurent." In *Baudrillard Live: Selected Interviews,* ed. Mike Gane, 180–190. London and New York: Routledge, 1993.

Baudry, Jean-Louis. "Ideological Effects of the Basic Cinematographic Apparatus." Trans. Alan Williams. *Film Quarterly* 28, no. 2 (Winter 1974–75): 39–47.

Belsey, Catherine. *Critical Practice.* London and New York: Methuen, 1980.

Benveniste, Emil. *Problems in General Linguistics.* Trans. Mary Elizabeth Meek. Coral Gables, Fla.: University of Miami Press, 1971.

Bolter, Jay David. *Writing Space: The Computer, Hypertext, and the History of Writing.* Hillsdale, N.J.: Lawrence Erlbaum Associates, 1991. A hypertext version of this work, copyrighted 1990 and published by Eastgate Press in Cambridge, Mass., also is available.

Booth, Wayne C. *The Rhetoric of Fiction.* Chicago: University of Chicago Press, 1961.

Borch-Jacobsen, Mikkel. *The Freudian Subject.* Trans. Francois Roustang. Stanford, Calif.: Stanford University Press, 1988.

————. "The Freudian Subject, from Politics to Ethics." Trans. Richard Miller, in *Who Comes After the Subject?* ed. Eduardo Cadava, Peter Connor, and Jean-Luc Nancy, 61–78. New York and London: Routledge, 1991.

Borges, Jorge Luis. *Labyrinths: Selected Stories and Other Writings.* Ed. Donald A. Yates and James E. Irby. New York: New Directions, 1964.

Bradford, M. E. "Addie Bundren and the Design of *As I Lay Dying.*" *Southern Review* 6, no. 4 (Autumn 1970): 1093–1099.

Cadava, Eduardo, Peter Connor, and Jean-Luc Nancy, eds. *Who Comes After the Subject?* New York and London: Routledge, 1991.

Calvino, Italo. *If on a winter's night a traveler.* Trans. William Weaver. New York: Harcourt Brace Jovanovich, 1981.

Canfield, J. Douglas. *Word as Bond in English Literature from the Middle Ages to the Restoration.* Philadelphia: University of Pennsylvania Press, 1989.

Carleton, David L. "A Mathematical Analysis of the Perspective of the *Arnolfini Portrait* and Other Similar Interior Scenes by Jan van Eyck." *Art Bulletin* 64, no. 1 (March 1982): 118–124.

Carroll, David. *The Subject in Question: The Languages of Theory and the Strategies of Fiction.* Chicago: University of Chicago Press, 1982.

Chown, Jeffrey. *Hollywood Auteur: Francis Coppola.* New York: Praeger, 1988.

Collier, James M. "Perspective in the *Arnolfini Portrait.*" *Art Bulletin* 65, no. 4 (December 1983): 691.

Computer Underground Digest. Electronic journal/newsletter. 6, no. 69 (July 31, 1994); 7, no. 13 (February 15, 1995); 7, no. 24 (March 26, 1995); 7, no. 31 (April 9, 1995).

Conrad, Joseph. *Heart of Darkness.* In *Joseph Conrad, Heart of Darkness: A Case Study in Contemporary Criticism,* ed. Ross C. Murfin. New York: St. Martin's, 1989.

————. *Lord Jim.* New York: Modern Library, 1931.

Coover, Robert. "The End of Books." *New York Times Book Review,* June 21, 1992, pp. 1, 23–25.

————. "Hyperfiction: Novels for the Computer." *New York Times Book Review,* August 29, 1993, pp. 1, 8–12.

Coppola, Francis Ford, dir. *One from the Heart* (film). Written by Armyan Bernstein and Coppola. Sets by Dean Tavoularis. Cinematography by Ronald V. Garcia and Vittorio Storaro. Zoetrope, 1982.

Coward, Rosalind, and John Ellis. *Language and Materialism: Developments in Semiology and the Theory of the Subject.* London: Routledge and Kegan Paul, 1977.

Cowie, Peter. *Coppola.* New York: Scribners, 1990.

Crane, Gregory, editor in chief. *Perseus 1.0, Interactive Sources and Studies on Ancient Greece* (CD-ROM, videodisc, and user's guide). New Haven, Conn.: Yale University Press, 1992.

Culler, Jonathan. *On Deconstruction, Theory and Criticism after Structuralism.* Ithaca, N.Y.: Cornell University Press, 1982.

Daix, Pierre. *Picasso: Life and Art.* Trans. Olivia Emmet. New York: HarperCollins/Icon Editions, 1993.

Danto, Arthur C. "Photography and Performance: Cindy Sherman's Stills." In *Cindy Sherman, Untitled Film Stills.* New York: Rizzoli, 1990.

Delany, Paul, and George P. Landow, eds. *Hypermedia and Literary Studies.* Cambridge: MIT Press, 1991.

Derrida, Jacques. "Deconstruction and the Other." Dialogue with Richard Kearney, in Richard Kearney, *Dialogues with Contemporary Continental Thinkers: The*

Phenomenological Heritage, trans. Richard Kearney, 105–126. Manchester: Manchester University Press, 1984.

——. "'Eating Well,' or the Calculation of the Subject: An Interview with Jacques Derrida." Interview by Jean-Luc Nancy, trans. Peter Connor and Avital Ronell, in *Who Comes After the Subject?* ed. Eduardo Cadava, Peter Connor, and Jean-Luc Nancy, 96–119. New York and London: Routledge, 1991.

——. *Margins of Philosophy.* Trans. Alan Bass. Chicago: University of Chicago Press, 1982.

——. *Of Grammatology.* Trans. Gayatri Chakravorty Spivak. Baltimore: Johns Hopkins, 1984.

Faulkner, William. *As I Lay Dying.* New York: Vintage/Random House, 1957.

Ferrer, Daniel. "*In omnis iam vocabuli mortem*: Representation of Absence, the Subject of Representation and Absence of the Subject in William Faulkner's *As I Lay Dying*." Trans. Geoff Bennington. *Oxford Literary Review* 5, nos. 1–2 (1982): 21–36.

Foucault, Michel. *This Is Not a Pipe.* Berkeley: University of California Press, 1982.

——. "What Is an Author?" Trans. Josue V. Harari. In *Textual Strategies, Perspectives in Post-Structuralist Criticism*, ed. Josue V. Harari. Ithaca, N.Y.: Cornell University Press, 1979.

Freud, Sigmund. *The Standard Edition of the Complete Psychological Works of Sigmund Freud.* Vol. 21. Ed. and trans. James Strachey in collaboration with Anna Freud. London: Hogarth, 1961.

Gaggi, Silvio. *Modern/Postmodern: A Study in Twentieth-Century Arts and Ideas.* Philadelphia: University of Pennsylvania Press, 1989.

Gibson, William. *Neuromancer.* New York: Ace, 1984.

Gombrich, E. H. *Art and Illusion: A Study in the Psychology of Pictorial Representation.* New York: Random House, 1965.

Goodman, Nelson. *The Languages of Art.* Indianapolis: Hackett, 1976.

Grundberg, Andy. *Mike and Doug Starn.* Intro. Robert Rosenblum. New York: Abrams, 1990.

Haraway, Donna. "A Manifesto for Cyborgs: Science, Technology, and Socialist Feminism in the 1980s." *Socialist Review* 80 (March–April 1985): 64–107.

Harbison, Craig. "Realism and Symbolism in Early Flemish Painting." *Art Bulletin* 66, no. 4 (December 1984): 588–602.

——. "Sexuality and Social Standing in Jan van Eyck's Arnolfini Double Portrait." *Renaissance Quarterly* 43, no. 2 (Summer 1990): 249–291.

Harpold, Terence. "Threnody: Psychoanalytic Digressions on the Subject of Hypertexts." In *Hypermedia and Literary Studies*, ed. Paul Delany and George P. Landow. Cambridge: MIT Press, 1991.

Heath, Stephen. *Questions of Cinema.* Bloomington: Indiana University Press, 1981.

Heim, Michael. *Electric Language: A Philosophical Study of Word Processing.* New Haven, Conn.: Yale University Press, 1987.

Held, Julius. *Rubens and His Circle.* Princeton, N.J.: Princeton University Press, 1982.

Irigaray, Luce. *Speculum of the Other Woman.* Trans. Gillian C. Gill. Ithaca, N.Y.: Cornell University Press, 1985.

Jameson, Fredric. *Postmodernism, or The Cultural Logic of Late Capitalism.* Durham, N.C.: Duke University Press, 1991.

Johnson, Barbara, ed. *Freedom and Interpretation: The Oxford Amnesty Lectures 1992.* New York: HarperCollins, 1993.

Joyce, James. *The Portable James Joyce.* Intro. and notes by Harry Levin. New York: Viking, 1962.

Joyce, Michael. "Afternoon, a story" (hypertext). Cambridge, Mass.: Eastgate Systems, Inc. 1987.

———. "Siren Shapes: Exploratory and Constructive Hypertexts." *Academic Computing* (November 1988): 10–14, 37–42.

Kantor, Andrew. "House Passes Net Censorship Bill." *Internet World* (March 1996): 16.

Kracauer, Siegfried. *From Caligari to Hitler.* Princeton, N.J.: Princeton University Press, 1947.

Kristeva, Julia. *Revolution in Poetic Language.* Trans. Margaret Waller. New York: Columbia University Press, 1984.

———. "Woman Can Never Be Defined." Trans. Marilyn A. August, in *New French Feminists,* ed. Elaine Marks and Isabelle de Courtivron, 137–141. First published in *Tel Quel,* Autumn 1974.

Lacan, Jacques. *Ecrits: A Selection.* Trans. Alan Sheridan. New York: Norton, 1977.

Landow, George P. *Hypertext: The Convergence of Contemporary Critical Theory and Technology.* Baltimore: Johns Hopkins, 1992.

Lanham, Richard A. *The Electronic Word: Democracy, Technology, and the Arts.* Chicago: University of Chicago Press, 1993.

Lapsley, Robert, and Michael Westlake. *Film Theory: An Introduction.* Manchester: Manchester University Press, 1992.

Lecercle-Sweet, Ann. "The Chip and the Chink: The Dying of the 'I' in *As I Lay Dying.*" *Faulkner Journal* 2, no. 1 (Fall 1986): 46–61.

Lemonick, Michael D. "The Net's Strange Day." *Time,* February 19, 1996, p. 55.

Levy, Steven. "Now for the Free-for-All." *Newsweek,* February 12, 1996, pp. 42–44.

Linker, Kate. *Love for Sale: The Words and Pictures of Barbara Kruger.* New York: Abrams, 1990.

Lyotard, Jean-François. *Heidegger and "the jews."* Trans. Andreas Michel and Mark S. Roberts, intro. David Carroll. Minneapolis: University of Minnesota Press, 1990.

———. *The Postmodern Condition: A Report on Knowledge.* Trans. Geoff Bennington and Brian Massumi. Minneapolis: University of Minnesota Press, 1984.

Marks, Elaine, and Isabelle de Courtivron, eds. and intros. *New French Feminisms.* New York: Schocken Books, 1981.

McCorduck, Pamela. *The Universal Machine: Confessions of a Technological Optimist.* New York: McGraw Hill, 1985.

Metz, Christian. *The Imaginary Signifier: Psychoanalysis and the Cinema.* Trans. Celia Britton, Annwyl Williams, Ben Brewster, and Alfred Guzzetti. Bloomington: Indiana University Press, 1982.

Miller, Jacques-Alain, Jean-Pierre Oudart, and Stephen Heath. "Dossier on Suture." *Screen* 18, no. 4 (1977–78): 23–76.

Moi, Toril. *Sexual/Textual Politics: Feminist Literary Theory.* London and New York: Routledge, 1985.

Montrelay, Michele. "Inquiry into Femininity." *m/f,* no. 1 (1978): 83–101.

Morrissey, L. J. "The Tellers in *Heart of Darkness*: Conrad's Chinese Boxes." *Conradiana: A Journal of Joseph Conrad Studies* 13, no. 2 (1981): 141–148.

Moulthrop, Stuart. "Dreamtime" (hypertext). *Perforations,* no. 3 (Spring/Summer 1992).

———. "Reading from the Map: Metonymy and Metaphor in the Fiction of 'Forking Paths.'" In *Hypermedia and Literary Studies,* ed. Paul Delany and George P. Landow. Cambridge: MIT Press, 1991.

———. *Victory Garden* (hypertext). Cambridge: Eastgate Systems, Inc. 1991.

———. "You Say You Want a Revolution? Hypertext and the Laws of Media." *Postmodern Culture: An Electronic Journal of Interdisciplinary Criticism* 1, no. 3 (May 1991).

Mulvey, Laura. "A Phantasmagoria of the Female Body: The Work of Cindy Sherman." *New Left Review,* no. 188 (July/August 1991): 136–150.

———. "Visual Pleasure and Narrative Cinema." In *Movies and Methods, Volume II,* ed. Bill Nichols. Originally published in *Screen* 16, no. 3 (Autumn 1975).

Nelson, Theodor Holm. *Literary Machines 93.1.* Sausalito, Calif.: Mindful Press, 1993.

Nichols, Bill, ed. *Movies and Methods: An Anthology.* Berkeley: University of California Press, 1976.

———. *Movies and Methods: An Anthology, Volume II.* Berkeley: University of California Press, 1985.

Norris, Christopher. *Uncritical Theory: Postmodernism, Intellectuals and the Gulf War.* Amherst: University of Massachusetts Press, 1992.

Ong, Walter J. *Orality and Literacy: The Technologizing of the Word.* London: Methuen, 1982.

Owens, Craig. "The Discourse of Others: Feminists and Postmodernism." In *Postmodern Perspectives: Issues in Contemporary Art,* ed. Howard Risatti, 186–207. Englewood Cliffs, N.J.: Prentice Hall, 1990. Originally published in *The Anti-Aesthetic: Essays on Postmodern Culture,* ed. and intro. Hal Foster. Port Townsend, Wash.: Bay Press, 1983.

Panofsky, Irwin. *Early Netherlandish Painting,* vol. 1. New York: Harper and Row, 1971.

———. "Jan van Eyck's 'Arnolfini' Portrait." In *Modern Perspectives in Western Art History,* ed. Eugene Kleinbauer, 193–203. New York: Holt, Rinehart and Winston, 1971. Originally published in *Burlington Magazine* 64 (1934): 117–127.

Paulson, William. "Computers, Minds, and Texts: Preliminary Reflections." *New Literary History* 20, no. 2 (Winter 1989): 291–303.

Pecora, Vincent. "*Heart of Darkness* and the Phenomenology of Voice." *ELH* 52, no. 4 (Winter 1985): 993–1015.

Peirce, Charles Sanders. "Logic as Semiotic: The Theory of Signs." In *Philosophical Writings of Peirce,* ed. and intro. Justus Buchler. New York: Dover, 1955.

Reed, Ishmael. *Mumbo Jumbo.* New York: Macmillan, 1972.

Risatti, Howard, ed. *Postmodern Perspectives: Issues in Contemporary Art.* Englewood Cliffs, N.J.: Prentice Hall, 1990.

Rubin, William. *Pablo Picasso: A Retrospective.* Chronology by Jane Fluegel. New York: Museum of Modern Art, 1980.

Rush, Richard, dir. *The Stunt Man* (film). Written by Lawrence B. Marcus, Richard Rush, and Paul Brodeur. Based on the novel by Paul Brodeur. Cinematography by Mario Tosi. Twentieth Century-Fox, 1980.

Salvatori, Mariolina. "Italo Calvino's *If on a winter's night a traveler.* Writer's Authority, Reader's Autonomy." *Contemporary Literature* 27, no. 2 (Summer 1986): 182–212.

Saussure, Ferdinand de. *Course in General Linguistics,* ed. Charles Bally and Albert

Sechehaye in collaboration with Albert Riedlinger. Trans. Wade Baskin. New York: McGraw-Hill, 1966.

Schabacker, Peter H. "De Matrimonio ad Morganaticam Contracto: Jan van Eyck's 'Arnolfini' Portrait Reconsidered." *Art Quarterly* 35, no. 4 (Winter 1972): 375–398.

Scholes, Robert. *Fabulations and Metafiction.* Urbana: University of Illinois Press, 1979.

Seidel, Linda. "Jan van Eyck's 'Arnolfini Portrait': Business as Usual?" *Critical Inquiry* 16, (Autumn 1989): 54–87.

Serebrennikov, Nina Eugenia, Karen-edis Barzman, Todd P. Olson, Meir Joel Wigoder, Terence Diggory, and Steven Z. Levine. "Agency in Art History." Session of the College Art Association Eighty-third Annual Conference, January 25–28, 1995, San Antonio, Texas. Tapes of this and other sessions of the CAA conference are available from Audio Archives International, Inc., La Crescenta, California.

Sherman, Cindy. *Untitled Film Stills.* New York: Rizzoli, 1990.

Silverman, Kaja. *The Subject of Semiotics.* New York: Oxford University Press, 1983.

Smagula, Howard. *Currents: Contemporary Directions in the Visual Arts.* Second edition. Englewood Cliffs, N.J.: Prentice Hall, 1989.

Sontag, Susan. "Fascinating Fascism." In *Movies and Methods,* ed. Bill Nichols, 31–43. Originally published in *New York Review of Books,* February 6, 1975.

Sorapure, Madeleine. "Being in the Midst: Italo Calvino's *If on a winter's night a traveler.*" *Modern Fiction Studies* 31, no. 4 (Winter 1985): 702–709.

Spalter, Anne Morgan, Annette Weintraub, Bonnie Mitchell, Elizabeth Licata, and Brian Wallace. "The Computer and the Visual Arts: A Revolution in Progress." Session of the College Art Association Eighty-third Annual Conference, January 25–28, 1995, San Antonio, Texas. Tapes of this and other sessions of the CAA conference are available from Audio Archives International, Inc., La Crescenta, California.

TAP-INFO. Internet distribution list of the Taxpayer Assets Project, founded by Ralph Nader. May 7, 1994.

Trethewey, Eric. "Language, Experience, and Selfhood in Conrad's *Heart of Darkness.*" *Southern Humanities Review* 22, no. 2 (Spring 1988): 101–111.

Venturi, Robert, Denise Scott Brown, and Steven Izenour. *Learning from Las Vegas: The Forgotten Symbolism of Architectural Form.* Cambridge: MIT Press, 1986.

Vertov, Dziga. "Kinoks-Revolution." Selections, in *Film Makers on Film Making,* ed. Harry M. Geduld. Bloomington: Indiana University Press, 1969.

Ward, John L. "On the Mathematics of the Perspective of the *Arnolfini Portrait* and Similar Works of Jan van Eyck." *Art Bulletin* 65, no. 4 (December 1983): 680–686.

Wiener, Jon. "What Happened at Harvard." *Nation,* September 30, 1991, pp. 384–388.

Wheeler, Elizabeth A. "Bulldozing the Subject." *Postmodern Culture: An Electronic Journal of Interdisciplinary Criticism* 1, no. 3 (May 1991).

Yeats, William Butler. *Selected Poems and Two Plays of William Butler Yeats,* ed. and intro. M. L. Rosenthal. New York: Macmillan, 1962.

Zimmer, Carl. "Floppy Fiction." *Discover* 10, no. 11 (November 1989): 34–36.

Index